AMERICAN
UNITARIAN
CHURCHES

AMERICAN UNITARIAN CHURCHES

ARCHITECTURE OF A

DEMOCRATIC RELIGION

ANN MARIE BORYS

University of Massachusetts Press

Amherst and Boston

Copyright © 2021 by University of Massachusetts Press
All rights reserved
Printed in the United States of America

ISBN 978-1-62534-603-2 (paper)

Designed by Sally Nichols
Set in Alegreya
Printed and bound by Books International, Inc

Cover design by Frank Gutbrod
Cover photo by Ann Marie Borys, interior of Unitarian Church of Arlington, VA.
Courtesy of the photographer.

Library of Congress Cataloging-in-Publication Data

Names: Borys, Ann Marie, author.
Title: American Unitarian churches : architecture of a democratic religion /
Ann Marie Borys.
Description: Amherst : University of Massachusetts Press, [2021] | Includes
bibliographical references and index.
Identifiers: LCCN 2021016938 (print) | LCCN 2021016939 (ebook) |
ISBN 9781625346032 (paperback) | ISBN 9781613768785 (ebook) | ISBN
9781613768792 (ebook)
Subjects: LCSH: Unitarian church buildings—United States. | Democracy and
architecture—United States. | Church architecture—Social aspects—United
States. | Architecture and society—United States. Classification: LCC NA4829.
U55 B67 2021 (print) | LCC NA4829.U55 (ebook) DDC 726.50973—dc23

LC record available at https://lccn.loc.gov/2021016938

LC ebook record available at https://lccn.loc.gov/2021016939

British Library Cataloguing-in-Publication Data
A catalog record for this book is available from the British Library.

To Leigh, Michael, and Daniel

CONTENTS

ACKNOWLEDGMENTS

Work on this project began to take shape through the process of visiting many churches and their archives. Although there are far too many to name, I am indebted to the friendly staff members that allowed me to wander, to photograph, and to page through boxes and binders of material. I thank the archivists and congregational historians of Unitarian Universalist (UU) churches for their interest and care in preserving records of congregational life over time. Still others that I was not able to visit generously sent information when queried. The consistent attitude of openness, interest, and willingness to help gave me yet another reason to admire the UU ethos.

I thank Andrea Greenwood and Mark W. Harris, ministers of First Parish of Watertown, Massachusetts, at the time, and authors of a cornerstone book in my research, for meeting with me early in my adventure, and for Andrea's continued support. I was also graciously received by Jon Luopa, minister of University Unitarian Church in Seattle. They all shared their enthusiasm and joy in the places they had served.

A huge thanks for handling major production requirements for the illustrations goes to Joshua Polansky, director of the Visual Resources Center in the College of Built Environments at the University of Washington, and also to Alissa Tucker for expertly producing all of the necessary floorplans. Thanks are also due to the College of Built Environments for generous assistance with publication costs, including the 2020 Johnston-Hastings Endowment for Publication Support; and to a number of colleagues in the Department of Architecture who have given advice and inspiration when it was most needed. I am also grateful to Matt Becker and everyone else at UMass Press for finding merit in my project and for expert guidance.

I am most grateful to all family members and friends who have offered encouragement along the way, with a special mention of my daughter, Leigh, for sharing an interest in Unitarian communities.

AMERICAN
UNITARIAN
CHURCHES

INTRODUCTION

The idea of "architecture and democracy" or a distinctly "democratic architecture" is a persistent interest in American culture, yet it remains elusive. There is no simple or singular response to the question of how architecture can express or reflect democracy—democracy as a form of government, or democracy as an orientation or way of life. That is one reason the question continues to recur. The last decade has brought rapid change to the discipline and practice of architecture along with social challenges, many of which require forward thinking and the creation of new architectural possibilities. But rapid change also raises the need to revisit open questions with fresh perspective. Several scholars have recently raised anew the issue of democracy and architecture.[1] Their questions and observations combine to create a speculative realm offering multiple paths toward an understanding of the relationship between architecture and democracy.

The architecture of American Unitarian churches provides an opportunity to examine the relationship between a fiercely democratic community and its spatial expression. Unitarian churches have demonstrated a striking degree of architectural innovation throughout the nineteenth and twentieth centuries, accompanied by a pattern of critical self-reflection on community values. Consequently, their buildings both record and reflect significant sociopolitical change in America. Consistently careful attention to the design process has established a high degree of connection between stated intentions and built forms. From the beginning of the nineteenth century, Unitarians concerned themselves with the promotion of a distinctively American culture, and they put the democratic ideal foremost over any theological position. Furthermore, the Unitarian community mirrors the tension in American society between individualism and social cohesion. These characteristics suggest that Unitarian church architecture is particularly suitable as a source not only for understanding the relationship between a particular community and its spatial realm but for revealing the capacity of architecture to reflect changes in American democratic ideals.

WHAT IS AMERICAN UNITARIANISM?

Although varieties of Unitarianism existed in Eastern Europe and then England and Wales from the sixteenth century onward, historian Mark W. Harris states that "Unitarianism as it is known in North America is not a foreign import."[2] Today it is a liberal humanistic religion that embraces all forms of spiritual practice and compels individuals to determine their own spiritual beliefs. It is sometimes mistaken for a New Age movement. However, American Unitarianism stretches back to the Congregationalist descendants of the New England Puritans. Its roots can be traced to the social and religious changes in the American colonies of the mid-eighteenth century. But its coherent establishment came on the heels of the American Revolution, with the dates 1784, 1796, 1804, and 1819 marking several key moments in its evolution.[3] The origins of American Unitarianism coincided with the foundation of the United States as a democratic experiment, and its moral and ethical outlook was based on the same Enlightenment philosophies.

The Puritans, separatists from the Church of England, settled New England from 1620 to about 1640.[4] Population growth thereafter in the colonial era largely descended from this group. Their religious practice, Congregationalism, was a strict form of Calvinism. Throughout the seventeenth century they did not allow any newcomers with different religions to settle among them. In the eighteenth century, an internal rift arose between an evolving theology that was responsive to social and intellectual developments and a theology that adhered to the world-view of the original Puritan settlers. By the end of the century, this internal divergence of theologies, which had increased over several decades, became acute. In choosing ministers, congregations could either follow reform-minded Calvinists who believed that the salvation of individuals, born in sin, had already been determined by God, or instead welcome liberal ministers influenced by Enlightenment philosophies who replaced the idea of the depravity of humans with their dignity and free will. The liberal faction only took shape as a separate denomination, Unitarianism, in the 1820s, while the conservatives retained their identity as Congregationalists. By then, though, most New Englanders had chosen between these radically different beliefs.

In its formative stage, American Unitarianism had no identity, name, or agreed upon set of beliefs. The liberal ministers expressed a variety of views that did not follow any single doctrine—only its distinctions from Calvinist theology and embrace of Enlightenment philosophies on questions of human nature and intellect gave it some coherence. This liberal Congregationalist-turned-Unitarian ideology developed in the same milieu of Enlightenment philosophies of reason and humanism that informed the articulation of democratic principles against the authority of a monarch in the founding of the United States. The founders applied their convictions vocally in the civic realm, but that same philosophy caused them to uniformly reject conventional religious institutions and dogma. John Adams determined that the liberal Unitarian religion was a denomination based on his own views of reason and freedom. George Washington, Benjamin Franklin, James Madison, and Thomas Jefferson are usually described as deists or free-thinkers; none belonged to a church or claimed a particular affiliation, but their views had much in common with Adams and other Unitarians among the founders. In fact, though Jefferson did not identify with a religion, he explored Unitarian views in correspondence with Joseph Priestley. Jefferson found Unitarianism so consistent with the principles of the founding ideologies that he expected Unitarianism to become the dominant religion of this country. He stated late in life, "I trust there is not a young man now living in the United States who will not die a Unitarian."[5]

As it emerged as a distinct denomination, according to one leading religious historian, Unitarianism was not "just an eighteenth century religion of the Enlightenment carried forward. . . . Unitarians too had become Americans in the tumults of Revolution, political construction, and social reordering." Their debates eventually yielded a coherent statement of beliefs in a sermon by Boston minister and Harvard professor of divinity William Ellery Channing (1780–1842) in 1819. He provided a clear set of beliefs in his sermon "Unitarian Christianity," the central core of which was based on reason: the unity of God and his benevolence toward man, the superior humanity of Jesus, and the moral nature of human conscience. More commonly known as the "Baltimore Sermon," it is still appreciated today as a "masterpiece of rhetorical adaptation as well as religious exposition."[6] And though Unitarianism continued to be characterized by struggles, debates, and schisms, the core beliefs that held through to the end of the nineteenth century remained close to Channing's statement. One reason may be that the identity of Americans aligned with them so well. Historian Stow Persons believes that "the secret of Channing's success . . . lay in his capacity to appeal to the rising humanitarian spirit of democratic America. . . . The objectives of Channing's [Christian] revolution were also essential ideals of democracy."[7] And Channing's Baltimore Sermon remains the *de facto* founding statement of American Unitarian beliefs to this day.

Although Jefferson's prediction did not come true, Unitarian values and ideas have had a major role in shaping American culture through Unitarian intellectuals and artists. In the first half of the nineteenth century, Harvard College was primarily a theological institution, and it was dominantly Unitarian from 1804 onward. Harvard graduates claimed the Unitarian pulpits in the Boston area and throughout New England. As a group, under the influence of a shared education, they were disinclined to focus their Christian leadership on doctrinal debate.[8] They turned instead to the development of literary and artistic culture as a means to elevate New England social norms as well as further cultural independence from Britain in the postcolonial period. By founding and developing the Boston Athenæum and by eventually transforming Harvard University from a divinity school to a liberal arts university, they promoted intellectual culture in the new American society. Nineteenth-century Unitarians such as Ralph Waldo Emerson, Henry David Thoreau, Nathaniel Hawthorne, Henry Wadsworth Longfellow, and Herman Melville were central to the first expressions of the new national psyche. Of course, the country grew rapidly with the advent of the railroad, and Boston did not retain its premier cultural position for long. But Unitarians continued to promote the arts, education, and civic institutions as hallmarks of a democratic society. Art historian Sally Webster concludes from an analysis of the iconography of 1896 murals in the Library of Congress, a public institution dedicated to the provision of access to knowledge as essential to the advancement of democracy, that "Harvard/Unitarian ideals are literally embedded in the walls."[9]

While New England would remain the only region of the country with a large concentration of Unitarian congregations, new congregations continued to be established in major population centers during the westward expansion of the nineteenth century. And individual Unitarians were prominent in major cultural movements: transcendentalism, abolition, women's suffrage, public education, founding of colleges and universities, and the urban and social reforms of the Progressive Era. While Unitarians did spread throughout the country, the denomination did not match the growth of other Protestant denominations in the later nineteenth and twentieth centuries. After lengthy parallel development with many shared views and affinities, the Unitarians merged in 1961 with the Universalists, a similarly small denomination with origins in eighteenth-century colonial society. A succinct description of the merger in religious terms would be that the resultant Unitarian Universalist (UU) legacy was that it could offer "a sweeping answer to creeds that divide the human family, [since] Unitarianism proclaims that we spring from a common source; Universalism, that we share a common destiny."[10] In more practical terms, the number of churches rose from around six hundred to just over a thousand.[11] That number has remained fairly constant, while membership rose in the 1960s by about 15 percent. Membership subsequently declined in the late 1970s and only reached its 1961 level again in the mid-1990s, a level that has been more or less retained for the last twenty-five years. The denomination's more recent impact on American culture has been in the promotion of humanism and in social activism.

UNITARIAN CONTRIBUTION TO AMERICAN ARCHITECTURE

The cultural contribution of Unitarians can also be seen in the realm of architecture. In 1982, the *New York Times* architecture critic Paul Goldberger reflected on the difficulty of designing authentically spiritual space:

> For the struggle to express the inexpressible—to create what Le Corbusier called, in reference to his great chapel at Ronchamp, France, "ineffable space"—is one that has yielded few successful results in our time or in any other. The extraordinary balance between the rational and the irrational that characterizes Ronchamp, or Frank Lloyd Wright's Unity Temple in Oak Park, Ill., or Louis Kahn's Unitarian Church in Rochester, N.Y., or Bernard Maybeck's Christian Science Church in Berkeley, Calif., to name four of the greatest religious structures of this century, is not something that can be made by formula, and it is not something that can be dictated by style.[12]

Goldberger's short list of great modern religious space includes three American buildings, of which two are Unitarian churches and the third was designed by a Unitarian architect, Bernard Maybeck. Frank Lloyd Wright's Unity Temple in Oak Park, Illinois (1906), and Louis I. Kahn's First Unitarian Church of Rochester, New York (1959), attained the highest level of innovation and influence. While these two buildings have stimulated an impressive amount of architectural scholarship, relatively little of it has focused on the denominational characteristics in any great depth. The exceptions are Joseph Siry's *Unity Temple and the Architecture of a Liberal Religion*, and the chapter on the First Unitarian Church of Rochester in Sarah Williams Goldhagen's *Louis Kahn's Situated Modernism*.[13] Some of the more cursory commentary suggests that Unity Temple became an archetype for subsequent Unitarian church design. And some count among Kahn's innovations at Rochester his rejection of Unity Temple as a model. However, a full survey of Unitarian architecture does not support these conclusions. Vincent Scully, the Yale University architectural historian who wrote about the church in Rochester before it was even completed, avoids a formal connection and proposes instead that the Wright and Kahn designs each touch something elemental about architecture itself.[14]

The only other existing literature that attempts a denomination-based view of American Unitarian church designs are chapters within larger studies.[15] The book *Modern Church Architecture: A Guide to the Form and Spirit of 20th Century Religious Buildings* by Albert Christ-Janer and Mary Mix Foley presents denomination-based interpretations of a substantial number of modern designs.[16] It is divided between Catholic and Protestant examples, and the Protestant section is further subdivided by denominations, including Unitarian. However, only two examples are featured. A chapter in Andrea Greenwood and Mark W. Harris's *An Introduction to the Unitarian and Universalist Traditions* is devoted to architecture, art, and music. They suggest that a strong visual and spatial tradition exists, but there are no illustrations. Their treatment of church form from the New England meetinghouse to the designs of Frank Lloyd Wright and a contemporary of his, Boston architect Edwin J. Lewis Jr., focuses on the mainstream stylistic movements and the social ideas that fueled deviation from them. Most importantly, Greenwood and Harris highlight the potential for architecture to make an internal Unitarian tension between "the elite and the folk" elements visible.[17]

While a denominationally based study might be expected to reveal a formal tradition, no single element or typology emerges as a key to Unitarian architectural expression. For the most part, variety and innovation have been highly valued. But an even more significant factor that has denied the development of a spatial typology or paradigm is a pattern of congregational renewal and reinvention. Many congregations trace lengthy histories by means of their successive buildings, and these reveal a strong tendency of a progressive religious community to always look forward rather than backward. There is a strong desire expressed for each new structure to be up-to-date with its time and place.

A dramatic example can be seen in the case of First Church in Boston. First Church was the covenant of the community of religious dissenters led by John Winthrop from Boston, Lincolnshire, England, that settled on the Shawmut Peninsula in 1630.[18] They built their first meetinghouse in 1632 on a site that later became State Street—there is still a sign in a commercial doorway that marks the spot. The congregation moved to a second structure on Cornhill (later Washington Street) in 1639. When it burned down in 1711, they replaced it with a third, larger meetinghouse of brick that was used for nearly one hundred years. A fourth building was constructed on Chauncy Street in 1807 in a Federal style because the Washington Street location had become a busy commercial area. Sixty years later the congregation decided to further escape downtown congestion; they built their fifth home in the newly reclaimed area of the Back Bay.

This was an up-to-date Gothic Revival church designed by Henry Van Brunt whose tower still stands at the corner of Marlborough and Berkeley Streets (fig. 2.3). Along Berkeley Street, there is an arcaded porch with a rose window above. On the Marlborough Street side, however, a modern concrete and glass structure is tucked behind the tower (fig. 6.1). The Gothic Revival building was a hundred years old when it was destroyed by fire in 1969 and the congregation chose Paul Rudolph to design its replacement. Its concave geometry surrounds a small sunken court, providing a moment of urban repose in the busy Back Bay and a reminder of the colonial commons. These disparate elements, the Gothic facade and the modern structure behind it, are still the home of First Church. The sequence of buildings is memorialized by a plaque in the Gothic arcade; it tells a story of one congregation that is also true of their denomination. While embracing progressive change in theology, worship, and architecture, the community has maintained continuity for over four centuries.

A primary aim of this book is to expose a culture of architectural excellence in what is generally perceived as a marginal movement in American religion. Most architects are aware of Unitarianism because of Wright's and Kahn's iconic designs. However, few architects know that they were preceded by leading designers of the nineteenth century, including Charles Bulfinch, Robert Mills, Frank Furness, and H. H. Richardson. Into the twentieth century, Bernard Maybeck, Pietro Belluschi, Edward Durrell Stone, Joseph Esherick, and Victor Lundy were also among those commissioned. If Unitarians were a large and wealthy denomination, this might not be particularly remarkable. However, Unitarians remained a small denomination, suggesting a kind of architectural activism with cultural impact.

Another important goal is to understand how the beliefs and cultures of Unitarian congregations seem to have prompted notable creativity and innovation in their buildings. Although the stories of the Wright and Kahn buildings have been well told, and formal aspects of the designs have been compared, similarities in the relationships to their clients during the design process have not been examined. These and several other projects show a high degree of sympathy between the architect and the congregation, and that designs for Unitarian churches are often important milestones within the architect's oeuvre. Unitarian beliefs have evolved continuously for two centuries; the architecture of each era is framed within major shifts in theology. Just as Unitarians were consistently progressive in their view of the world, they also continuously adopted change in architectural expression. The book traces these parallel evolutions.

A central question the book confronts is the basis of design for American Unitarian churches in the twentieth century. Church design is generally an area where historical precedent sets a lot of design parameters. And when that is not the case, the ritual practices, beliefs, and need for specific symbolic expression can guide architectural design. Twentieth-century Unitarians have generally allowed for free forms of worship, so what is the basis of church design for a religion without liturgy or creed? This book demonstrates that the architecture of a church for an "ethical religion" is allied with secular civic institutions but is more optimistic and aspirational in expressing core American values and ideals.[19] American Unitarian churches express their faith in freedom and democracy.

This study situates architectural production in the context of American Unitarian ideas and beliefs as they have evolved from William Ellery Channing's 1819 Baltimore Sermon, the first defining statement of Unitarian beliefs. As faith in a deity faded in the twentieth century, modern Unitarians focused on the values of democracy and individual freedom that were central to Unitarianism and to American culture at large from their shared beginnings in late colonial and early republican times. Ultimately, this book shows that Unitarian history, rather than marginal, is in fact woven into American history, and that the architecture of their churches is an architecture of democracy.

As Stow Persons, scholar of American intellectual history, explains, it is denominationalism that makes American religion democratic.[20] Inherent features such as choice and toleration replaced earlier views that social stability required a homogeneous faith community. Although this belief was already in decline at the time of the American Revolution, it was the Unitarian split from conservative Congregationalists in the decades that followed which ultimately deprived local governments of their right to tax all townspeople for Congregationalists' benefit. As Unitarianism evolved throughout the nineteenth century, it became "a faith prepared to spiritualize the secular, and to consecrate the common life, unhampered by authoritarian ideal or other-worldly considerations," and it was therefore an "authentic religion for democracy."[21]

NOTES ON NAMES AND TERMS

This study is focused on the Unitarian story in America, which means essentially from 1800 forward, when Unitarianism was defined and gained institutional presence. However, the book starts with the colonial period in order to fill in the background and to establish some limits to the relevance of the colonial meetinghouse on later churches. The narrative travels forward to about 1970, when just over two decades of major postwar church construction were completed. Since the 1961 merger of Unitarians and Universalists occurred so close to the end of my study period, I refer to the denomination as Unitarian rather than Unitarian Universalist, or UU, throughout. Most Unitarian congregations subsequently changed their names, adding "Universalist," and many congregations have had internally driven name changes over time as well. I have generally used the names of churches at the time of their construction, or else the longest-standing name in documents.

Studies of religious architecture inevitably confront problems of vocabulary—terms that are used differently by sources and terms that shift their meanings over time. A general readership might identify the terms "meetinghouse," "church," and "temple" with specific religious traditions—Quaker, Christian, and Jewish in contemporary America. Architects tend to identify these terms with certain physical forms or spatial qualities. But from a religious perspective, it is helpful to remember a simple distinction: whether a particular building is fundamentally understood as a "house of god," or *domus dei*, or a "house of god's people," or *domus ecclesiae*. Historically in the Jewish and Christian traditions, a temple was the former and a church or synagogue was the latter. They were meeting houses, buildings in which to meet for communal worship. However, over time, the Christian church, whose sole use was for religious practice, took on the aura of the holy; it is often referred to as "God's house." The fluidity of these terms should make us skeptical of interpreting statements about architectural intentions that may reference both "church" and "temple" freely.

The term "meetinghouse" can be similarly confusing rather than clarifying. The meetinghouse had two purposes for the dissenting Protestants that first used it in North American settlements. One was to reestablish the true nature of the church, a reminder that no god dwelled there in their belief system, and to highlight its plainness. The other was to convey the fact that a single building was erected for all public gatherings, both civil and religious. As is shown here, there were a variety of architectural forms for the New England meetinghouse, and a few Unitarian congregations today still call their buildings a meetinghouse, though their forms are even more different than those of earlier centuries. However, architectural use of the term usually refers to one thing—the earliest forms of the colonial meetinghouse. For architects, the word infers a shape and probably also a seating arrangement within the spatial volume. These different contextual meanings are often unknown and can lead to confusion.

Another vocabulary problem that arises related to the distinction between *domus dei* and *domus ecclesiae* is the name of the space in which the congregation gathers for worship. Within that understanding, it would be a "sanctuary" in a *domus dei*, an "auditorium" in a *domus ecclesiae*. However, these terms are both used by various Unitarian congregations, and architects may use them interchangeably. Some congregations in the twentieth century wanted a place of worship that was spiritually evocative; for these the term "sanctuary" seems appropriate. Others wanted rooms that would be comfortable for a variety of uses that might not be spiritual in nature, so these seem best described as auditoria. I have used whatever term is on the published plans or in congregational descriptions when these are available.

Finally, there are a number of different words used for the other major space in the Unitarian churches studied, the social hall. That term sometimes alternates with "fellowship hall" and occasionally "multipurpose room." These are the best words for the larger social rooms of the twentieth century, ones roughly equivalent to the space for worship in which community meals could be served. Smaller social spaces might be called "parlor," "lounge," or "living room"—they would have comfortable seating and usually a fireplace.

INQUIRY: THE NATURE OF THE AMERICAN UNITARIAN CHURCH

This book is divided chronologically between the nineteenth and twentieth centuries, roughly speaking. The first part consists of three chapters tracing nineteenth-century developments of Unitarian identity and cultural leadership as integral to the socioeconomic development of the United States and its continuous westward expansion. Unitarians were central to major movements in American culture on the whole, and congregations were founded in most major cities across the continent. The second part is mainly focused on a resurgence of Unitarian cultural vitality in the post–World War II decades after a period of semi-decline and war. By this time, Unitarians no longer had the same sort of cultural influence in a far more complex American society. But the same progressive spirit continued to drive their own values and beliefs, as well as their architectural intentions.

Chapter 1 reviews the varieties of meetinghouses of the colonial and early American periods and situates two that have become iconic (one for architectural reasons and one for historic and patriotic associations). There have been a number of excellent architectural histories of the meetinghouse, so this does not repeat that literature. It does draw inspiration from the most recent one by Peter Benes, who refutes the oversimplified myths of New England meetinghouses in sociological and experiential terms.[22] This chapter questions the narrow architectural understanding of the meetinghouse, and a tendency in the interpretation of modern Unitarian churches to automatically invoke "the meetinghouse."

The next chapter traces the cultural history of Unitarianism in America in the nineteenth century, when it was more central to American culture as a whole. Architecturally, Unitarians were in step with other Protestant denominations and readily took advantage of developments of nineteenth-century architecture as it was reaching its first maturity. Of particular interest is the connection between both of the first two architects credited with an original American style and Unitarianism. Chapter 3 focuses on more marginal but extremely significant developments in later nineteenth-century Unitarian church architecture: social progressives in the Midwest, including women ministers, women architects, and the beginnings of a new sensibility in the cultural outpost of San Francisco. These were various threads of resistance to standard church design. The chapter ends with the icon of Unitarian antichurch, Wright's Unity Temple in Oak Park, in order to frame that well-known building in a new light.

Chapter 4 initially describes the main developments in the Unitarian denomination in the first half of the twentieth century and the more conservative approach to church architecture that took hold. It then proceeds to the post–World War II era when new church construction was booming. This chapter focuses on the variety of site conditions that the expanding American cities offered, and the response of church form and character to its context. Chapter 5 narrows to an interior focus on the same churches to examine, first and foremost, the ways that the sanctuary design achieved provision of a spiritual space for a religion without creed or liturgy. It also looks at the sanctuary as part of a larger social organism, how the whole building is experienced, and what it expresses.

The final chapter considers the process that congregations undertook with their architects to achieve a building that expressed their values and beliefs. It looks in detail at some of the ways a congregation understands its individual identity within the scope of Unitarian history. Using the related concepts of humanism and democracy as ways of understanding individuals and communities, the chapter proposes that a spirit of creative imagination based in a culture of literacy and the collective will to always look forward rather than back animates the architecture of Unitarianism.

PART I

UNITARIANISM AT THE CENTER

FIGURE 1.1. First Church, Peterborough, New Hampshire, 1825, an example of the third type of New England meeting-house, centrally located on the commons. Photograph by author.

CHAPTER ONE

The Myth of the Meetinghouse

The mind does not receive everything from abroad. Its great ideas arise from itself, and by those native lights it reads and comprehends the volumes of nature and revelation. The elements of the idea of God we gather from ourselves. Power, wisdom, love, virtue, beauty, and happiness, words which contain all that is glorious in the universe and interesting in our existence, express attributes of the mind, and are understood by us only through consciousness.

—William Ellery Channing, "Discourses"

FROM MEETINGHOUSE TO CHURCH ON THE GREEN

The meetinghouse is widely recognized as the earliest architectural form for worship in colonial New England. It is readily accepted as the most authentic, or original, architectural expression of Protestant denominations that descended from the New England Puritans, the Congregational and American Unitarian traditions.[1] Numerous interpretations of twentieth-century Unitarian church designs suggest inspiration in the meetinghouse. However, the early meetinghouses of New England were not religious buildings in the usual sense—purpose-built for worship. Rather, they were a distinctive social institution from an era when church and state were integrated. The meetinghouse of the Puritans was a place of assembly for both civic and religious functions. It was initially the only public building in each village, and it was paid for by taxes required of all households, as was the salary of the minister. In the seventeenth century, attendance at town meetings and religious services was mandatory for all townspeople. The functions of the meetinghouse varied throughout the week and were signaled by different flags, drumbeats, or bell peals. Most importantly, it was never considered by its users to be a "sacred" or holy space in the manner of a church.[2] The community of members were the church, and the meetinghouse was merely a building for assembly. It was a fixture in New England villages, towns, and cities from 1630 until about 1830, and across that time frame it had at least three distinct architectural forms.[3]

In architectural terms, mention of the "Puritan" meetinghouse generally refers to its earliest form, a relatively compact two-story rectangular, or sometimes square, space with a raised pulpit opposite the main entrance and a gallery wrapped around the other three sides. The exterior form is closely associated with domestic architecture of the time, a simple rectangular wood frame structure with windows evenly spaced in two ranks around the perimeter. The meetinghouse would stand out from neighboring houses by its slightly larger size, regularity of windows, rooftop cupola, and when possible, a favored location on a slightly elevated site.[4]

Any mention of the colonial meetinghouse in an architectural context inevitably points to the poetically named Old Ship in Hingham, Massachusetts, to illustrate its form (fig. 1.2). Old Ship is in remarkably good shape for a timber building dating from the seventeenth century, and it is still in use today.[5] Built in 1681, Old Ship's original dimensions were forty-five feet by fifty-five feet; it was enlarged twice in the eighteenth century, and the original benches were replaced by box pews. Its exterior walls rise two stories, and regularly spaced windows light the main floor and a gallery on three sides. A hipped roof rises to a central cupola. The main entry was moved to the center of the longer side in the first renovation, and the pulpit moved as well to face the entry across the short axis of the plan.[6] This arrangement is sometimes mistaken for a defining characteristic of the New England meetinghouse.

Old Ship is the only remaining example of the type of meetinghouse common from about 1630 to 1710. Evidence of numerous similar seventeenth-century structures survives only in the form of drawings. Starting in the early 1700s, they were gradually replaced by a new style that was more elongated in its plan proportions and was spanned by a simple double-pitched roof rather than a hipped form. The change was likely due to the need for a larger space and the ease of framing a roof over the resultant rectangular area. The main entry was always on the long side, sometimes placed in a protruding vestibule, but there were often multiple doors. If there was a bell tower attached, it would be usually appended on one end. The interior arrangement remained unchanged, but its character was slightly more

FIGURE 1.2a. Old Ship Meetinghouse, Hingham, Massachusetts, 1681, exterior view. Photograph by author.

FIGURE 1.2b. Old Ship Meetinghouse, interior view. Photograph by author.

refined. Among the many examples from this era remaining intact, Rocky Hill in Amesbury, Massachusetts, is representative. The main door enters a protruding square vestibule with stairs to the gallery, but there is no bell tower.

Perhaps the most significant change in colonial meetinghouse form from an architectural point of view was the migration of the cupola for the bell from the roof to an independent tower when the double-pitched roof replaced the hipped roof. An end tower accentuates the directionality of the new roof type and made the Congregational meetinghouse much closer in appearance to Anglican churches, which had begun to appear in Boston to serve representatives of the British government in the colonies. In these, the entry was prominently located in the protruding tower on the gable end of the structure, and the interior space was organized by the long axis of the roof. Among them, the famous Old North Church in Boston provides a well-preserved example.

The last phase of meetinghouses built by the descendants of the Puritans occurred between 1790 and 1830.[7] The meetinghouse underwent a final and more radical architectural change while in social terms it continued to function for both civic and religious assembly. It was transformed from a laterally oriented space into a longitudinally oriented one, a difference that architecturally aligned the meetinghouse with the formal arrangement of a church. The change began with a rearrangement of interior elements in some of those meetinghouses having a square bell tower on their short ends. This was adapted to become the main entry, and the interior arrangement of galleries, pulpit, and seating was rotated to the longitudinal axis, bringing interior and exterior into better correspondence. Once this arrangement became common, most new construction was designed in this way as well.

There were numerous factors that contributed to the adoption of a more church-like form by the congregations whose origins and traditions were separatist. Among them, the increased presence of Anglican churches and other denominations in New England presented an aesthetic challenge to meetinghouse builders. It was increasingly important to forsake their residential character for greater presence and distinction.[8] By the time of the American Revolution, some of the harshness of early colonial life had eased, and cultural expression was richer.[9] A wider mix of society was emigrating from northern Europe, and some American-born colonists traveled to England or Europe. Along with increased wealth and leisure, tastes became more sophisticated. As new meetinghouses were built with the longitudinal arrangement, a wider phenomenon of bringing more refinement to all new buildings was underway. The meetinghouses of both factions of Congregationalists forsook their extreme architectural simplicity, adopting modest classical motifs. At the same time, some bell towers acquired a spire over the cupola.

Charles Bulfinch (1763–1844), a self-educated gentleman-architect and a Unitarian, was beginning his practice in Boston at the time that interest in classical refinement was growing. After obtaining two degrees at Harvard, he traveled to England and France, arriving back in 1787. His first church design, the Hollis Street Church in Boston, showed his ability with the neoclassical forms he had studied abroad: he successfully combined a pedimented portico with flanking towers without following any specific model (fig. 1.3a). Its classical monumentality was of a new order for Boston. While this design received favorable attention at the time, another that he undertook shortly afterward for Pittsfield, Massachusetts (1789), would have more importance in the long run, for it was the first manifestation of a new paradigm.[10] Neither this building nor the next that he built in Taunton, Massachusetts, soon after has survived. However, a close copy by others built in Salisbury, Connecticut, in 1800 is still in use (fig. 1.3b). Unlike the Hollis Street Church, this design had clear continuity with the meetinghouse tradition but achieved new architectural expression as a church. Instead of a door simply placed in a square bell tower, the entrance was articulated as a gabled building block roughly half the width of the church and not quite as tall. The square base of the tower was mounted above it but set back from the face to straddle the joint between the main body of the church and the entry bay. The nested gable ends of the two rectangular masses were completed in a way that suggested pediments. Other classical allusions included quoining at the corners, a classical frame for the door, and a Palladian window above it. The influence of Christopher Wren, James Gibbs, and their followers in London is unmistakable, but the composition was novel for an American meetinghouse.

Bulfinch's synthesis of the major elements in Pittsfield was repeated, with different degrees of variation, in many New England towns over two decades. The influence of his meetinghouse-turned-church form with classical elements was multiplied by Asher Benjamin (1773–1845). Benjamin's widely consulted pattern book *The Country Builder's Assistant* of 1797 included a design for a church that was quite close to Bulfinch's design for Taunton. Similar designs were executed by Benjamin himself in towns in Massachusetts, New Hampshire, and Vermont. Other builders, such as Lavius Fillmore, Ithiel Town, David Hoadley, and Isaac

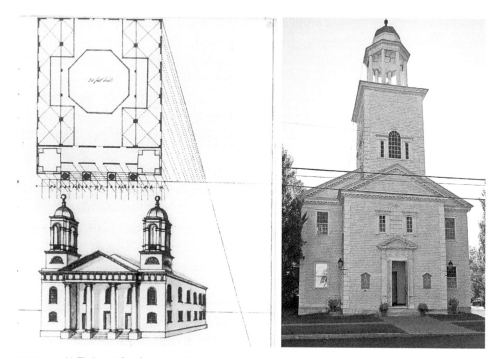

FIGURE 1.3a. Hollis Street Church, Boston, Massachusetts, plan and perspective by Charles Bulfinch, 1787. Library of Congress, Prints & Photographs Division, www.loc.gov/item/97504949/.

FIGURE 1.3b. Congregational Church, Salisbury, Connecticut, 1800. Photograph by author.

Damon contributed to populating New England with a large number of white steepled churches exhibiting rich variety and yet, nonetheless, clearly adhering to a single model. To give a sense of the impact, around 250 towns had a church of this description either through renovation or new construction; some were later updated but many remain in their original form.

The general adoption of the new pediment-and-steeple form occurred simultaneously with the gradual division of Congregationalism and the establishment of Unitarianism as a separate denomination.[11] There was no single breaking point, but congregations individually came to the conclusion in the decades following the Revolution that their differences were too great to go on worshipping together; minority factions had to leave and build a new church. The more conservative faction retained the Congregational identity and sought to reform it to former moral standards while liberals succeeded in articulating their ideas and a distinct religious identity. This was also concurrent with the gradual disestablishment of Congregationalism as a state-sponsored religion in New England states, although the last to do so was Massachusetts, which held out until 1833.

This new meetinghouse form became, for a short time, the dominant image of an "American" church—the steepled and pedimented white church on the town common or village green. John Stilgoe concluded that the town as a community—a social and spatial structure—was still focused in the early nineteenth century on divinity, which in turn was most clearly symbolized by the central meetinghouse.[12] However, Benes finds that our grander idea of the meetinghouse as a "symbol of permanence, stability, democracy, and . . . an orderly network of 'primitive' Christian communities" was a result of myth-making by parish and town historians in the later nineteenth century.[13] Through them, the meetinghouse bell and its spire came to represent an era of community stability, central to democratic village social structures that were unified geographically by the sound of the bell. Although these simplistic notions of the New England meetinghouse have been challenged by more detailed studies of their social and physical complexity, the ubiquitous physical presence of the crisply defined architectural elements—porch or narthex, belfry and spire, rectangular body—continues to evoke an imaginary ideal.

EARLY AMERICAN UNITARIAN CHURCHES IN OTHER CONTEXTS

The New England meetinghouse was the main architectural expression integral to the emergence of Harvard-centered American Unitarianism, and the meetinghouse reached its final form just as Unitarianism itself reached its clear definition. This happened also to be the moment when professional architects were having their first presence and impact in American culture. The iconic form of the New England church is equally attributable to two figures who were not professionally trained, Charles Bulfinch and Asher Benjamin, but who were able to establish themselves as professionals. Bulfinch was a Harvard graduate; though self-taught in architectural design, he benefited from direct study of English and French neoclassicism. Benjamin began as a craftsman—an American Palladio—but eventually surpassed the knowledge and skill of a master craftsman. They each achieved professionalism through the design of successful, innovative, and influential buildings, and in the case of Benjamin, through teaching and publishing.

The emergence of professionals in the post-revolutionary period—both native and immigrant—meant that church form would no longer be necessarily limited to the continuities of builder and craftsman knowledge transmission and tradition.

Although Bulfinch's designs for Pittsfield and Taunton played an important role in the development of the typical New England church, none of the five churches he built in Boston adhered to the type. Of these, two are noteworthy in terms of Unitarian church form. Hollis Street Church (1787) and the New South Church (1814) had quite different exterior forms and expressions but shared important interior spatial qualities. Hollis Street was an early example of a full Doric portico, with a deep porch under its roof. Almost as tall as the body of the church behind it, the portico was flanked by two towers that masked the joint between the porch and the wider church. At New South, the portico was more three-dimensional—it projected from one side of an elongated octagonal plan. Under its pitched roof, an open columnar porch preceded a vestibule that was surmounted by an attic story and a tower inspired by London's St. Martin in the Field. According to architectural historian Harold Kirker, it was Bulfinch's most admired church design.[14]

The church interiors were somewhat similar but unlike any other Unitarian churches at the time. Both had elements that implied a Greek cross within the regular geometry of the exterior walls, clearly inspired by Wren's St. Stephen Walbrook. In the case of Hollis Street, the church plan was a square measuring sixty feet on each side. Galleries along each side were supported by small Doric columns, while the ceiling was supported on four taller Ionic columns. An almost forty-foot diameter dome on an octagonal drum was also supported by a series of vaults defining the arms of the cross. At New South Church, a Greek cross fit more readily into the octagonal geometry. Unfortunately, the central circle of the ceiling was flattened due to a concern for acoustics on the part of the minister. It is not clear if Bulfinch thought that the centralized geometry had some particular qualities or meaning that made it suitable for these Unitarian congregations, or if he was merely following Wren's experimentation and willful variety in the late seventeenth-century churches of London. He might have seen the use of octagonal geometries in some English Unitarian chapels but seems to have been more guided by the mastery of Wren.[15]

Bulfinch returned to the third meetinghouse typology for his last two church designs, one in Lancaster, Massachusetts (1816), and one in Washington, DC (1821). In both, he used an attic story to make the joint between the lower entrance portico and the main church mass. Lancaster was relatively unusual for its masonry, rather than frame, construction. But to some extent, it was a further refinement of the motifs of New South in Boston. In this case, the four pilasters of the portico frame three plain arches leading to an open porch, and the belfry was simplified as a set of stacked units rather than a continuous vertical element. Its complexity arose from the integration of the porch and tower with a rectangular church with a double pitched roof. When Bulfinch moved to Washington to become the architect of the U.S. Capitol in 1818, he joined with several other New England Unitarians to found a church of their own.[16] They acquired a lot at the corner of Sixth and D Streets, NW, and Bulfinch provided the design for a church somewhat similar to that for Lancaster. It became the home of Washington Unitarians up to the Civil War.

Unitarianism in Philadelphia had another provenance altogether. Joseph Priestley, scientist and British Unitarian theologian, first settled in Philadelphia when he fled persecution in England in 1794. He founded the First Unitarian congregation there in 1796—before American Unitarianism had achieved its full identity in New England.[17] (First Unitarian would eventually assimilate when Harvard-trained William Henry Furness took the pulpit in 1825.) The congregation continued to grow even after Priestley had moved on, and they were ready to build their first church in 1812. Robert Mills (1781–1855) was engaged in building a Baptist church on Samson Street at the time, and the congregation hired him to design theirs for a site on the corner of Tenth and Locust.[18] His design for the Unitarians was octagonal, perhaps based on what Priestley had said of English Unitarian meetinghouses. Or Mills may have proposed it due to the success of his circular Baptist church design, especially in terms of acoustics. The only extant Mills drawing of an octagonal church was made over ten years later but is believed to have represented his Unitarian church design (fig. 1.4a). The octagon was approximately seventy feet in diameter and topped by a saucer-shaped dome; rectangular bays extended outward on the four cardinal points with one of them providing the entry. Unfortunately, this building was outgrown within ten years of its construction, and William Strickland (1788–1854) was commissioned for a replacement.[19] Strickland's building was demolished in 1885; the few remaining images show an exterior that was quite severe: a Doric porch fronted a plain rectangular block (fig. 1.4b). Most unusually, there were no windows on the main facade, and a single entry door was the only opening in the long wall. The shorter sides had two stories of evenly spaced windows. It is easy to imagine a meetinghouse arrangement of galleries on the interior, but it seems incongruous with the

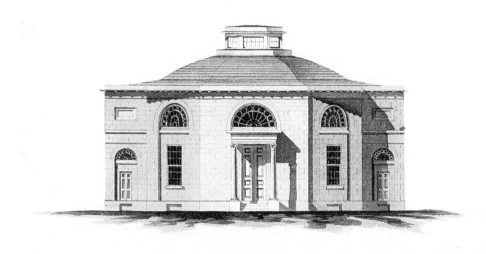

FIGURE 1.4a. First Unitarian Church, Philadelphia, Robert Mills, 1812. This Mills drawing is believed to be the design of the congregation's first building. Robert Mills Papers (1135.00), South Carolina Historical Society, Columbus.

FIGURE 1.4b. First Unitarian Church, Philadelphia, William Strickland, 1827. This is the congregation's second building. From *Views in Philadelphia and Its Vicinity—Engraved from Original Drawings* (1827), Flickr's The Commons.

time. It may be that the congregation or Strickland himself was conforming to a Quaker context.

In Baltimore, a more monumental centralized scheme than the Mills design was built by the first Unitarian congregation there. Transplanted New Englanders started this congregation, but they were not the mainstream. They came from the King's Chapel congregation, a singular instance of Boston Unitarianism formed from an Anglican congregation and more aligned with the philosophies of Joseph Priestley than the Harvard theologians. Soon after the Baltimore congregation was established in early 1817, they commissioned Maximilian Godefroy (1765–c. 1838) to design their church. Although his name is less well-known now, Godefroy was a professionally trained architect with several important commissions to his credit and a reputation equivalent to his contemporaries Mills and Benjamin Henry Latrobe.[20] He had come to the United States in 1805 as an exile from the French Revolution and been drawn to Baltimore by other exiles who founded a Catholic seminary there. His design for the Unitarian congregation was a skillful interpretation of the Pantheon in the manner of French neoclassicism but also showed the influence of Latrobe's Baltimore cathedral nearing completion just around the corner.[21] A simple cubic mass intersects with a lower pedimented Tuscan portico; the pediment projects very slightly, while the deep recess of the loggia is carved into the block (fig. 1.5a). There are three doors into the auditorium, a Greek cross form with shallow arms. A National Register of Historic Places nomination report describes it as "a supremely rational building which is essentially a hemisphere set on a cube."[22] The central space was completed by a dome with a diameter of 53.5 feet. The dome, later hidden by the insertion of a barrel vault, is not quite hemispherical, springing from 49 feet to an apex at 80 feet, but its coffers link it to the Pantheon ideal (fig. 1.5b). While the style is austere, there are a number of figural elements, including a sculpted "Angel of Truth" in the pediment. The architect cited several sources from Renaissance Rome for various features, drawn by him from a 1798 publication by Charles Percier and Pierre François Léonard Fontaine.[23] Historian Robert Alexander traces a variety of influences in this design but concludes that Godefroy's synthesis and integration of the "Renaissance ordonnance of piers, arches, pendentives, and dome" made this design his masterpiece.[24]

Other early congregations outside of New England included Richmond, Virginia; Charleston, South Carolina; Savannah, Georgia; and New Orleans. In the case of Richmond, a small and plain wood-frame church was built in 1833, in use up to its abandonment in the first year of the Civil War. The Charleston

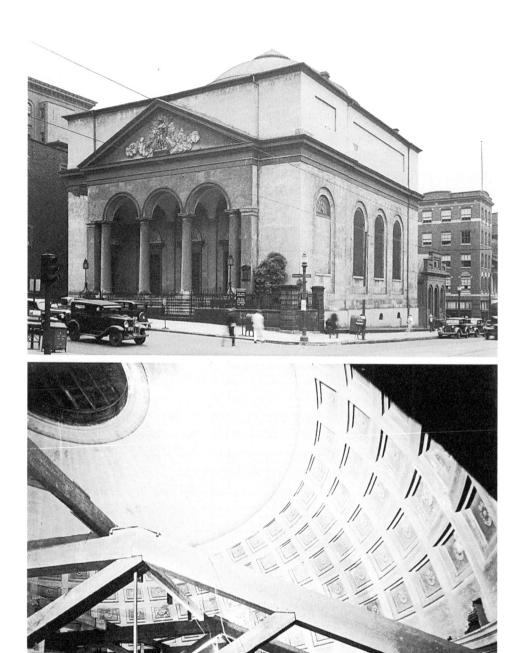

FIGURE 1.5a. First Unitarian (Independent) Church, Baltimore, Maximillian Godefroy. Library of Congress, Prints & Photographs Division, Historic American Building Survey, HABS MD, 4–BALT, 58–1.

FIGURE 1.5b. First Unitarian Church, interior view showing the original dome above a suspended plaster barrel vault constructed in 1893 to improve acoustics. Library of Congress, Prints & Photographs Division, Historic American Building Survey, HABS MD, 4–BALT, 58–4.

congregation had several identities and locations before formal identification as Unitarian in 1832.[25] For a time, it had two church buildings, one of which was the Robert Mills–designed Circular Church. However, it finally settled into its Archdale Street church, a building of the 1790s that was subsequently enlarged and renovated in 1854. Congregation member and architect Samuel Lee produced an English Gothic design that was left undamaged by the Civil War. However, only extensive restoration, necessitated by natural disasters in the later nineteenth century, has preserved its unique place in Charleston and in American Unitarian architecture.[26]

CONCLUSION: SIGNIFICANCE OF UNITARIANISM IN EARLY AMERICAN CHRISTIANITY

Interpretations of twentieth-century Unitarian church designs often refer to the meetinghouse as a possible, or likely, source of inspiration. This idea implies a natural inclination to reference an original or authentic architectural form that was singular to Puritans and, in slightly different form, Quakers. However, the question of an "original" or earliest architectural expression of American Unitarianism is not that simple. It is true that the Puritan meetinghouse of the iconic Old Ship variety was an antecedent to the dominant form of church when Unitarianism emerged from Congregationalism's controversies. The fact that Old Ship has been in continuous use since the seventeenth century, and still serving a Unitarian congregation, creates a reasonable notion that this building provides an archetype for American Unitarian church architecture. However, the congregation that built it was Puritan, not Unitarian. Historian Marian C. Donnelly reminds us that "the Puritan contribution to western architecture was not so much in ornament or the lack of it as in a building concept suited to the needs and purposes of the New England theocracy."[27] Their descendants created Unitarian Christianity in a post-revolutionary democracy, the period when New England was finally moving toward full separation of church and state through disestablishment of religion, and when congregations had to choose between conservative and liberal factions of Congregational Christianity. Architects today maintaining a nostalgia for a form of meetinghouse that only lasted for about the first fifty years of colonial settlement are not likely to be thinking of the Salem witch trials, but they should be.

Another iconic image from New England, the Federal style (or third style) meetinghouse, has also sometimes been taken to be the historically authentic architectural form of American Unitarian churches. Initially, it still functioned as a meetinghouse by serving both civic and religious functions, but the formal elements were church-like. This third style was the most prevalent form in the decades in which Unitarians established their fully independent identity. There were numerous factors that contributed to the adoption of a more church-like form by the congregations whose origin and tradition were separatist. Generally, it was increasingly important to forsake their residential character for greater presence and distinction.[28] From a visual standpoint, the third style meetinghouse remains a dominant image throughout the towns of New England; a slightly more monumental version was revived in the twentieth century.

More importantly, this potent architectural image surpasses its historical connections with the post-revolutionary New England Congregationalist culture and the emergence of Unitarianism. Despite clear derivation from British models, it became generalized as a symbol of American culture. The Unitarian meetinghouse of Groton, Massachusetts, was featured on the November 1942 cover of *Life* magazine as an "icon of American democracy" (fig. 1.6).[29] While the popular press mistakenly associated its architecture with "the Puritan Spirit," they used it to communicate to a broad spectrum of Americans a foundational ethos of individualism, bravery, and freedom. The Thanksgiving issue was closing out the first year of war, so it was intended to heighten moral courage and recall Yankee perseverance as a national source of pride and resolve. While their cover image was not, in fact, a Puritan meetinghouse, it served a purpose of tying a generalized idea of shared national religious (Protestant Christian) faith to the roots of the American spirit. They used the white-steepled Unitarian church on the green to symbolize something essential about the founding of this country and its democratic idealism.

The Groton church in the cover photo was the final church-like form of a two-hundred-year-old meetinghouse.[30] Its antecedent had been built in 1714 and enlarged twice by 1730. A second meetinghouse replaced it on the same site in 1755; this structure needed extensive rebuilding after a fire in 1794. It was another forty years, however, before the building acquired its iconic appearance. In 1839, the building was turned on its site and the shorter side became the main facade. A floor was added so that the continued use as a town hall could be separated from the worship space in the upper half. It maintained this dual purpose until a new town hall was built in 1859. The Unitarian congregation (now Unitarian Universalist) still gathers and worships in this building that was cast by *Life* as an inspirational symbol of America's fundamental spirit.

FIGURE 1.6. First Parish Church, Groton, Massachusetts, 1755. The current appearance is a result of renovations in 1839. Photograph by John Phelan, CC BY 3.0, https://creativecommons.org/licenses/by/3.0/deed.en.

Other prominent church buildings from the early period of American Unitarianism included Peter Harrison's King's Chapel, Charles Bulfinch's Hollis Street Church and his New South Church in Boston, the octagonal First Unitarian Church by Robert Mills in Philadelphia, and the neoclassical First Unitarian Church in Baltimore by Maximilian Godefroy. Unitarian congregations were not subject to a denominational definition of the form of worship or unified symbolic systems, so there was no religious or cultural pressure to conform to a particular architectural idea. The apparent uniformity of the New England meetinghouse in the eighteenth and early nineteenth centuries was a result of a craft culture of building construction, resource and technology limitations, and economic and moral minimalism, rather than an imposed idea with particular meaning and fit for the whole denomination. A variety of forms in the first decades of the nineteenth century arose with the emergence of architectural professionals taking the place of master craftsmen.

It is interesting to note that the church in Baltimore was never adopted as a precedent by any later congregation for its church design—it has both cultural significance and architectural distinction to its credit. This was the church in which William Ellery Channing delivered his denominational-defining sermon "Unitarian Christianity" on the occasion of the ordination of Jared Sparks. Its original title is often forgotten, and it is widely referred to as the "Baltimore Sermon." Furthermore, this building was probably the best and most complete architectural analogue of the philosophical reasoning of the Enlightenment that drove the Unitarian movement. Scholar Robert Alexander credits Godefroy with a skilled synthesis of his different sources and considers the church design to be Godefroy's most mature work. It is a neoclassical rendition of the centralized cross-in-square form of Renaissance humanism; it expresses the rationalism of pure geometry and spare classical ornament, along with the nobility of ancient civilization, though the architect's intentions were indirect. The Pantheon was a widely used model for neoclassical design, but it was uniquely suited to use for a Unitarian church. Of course, the Roman dedication to all the gods was not resonant to early nineteenth-century Unitarians; they were still Christian. But within fifty to seventy years, Unitarians would be exploring world religions as valid forms of belief, and within one hundred years would welcome all beliefs. Even though the dome's echo of the Pantheon would not have carried the same degree of meaning to the Unitarianism of 1820 as it does today, its more fundamental symbolism of unity was certainly highly appropriate.[31]

The Federal style meetinghouses and neoclassical designs of Bulfinch, Mills, and Godefroy offered the rationality of geometries and classical systems of ornament, as well as their abstract relation to nature, symbolic of human intelligence. They are an architectural expression of Channing's clarity in the midst of theological debates: a single deity, moral in the making of humanity as free and good; Jesus, a human sent by God as an example to follow in order to achieve salvation; and love for God, for Christ, and for fellow people as a spiritual path available to all.[32] To the congregations that built them, they were all meetinghouses, and the difference marked the progress from colonial vernacular to a more sophisticated cultural context with a professional class that could build more formally articulated houses for worship.

The central role of Unitarianism in the early American religious landscape, and in American culture more generally, has been largely overlooked. The denomination was outpaced in growth by other Protestant denominations in the late nineteenth and twentieth centuries. Historian Howard Mumford Jones connects the importance of humanism in the founding ideology of the country to central Unitarian beliefs; in both contexts, "It implies that every human being by the mere fact of his existence has dignity, that this dignity begins at birth, that the possession of this dignity, even if dimly realized by the possessor, is, or ought to be, the continuum of his life, and that to strip him of this dignity is to degrade him in so outrageous a way that we call the degradation inhumane."[33] We take for granted this core idea of American government but need to understand that of Christians, Unitarians alone prioritized this value over scripture. In the eighteenth century, the main argument for the dignity of humans was the capacity for reason. After the Revolution, it was more fully developed as free will and self-determination, the belief in "a sublime human potential." Noting that the Unitarian adoption of "commonsense republicanism" was eventually embraced by more orthodox Protestant denominations, Mark A. Noll observes that it was attributed to Unitarians because they "were also successful at maintaining themselves as the elite bearers of reason, good taste, benevolence, and refined sensibility in Boston, the center of New England's learned culture, they enjoyed an intellectual influence far out of proportion to their actual numbers."[34] If all of American Protestantism was in some degree influenced by the Revolution and the founding of American democracy, the adoption was most complete and most clearly expressed by Unitarians. And this, more than the "Puritan spirit" cited by the editors of *Life*, is what made their choice apt.

FIGURE 2.1. First Unitarian Church, Philadelphia, Frank Furness, 1883, interior view showing the rich Victorian color scheme. Photograph by author.

CHAPTER TWO

Originality, Not Origins

It is possible to have a church which shall be united, not on ceremonies, nor on a creed, but on study and labor, on loving and doing. The condition of admission should be the purpose to get good and do good.

—James Freeman Clarke, *Orthodoxy*

ROMANTICISM AND AMERICAN ORIGINALITY

In post-revolutionary America, Federal style and Greek Revival classically referenced Protestant churches joined early neoclassical government buildings as visual symbols of the mentality of Enlightenment views that had driven the political will for war and independence. The white steepled church form with classical pediments and either columns or pilasters came to dominate the townscape throughout New England. Subsequently, many perceived this form as a standard for American Unitarian church architecture due to their number and geographic proximity; there were a substantial number built within a fairly short timeframe. However, as demonstrated in the previous chapter, there was some variety of church forms even in the early years of Unitarian Christianity. And, as attitudes and interests inclined more and more toward Romanticism in the 1830s and 1840s, Unitarian churches were designed with increasing variety. This was concurrent with efforts toward westward expansion.

Even though Romanticism was another European import, American Romanticism also arose from changing social and economic conditions here. Historian Stow Persons argues, in fact, that those factors—continental exploration, increasing wealth and security, and an appreciation for individualism and nonconformity—made the American version of nineteenth-century Romanticism unique.[1] The idealism of democracy as a classless social system was fully elevated by Romantic writers and thinkers. The impact of Romanticism came just as the new republic had stabilized enough socially and politically to begin to cultivate the arts. At the same time, Americans' belief in individualism blossomed into a cult of personality, providing a welcoming context for creative artists.

Unitarianism would prove to continue to be adaptable to a changing world. While the Unitarian orientation was strongly wedded to the rationalism of the Enlightenment, there were aspects of Romanticism that aligned with its fundamental outlook. Likewise, though the most essential beliefs, and the denomination name, was settled by the wide acceptance of William Ellery Channing's Baltimore Sermon, there were many issues still subject to debate. His main tenets—the benevolence of a single god, and humanity's moral capacity and responsibility for their own actions and salvation—were the basis of a humanistic Christianity but one still accepting of the Bible as God's word. To some degree, the influential ministers of Boston (Channing and his peers) chose not to further codify a religious belief system, preferring to promote moral and ethical viewpoints for the lived world.[2] Thus there remained a clear tension between the liberal insistence on reason and the suggestions of the supernatural in the Bible. At the same time, Unitarians were setting themselves in opposition to the emotionalism of another wave of evangelism.

The faults of logic within the main idea of Unitarianism established by Channing's 1819 sermon were soon challenged. Ralph Waldo Emerson (1803–1882), son of a Unitarian minister, entered Harvard Divinity School in 1825, the same year that Unitarians first formed an organization, the American Unitarian Association.[3] Upon graduating, he was ordained at Boston's Second (Unitarian) Church in 1829. But his evolving views and the tragedy of his wife's death led him to resign after just three years. He continued to develop his personal philosophy through public lectures rather than sermons, eventually also publishing them as essays. Emerson shaped his own vision of spiritual truth, one that was known to individuals as a matter of instinct rather than empirically derived. Eventually taking its own shape and inspiring the Transcendentalist movement, much of his philosophy extended from the very Unitarian values he was raised and educated with: individualism, reliance on personal experience for knowledge, and the moral responsibility of free will. However, he openly opposed the dominant Unitarian theology of his time. Although he enraged the Harvard Divinity professors, representatives of the status quo, Unitarian ministers of the second generation, including George Ripley and Theodore Parker, were highly influenced by

Emerson's ideas. And although a renegade in his own time, much of Emerson's worldview became mainstream in Unitarianism in the later nineteenth century.

Emerson and those he inspired were charting new social positions enabled by the unique circumstances of early America. He was able to become an influential public figure without any institutional connection. There was a public appetite for new ideas, evident within religion in the second wave of revivals and new religious movements. Travel over greater distances grew easier with each decade, so public speakers, like itinerant "players" of previous centuries, could find new and ready audiences. As the frontier moved west, the recently settled territories were in themselves new forms of society, and Emerson's originality was welcome.

Boston's Unitarian ministers, the ones against whom Emerson rebelled, were actively involved in trying to transform the older social milieu of New England, to make it more sophisticated. Their promotion of knowledge and the arts created the conditions for a vibrant literary culture that dominated American arts in the first half of the nineteenth century. Joseph Stevens Buckminster led with the development of sermons addressing intellectual and moral growth rather than Bible study as a way toward spiritual growth. He professed a "vision that linked intellectual and artistic pursuits with religious and moral ones."[4] As the congregations prospered, ministers encouraged their leading citizens to support the publication of a monthly literary anthology and review, the *Atlantic Monthly*, and to found the Boston Athenæum, a library and cultural center. Even while historian Lawrence Buell challenges some "easy assumptions" that have attributed the rise of an original American literature to the Unitarian movement, he recognizes the general truth of the claim. He cites many conditions that support the thesis, especially the high level of education and social prestige among liberal Christians.[5]

ANTEBELLUM DISCORDS: TRANSCENDENTALISM AND THE SLAVERY QUESTION

The Transcendentalist movement is generally known for its importance to American literature, and for a philosophical intensity that some have seen as a broad cultural development in reaction to changing social conditions.[6] But it is equally important to understand that this "culturally defining movement was primarily a religious demonstration" and "at bottom a Unitarian [theological] dispute."[7] Historian David Robinson recounts a number of distinct quarrels that arose in reaction to new ideas in speeches and texts from the mid-1830s into the 1840s. Emerson's infamous "Divinity School Address" (1838) is only the most well-known. This scathing critique of the Unitarian status quo was pointedly delivered in a Unitarian institution to a Unitarian audience for the purpose of provocation. Even though Emerson had left the pulpit himself, and his criticism was rejected by Harvard professors, this speech eventually became central to Unitarian development. The other texts that contributed to the dispute were similar battles between an older generation of theologians who were conservative about the established compromise of Unitarianism, and a new generation that agreed with Emerson and wanted to further its liberal propositions.

Followers of Emerson who chose to stay within Unitarianism and to reform it along Transcendentalist lines adopted his vision of intuition's role in knowledge, especially knowledge of divinity. Theodore Parker (1810–1860) was the most important of this group. A statement of his beliefs as part of an 1841 sermon sparked another of the major open disputes between Transcendentalists and the Harvard establishment, one that finally led to his own ostracization. He replaced the scriptural and doctrinal basis of religion with a focus on "the divine life of the soul, love to God, and love to man."[8] His view of a natural religion, a "mystical conviction of the union of God, nature, and man," was not accepted by the mainstream in his lifetime, but he still attracted a significant following to his church in West Roxbury.[9] His extensive writing has had continued influence on Unitarian views and also beyond the religious context. Although shunned by mainstream Unitarian ministers at the time, he continued to preach until he contracted tuberculosis. He died in 1860 in Florence, Italy, where he had gone for rest and recovery. His radical ideas would become more mainstream after the Civil War.

James Freeman Clarke (1810–1888) was another Transcendentalist of Parker's generation that remained a Unitarian and supported the strengthening of the denomination.[10] His most intimate friend during his formative years was Margaret Fuller, whose name has wider recognition today as a central figure among the Transcendentalists. After leaving Harvard, he went west to Louisville, Kentucky, in the 1830s as a personal commitment to westward expansion of the denomination, and he encouraged others to make similar moves. When he returned to Boston, he started a new, church-less congregation based on his progressive ideas: fighting the social hierarchy in Unitarian congregations (in part, by eliminating pew rents), encouraging more socially mixed activities through open meetings that were distinct from religious services, and active participation in services by all through spoken prayer and lay readings, even by women. His preaching in Boston was initially only moderately successful, but he eventually gathered a strong following and became a denominational leader after the war. After decades of reliance on rented halls, he was able to build a permanent home for his Church of the Disciples in the South End neighborhood of Boston, dedicated in 1869.

Closer to the end of his career, he offered a new summary of Unitarian beliefs in five points. While not written until the mid-1880s, Clarke's views illustrate the development of Unitarianism in the context of nineteenth-century Romanticism. He set forth five essentials of a "new theology" in direct counterpoint to five core beliefs of Calvinism: the fatherhood of God, the fellowship of all people, the leadership of Jesus, salvation by character, and the continuity of human development (or progress of humankind).[11] Clarke's points took no position on the Bible or the divinity of Jesus; instead, people's responsibility for their own salvation and their obligations to one another and to humanity were at the center of his faith. They represent the degree to which Transcendentalism, once radical, had become acceptable to Unitarians.

The Transcendentalist movement pushed the moral stance of the Unitarian movement from introspection and individual free will toward greater social responsibility right when the institution of slavery became a matter of national debate. The leading figures among the Unitarian establishment were generally disinclined to engage in open social conflict. They were not "crusaders" by nature, and the fact that they were supported by congregations attended by the cotton merchants of Boston also made them reluctant to speak on the topic. They were slow to realize that the debate over the institution of slavery was not merely another political issue of the day and that failure to engage it was tantamount to abdicating the core humane philosophy of their religion. Channing, widely recognized as the leading light though having no position of authority, avoided the topic as long as he could—his own parents had enslaved people before the Revolution, and his wife's family "was deeply implicated in the North's complicity with slavery."[12] Eventually, though, his own moral sense caused him to denounce slavery with a lengthy argument published in 1835. He drew open criticism for it and angered many loyal friends and congregants—the expected outcomes he had been avoiding. His courage to finally take a stand was a source of inspiration to some, but for the remaining twenty-five years before the war Boston Unitarians remained divided.

William Henry Furness (1802–1896) had similar reasons for avoidance of the topic. But the situation in Philadelphia was far more volatile in the 1830s than in Boston.[13] As the first city north of the Mason-Dixon line, it was home to a growing population of former enslaved people. There was open racial violence, as well as a more robust abolitionist movement, partly due to the Quaker population. Influenced by Channing's views, and those of Lucretia Mott and Samuel May, Furness declared his opposition to slavery and his commitment to the fellowship of all people. From 1839 onward, he was adamantly and consistently outspoken against slavery despite the pleas of many or most congregation members and even his family to stop. He allied himself with the radical William Lloyd Garrison, participated in supporting the Underground Railroad, and took in his friend Senator Charles Sumner after he was assaulted on the floor of the U.S. Senate for his opposition to the Fugitive Slave Act. Through two decades Furness acted and spoke against the prevailing sentiments of his own congregation.

The public voice and willingness to take action that characterized those Unitarian ministers who were abolitionists led to a widespread perception that Unitarians were predominantly abolitionist, which was never the case.[14] Theodore Parker went beyond sermons and speeches. He was one of two Unitarian ministers among the six backers of John Brown's rebellion; the other was Thomas Wentworth Higginson. And William Henry Furness was among a small contingent that received Brown's body at a train station in Philadelphia after his execution in Virginia. But, in the end, Parker's abolitionist writings were the more lasting legacy. His words were echoed by Abraham Lincoln in the Gettysburg Address, and one hundred years later by Martin Luther King Jr. when he addressed the Unitarian Universalist Association General Assembly. Close to the end of "Don't Sleep through the Revolution," King paraphrased from an 1853 sermon of Parker's: "Look at the facts of the world. You see a continual and progressive triumph of the right. I do not pretend to understand the moral universe, the arc is a long one, my eye reaches but little ways. I cannot calculate the curve and complete the figure by the experience of sight; I can divine it by conscience. But from what I see I am sure it bends towards justice."[15]

In addition to the division in the North between those with a financial interest in the products of the southern slave economy and those viewing slavery as a strictly moral question, there was a divide between northern and southern Unitarians. The spread of Unitarianism in the South was initially sparked by Joseph Priestley's ideas rather than the predominant theologies and philosophies of New England Unitarians. But these distinctions were never that sharp, and there were ministerial connections that blur any sense of great differences. The histories and sympathies of congregations from the 1820s onward in Baltimore; Washington, DC; Charleston, South Carolina; Savannah; New Orleans; and Richmond, Virginia, are not easily generalized. However, the leading figures in Charleston and New Orleans exemplify their approach to the question of slavery. They felt that anti-slavery positions among northern Unitarians were at odds with the liberal attitude of allowing individual conscience to guide any moral question. While they refused to judge any enslaver, they advocated for humane treatment of enslaved people, including education, and they hoped that gradual social change would end slavery. They believed it was in the enslaver's self-interest to provide for the health and education of their enslaved people, and they included free Blacks and enslaved people in worship (fig. 2.2). The scholar John A. Macaulay exposes the way that they rationalized social contradictions: "As both slaveholders and church-goers, Southern Unitarians worked diligently for reform of the institution."[16] For them, improving the institution of slavery was considered to be a family matter and a moral duty, and they wanted to believe that most enslavers felt this moral compulsion. Northerners who had seen the living conditions of enslaved people for themselves knew that this benevolent reform was woefully inadequate.

Although split over slavery, northern Unitarians became more unified in the final decade leading to the Civil War, first in opposition to the Fugitive Slave Act and then in opposition to talk of secession. Lingering denominational disputes became less important, and from a larger perspective, Unitarians "were the most vital (and controversial) force in American intellectual life. . . . They accepted the social and industrial character" of the 1850s and they "tried to create a better world from it."[17] When the Civil War was over, leaders emerged that were more interested in strengthening the denomination as an organization than in arguing about beliefs. (The most radical believers split away to form the Free Religion movement.[18]) The New York minister Henry Bellows (1814–1882), having initiated and administered the U.S. Sanitary Commission during the war, was the central figure in promoting the values of denominational organization. Without it, he felt that the denomination would founder in the aftermath of the war and with the continuing geographic expansion of the country. His prewar sermon "The Suspense of Faith" indicated his pragmatic interest in changing the discourse from divisive issues of theology to common interests and a national identity.[19]

Historical judgement of the Unitarian position on slavery remains equivocal. Historian Daniel Walker Howe argued that the "Unitarian moralists," twelve first-generation Boston ministers, "contributed enormously to the development of American civilization," and that on major themes of modern intellectual history, they led the rest of the culture. However, they also "shattered themselves

FIGURE 2.2. First Unitarian Church, Baltimore, view of the enslaved people's gallery. Southern Unitarian ministers encouraged access to education and religion for enslaved people. Library of Congress, Prints & Photographs Division, Historic American Building Survey, HABS MD, 4–BALT, 58–6.

upon the rock of slavery."[20] Although Channing finally spoke out, other Harvard elders remained silent. It was the next generation that included the most notable abolitionists, such as Furness, Parker, and Clarke. A public tribute in the form of a statue of Unitarian minister Thomas Starr King stood in the U.S. Capitol Hall of Statues for over seventy years commemorating his effective antislavery and pro-Union advocacy in the San Francisco Bay Area from 1860 to his early death in 1864. He was given credit by Lincoln for keeping California in the Union.[21] The noteworthy words and deeds of the most consequential ministers of the time have given a false perception that Unitarians as a movement were antislavery, when in fact they were split to the same degree as the general population in the North.

THE ARCHITECTURE OF ROMANTICISM

In the realm of architecture, Romanticism fostered an interest in medieval traditions, especially Gothic, as a counterpoint to neoclassical rationalism. The earliest experiments with Gothic Revival in American church architecture occurred even while the proliferation of the Federal-style church was at its height.[22] Benjamin Latrobe famously offered his Catholic clients in Baltimore two designs for their national cathedral in 1804, the selected neoclassical design and a Gothic Revival option.[23] Charles Bulfinch designed the Federal Street Church in Boston in 1809 using Gothic motifs to satisfy the wishes of the minister. Bulfinch's client was William Ellery Channing—the minister who defined the rational basis of Unitarianism has also been described as "one of the earliest exponents of Romanticism in America."[24] But Bulfinch's early attempt at Gothic styling is an example of a Federal-style church in plan and massing that was merely given Gothic surface treatments. In this case, Gothic features were limited to its lancet-shaped windows, pinnacles on the belfry and spire, and shape of the ceiling.

The Episcopal Trinity Church in New Haven, designed by Ithiel Town in 1814, is given credit for being the first true Gothic Revival church in the United States, and there were at least three others built in the 1820s.[25] However, the full embrace of Gothic Revival, with its scholarly sources and meanings, ran from the mid-1830s up to the Civil War. The core of the movement came from within the Episcopal Church and its Anglican advocates in England.[26] Interest was growing in a somewhat more archaeological approach, partly aimed at shedding a sense of inferiority or provincialism. Richard Upjohn, John Notman, and James Renwick were among the architects who bolstered the still-foundering architectural profession by developing a more sophisticated academic knowledge of the varieties of Gothic architecture and the correct forms for a language of elements and details. Nevertheless, following Anglican-approved versions of a particular style of Gothic and subscribing to a degree of historical accuracy were a matter of denominational character and interests.

Gothic Revival would appear to be an odd choice for Unitarians, whose emphasis was on reason and the intellectualism that the clarity of the classical language exemplified. Among many things that can help to explain complex social phenomena, the simplest explanation was partly true—American Protestants adopted a historically Catholic style as a matter of keeping up with the latest fashion. Episcopalians were influenced by British Anglican practices, adopting trends that set new standards for beauty. But there were more specific reasons that it made sense for Unitarians to adopt the style so widely. One was a connection to literature. Unitarians of the early nineteenth century were highly literary, and the origins of Gothic Revival in poets' imaginary fantasies gave it a familiarity and strong appeal. The moral arguments for Gothic Revival published by English architect Augustus Welby Pugin and then by art critic John Ruskin would also have been influential. And the widely recognized connection between Gothic architecture and nature may have been equally important.[27] As ideas about nature in America were evolving from a threatening wilderness to a national myth of the American landscape, many embraced the Transcendentalist focus on nature as the source of truth and knowledge. Gothic Revival provided a church interior with arched wood trusses that could easily promote associations with natural environments.

Gothic Revival in the United States, Upjohn and his contemporaries notwithstanding, was never quite as tied to the question of archaeologically correct copies of medieval models as its counterpart in England was. Early examples of Unitarian adoption of Gothic in Salem and New Bedford, Massachusetts (1838), for instance, were not at all like the Episcopalian models but rather a medieval form based more on castles than cathedrals.[28] In these churches, heavy stone walls were topped with battlements, giving the appearance of strength. The style of the Salem church was described at its dedication as "neat and chaste" and judged as superior to any of Salem's other churches in terms of "beauty and elegance," though it was quite plain.[29] Similarly, the New Bedford church, designed by Andrew Jackson Downing and Russell Warren, was praised in the *Christian Register* as "exceedingly beautiful; one of the few good specimens of Gothic architecture which our country possesses . . . a credit to the liberality of the congregation who have erected it."[30] However, the only Gothic-inspired Unitarian church that was actually based on an ornate English model is in Charleston, South Carolina. The original building on the site dated to the revolutionary era, but it was enlarged and updated in 1852–54 by a local architect. Its interior was lavishly finished in plaster and lath to resemble the pendant fan vault ceiling of the Henry VII Chapel at Westminster Abbey.[31] Still, this elaborate version of Gothic reverie remained unique.

A sophisticated example of the many Gothic Revival churches built by Unitarian congregations in the Victorian Era can be seen in the First Church in Boston (fig. 2.3). The First Boston congregation dates back to 1630; its 1640 meetinghouse followed the typical Puritan form with a hipped roof. Centrally located on State Street, it was in use up to 1713. Two more up-to-date structures came with moves as Boston grew, first to Washington Street and then Chauncey Street. In 1868 the church moved once again to the corner of Berkeley and Marlborough Streets in the newly established Back Bay. The commission was won in a competition by Ware & Van Brunt, one of the premier firms in Boston at the time.[32] Henry Van Brunt (1832–1903) was a member of the congregation, and he likely would have discussed

FIGURE 2.3. First Church, Boston, Ware & Van Brunt, 1868. Photograph by Nathaniel L. Stebbins. Courtesy of Historic New England.

the design with the building committee in terms of his steadfast interest in two important ideals: the moral claims regarding Gothic architecture that Pugin and Ruskin had established, and the ways in which it celebrated American freedom from "the tyranny of historic precedent."[33] That is, it did not follow either a particular medieval model or an academically synthesized version of correctness.

Van Brunt opposed studied copies of past forms: "Architects become antiquaries when they feed exclusively upon the past, and are content to reproduce archaeological curiosities and copy shapes, however beautiful, of a fossil art without reanimating them with the breath and spirit of the present."[34] His design for First Boston illustrated his capacity for invention and for achieving an overall unity of the whole. It was a relatively monumental structure, but it was set low to the ground, with two arcades open to the streets. The base of a corner tower was pierced by a large open arch on each face. The height of the interior space was due to a tall and steeply pitched roof rather than tall exterior walls. It is easy to look at its design and think of it as something unremarkable, almost standard, but the Gothic Revival was subject to great variety, and in Van Brunt's design reached a beautiful but difficult simplicity.

The Gothic was a standard for churches of nearly all denominations during the period of westward expansion of Unitarianism. Early expansion established congregations in Louisville, Kentucky, and St. Louis, Missouri. Both of these pioneering congregations of the mid-1830s rebuilt in the later nineteenth century in the Gothic style. The Gothic Revival of the Victorian Era evolved as the use of new materials and new building types invited ever greater eclecticism.[35] Designs were no longer generated from a desire to demonstrate a competent grasp of the authentic medieval vocabulary of forms but became a matter of tone and character in how designers adopted and synthesized various elements of its language. It continued to be used in part because it had the capacity to visually distinguish churches from other buildings in the growing towns and cities across the continent; the Gothic idiom could be relied on for making a church look like a church. The Unitarian churches of West Roxbury, Massachusetts, and Milwaukee, Wisconsin, built at the end of the century, illustrate common Victorian-Era elements and variations (fig. 2.4).

For Unitarians, accepting the general cultural norm of the time may have been calculated to assert legitimacy as a denomination once they started building in the newly settled cities of the Midwest and West. They also wanted their church architecture to contribute positively to the civic landscape of the town or city. And in

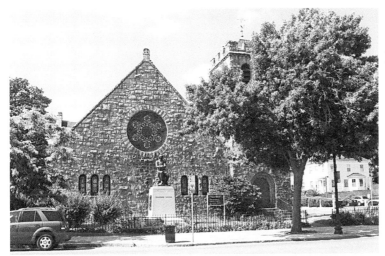

FIGURE 2.4a. First
Parish of West Roxbury,
Boston, Henry M. Seaver,
1900. Photograph by
John Phelan, CC BY 3.0,
https://creativecom
mons.org/licenses
/by/3.0/deed.en.

FIGURE 2.4b. First
Unitarian Church,
Milwaukee, Ferry &
Clas, 1892. Library of
Congress, Prints &
Photographs Division,
Historic American
Building Survey, HABS
WIS, 40–MILWA, 31–1.

some cases, its widely appreciated beauty was an appealing contrast to industrializing cities and hastily constructed frontier towns. However, it is important to
confront the contradictions that were also inherent in the adoption of Gothic forms.
Referring back to European tradition was inconsistent with the Unitarian desire
for intellectual integrity, and "the Gothic revival indicated a re-assertion of many

of the values that Unitarianism had struggled to overcome."[36] Many congregations accepted an overt expression of prosperity over the clarity and pragmatism of the iconic third-style meetinghouse. Congregations that had cycled through a number of buildings as needs evolved chose a greater sense of permanence with a more substantial Gothic structure. These tensions between Unitarian values and Gothic Revival church buildings would not go unchallenged; alternative styles emerged alongside the Gothic Revival in the last two decades of the nineteenth century.

Although Gothic Revival dominated nineteenth-century Romantic tendencies, other eclectic influences began to appear as well. One highly visible and influential departure from the Gothic deserves special notice: All Souls Church in New York City (1855). Its influence was not as a model that was adopted by others but in its unique daring. The wish for something fresh and innovative came directly from the congregation's minister, Henry Bellows.[37] He rejected a design that had already been commissioned by the congregational building committee. Instead, Bellows (with the financial backing of a sympathetic friend) brought British architect Jacob Wrey Mould (1825–1886) to New York in order to introduce more innovative design ideas like those being explored in the English circle of Owen Jones. In particular, Mould was interested in architecture that was accepting of the character of the contemporary world. He designed a domed Greek cross structure with a far more animated space than its contemporaries. Its iron trusses with lacey infill were the most ornamental feature of the otherwise plainly rendered interior. This was among the earliest uses of exposed iron in a religious building anywhere.[38] Far more dramatic, though, was the polychrome exterior that caused it to become known as the "Church of the Holy Zebra" (fig. 2.5). Although many found the stripes to be overbearing, they suit the overall character of the sharp clarity of massing. Bellows was pleased, finding it to have a "self-possession which neither ridicule nor blame could disturb, and a zeal" that was appropriate for a "Christian temple."[39] Bellows was not alone in judging the design as contributing something novel to the New York cityscape; he had gambled on Mould and had accomplished his goal. Mould was only twenty-seven years old when he arrived in New York, and his career spanned another quarter century. Although it included well-regarded residential and institutional projects and a good deal of public service, All Souls Church remained his most prominent work.[40]

AMERICAN ORIGINALITY: FURNESS

While Gothic-inspired churches of the later nineteenth century diverged from English models ever more significantly, the architecture was still derivative of European traditions. But from at least the 1840s, there were calls for the invention of a distinctly American architecture completely divorced from the historic styles of England and continental Europe. Emerson was only the strongest voice in the mid-nineteenth century to appeal for the expression of a unique American identity in the arts. He held himself to the same standard, promising in a letter to his oldest friend, William Henry Furness, to "begin the world anew with every word and speak as a rational man to a rational man."[41] Furness was Emerson's schoolmate from childhood through college, and the two remained friends through letters and visits their whole lives.

FIGURE 2.5. All Souls Church, New York City, Jacob Wrey Mould, 1855. Photograph from the collection of the New-York Historical Society.

Furness was the charismatic minister of the First Unitarian Church of Philadelphia for fifty years. Arriving from Boston in 1825, he became a leader in Philadelphia's nineteenth-century social culture, though he bristled against its Quaker conservatism. The appeal of his oratory drove rapid congregational growth and even kept the congregation healthy through two decades of objections to his abolitionist preaching. Furness was both a scholar and an activist, with a habit of "standing for those outside of genteel society." He studied the Bible as a historic (human-made) text rather than divine revelation, and published books on the historical life of Jesus and on the Gospels as literature. His views placed him among the Transcendentalists, but his distance from Boston and his less strident temperament kept him out of those controversies. He shared Emerson's views on the importance of individual creativity and the development of authentic American art forms. Furness's views specific to architecture are known from his address to the annual meeting of the American Institute of Architects in 1870. Although he acknowledged that the culture and tastes of clients could be a limiting factor on the artistic freedom of the architect, he nevertheless implored architects to reject historical styles and conventions and to create "new orders of architecture" suitable to American materials, needs, and imaginations.[42] His youngest son, Frank Furness (1839–1912), had recently returned from New York to start his own architectural practice, and he would be the one to fulfill this vision of creative imagination and originality in architecture.

Frank Furness was not only raised by a progressive Unitarian minister; he also had Ralph Waldo Emerson, a frequent visitor to the Furness house, as something like an uncle. Frank fully absorbed the faith in bold artistic intuition that was his inheritance. His only formal training in architecture consisted of several years in the New York City atelier of Richard Morris Hunt just before and for a short while after his service in the Civil War.[43] Hunt had trained at the École des Beaux-Arts in Paris and had set his New York office up as a teaching atelier in the tradition of the Parisian masters. The positive impacts of this training on Furness, explored in detail by biographer James F. O'Gorman, were classical ordering and proportions, disciplined plans, and a fusion of English and French historicism, as well as access to the works of Eugene-Emmanuel Viollet-le-Duc and Ruskin.[44] But his formal training's limited timeframe also indicates that Furness had the capacity to learn directly from books and buildings. In looking at the two churches Furness designed for Unitarians, they are best appreciated in the context of his personal drive to create something wholly original, which was a theme of his upbringing;

his freedom from the conforming tendencies of a formal education; and his apparent native talent, indicated by his ability to move from his limited education to the production of complex projects.

Furness's father gave him both the philosophical imperative for artistic originality and the means: access to clients from his congregation who were equally convinced of the need for an American architecture. His Unitarian clients were especially important to three project areas—residential, social welfare institutions, and railroad stations. Congregation members also commissioned two churches. The earlier of the two was his first independent commission after returning to Philadelphia from New York, undertaken before he established a regular practice with two partners. It was commissioned by a splinter group founding a second Philadelphia Unitarian congregation in Germantown after the war. Not surprisingly, there was nothing of the audacious Furness in his first work, but it was not without invention.

The exterior of the church was relatively straightforward—a somewhat spare rendition of Gothic Revival, notable mainly for its quiet restraint considering the exuberance of his later works (fig. 2.6a). It is interesting to note that the nature of Gothic was well-suited to allow for some irregularities in form, but Furness's design was forthrightly symmetrical. Furness had no personal experience working on church design—Hunt's office did not have those commissions while Furness was there. But he would have certainly been familiar with highly regarded examples of Gothic Revival churches in Philadelphia. St. Mark's, located about six blocks west of his father's church in central Philadelphia, was designed by one of the recognized experts in Gothic revival, John Notman, in 1847. Structurally speaking, it was more of a Romanesque rendition of a basilica, but the articulation and ornament were Gothic. The structure and plan were based on uniform bays; the only irregular element was a tower placed along one flank with a portal facing the street, an arrangement necessitated by a mid-block location. The smaller St. James the Less (1849) was also a basilica plan, but the nave and side aisles were gathered under a double pitch roof. It is described by architectural historian Phoebe Stanton as being particularly influential on subsequent Philadelphia church design.[45] Through a series of mistakes, this church was built relatively faithfully from plans of an actual thirteenth-century structure in England, so the masonry was thicker than other churches of the period. The walls' visibly weighty character would have no doubt appealed to Furness. The sparse simplicity of its massing was clearly echoed by Furness's design for Germantown.

FIGURE 2.6a. Unitarian Society Church, Germantown, Pennsylvania, Frank Furness, 1869, exterior view. Photographs of Unitarian Universalist Churches, bMS 15001, Andover-Harvard Library, Harvard Divinity School, Cambridge, Massachusetts.

FIGURE 2.6b. Unitarian Society Church, interior view. Original image by D. Sargent Bell, photograph of historic print by Joanne David, courtesy of the Unitarian Society of Germantown, Pennsylvania.

Although the 1869 design for the Germantown church seems rather ordinary, a few elements made it distinct. Furness rejected the basilican plan, preferring to unify the interior space. The long dimension of the hall-like nave had six bays, and the width was slightly greater than half the length. Two arms extended the space of the fourth and fifth bays outward to form a shallow transept under lower roofs. Beyond the transept, the sixth bay was merged into a half-octagon. At the time, squared-off end walls were the norm, often as an extended rectangular chancel space narrower than the nave. Furness's full-width octagonal apse may have been inspired by Jacob Mould's 1858 design for the Second Unitarian Church in Brooklyn; it was otherwise quite unique. (Commentary on Mould's design was that it was the "first departure from conventional church design in Brooklyn.")[46] It worked together with the unusually low spring points of the arced trusses to create a strong impression of a continuous space under a dominant roof (see fig. 2.6b). There was minimal awareness of vertical walls, giving an unusual sense of groundedness in a Gothic nave. The congregation was held together under a surprisingly expansive pseudo-vault created by the shape of the trusses. The proportions of this simple, unified space were unorthodox, to say the least, within the Gothic language.[47] Unfortunately, the building was razed in 1928.

The main door was in the center of the nave's west wall, and one of the transept arms formed an additional portal to make use of the corner site. The axial entry of the main door did not lead to the usual central aisle; a bank of pews occupied the center of the space, and the circulation was split into two aisles on either side. Either the budget or the suburban site did not support a full corner tower, so a place for a bell was made by a vertical extension of the front wall. A final notable decision was to set the church on a bermed plinth. This may have been necessitated by soil or water table conditions, or it may have been in order to create a double cascade of steps at each entry that echoes the stepped faces of the buttresses, and the only relief in this planar composition. These relatively small irregularities demonstrated an approach that was seeking character in the shaping of space and expression through the function and correspondence of elements.

Furness's project roster included other Gothic Revival churches that are fairly conventional, but they are attributable to his partner George Hewitt, who had trained in the office of John Notman.[48] Only one church of Furness design came between his two Unitarian churches, which were separated by fifteen years. The Church of the Redeemer for Seamen and Their Families in Philadelphia (1878) was a chapel built together with a school in a single structure. The exterior was residential in scale and many details. It is mainly notable that the interior space of the squarish chapel had low and spreading proportions in section that were similar to the Germantown church.

Furness's second design for a Unitarian church was executed at the height of his career in 1883. He had been consciously pursuing a unique American expression in his work, fulfilling the call for artistic originality. He had developed a vocabulary of elements that were not in themselves brand new but which he used in unconventional ways. He also combined traditional masonry construction with new materials such as iron and glass. His most daring designs exhibited unique compositions of these elements into the whole. His interest in variety was also developed through color, texture, and ornament. The commission for his second Unitarian church came around ten years after his competition-winning design for the Pennsylvania Academy of Fine Arts had established his style as fully accepted into the cultural norms of the city.

Historians and critics have judged this new commission, the First Unitarian Church and Parish House of Philadelphia, to be among his best works. It combined his capacity for invention and wit with the less energetic character of his social institutions.[49] The congregation had naturally turned to the son of their emeritus minister when they needed a new building. But his reputation as the leading designer in Philadelphia at the time also suited a congregation that had employed both William Strickland and Robert Mills. Philadelphia had expanded westward during the nineteenth century to finally fill the grid established by William Penn, so the congregation had to relocate west of the city center to obtain a lot ample enough for the larger church they now needed. Furness placed the church directly on Chestnut Street, one of the continuous east-west streets spanning the city, and logically located the required parish house behind it facing the narrower cross street, Van Pelt. The basic elements of the church facade—a corner tower, an entry arcade, and a gable end with a round window—were composed in familiar relationships, but their massing and articulation made them exceptional (fig. 2.7).

This church has been described as fundamentally Gothic, but in reality it cannot be identified with any particular tradition.[50] The roof is not the usual Gothic Revival double pitched roof extending between two masonry end walls; it is more complex. The main roof is actually hipped, with large gabled dormers projecting on the long axis to complete the length of the nave. The difference in the width of the dormer and the full nave foreshadows the sectional qualities of the

FIGURE 2.7. First Unitarian Church, Philadelphia, Frank Furness, 1883, exterior view before the corner tower was demolished. Photograph courtesy of the Philadelphia Historical Commission.

hammer-beam ceiling within. The nave roof is bisected by wide transept roofs, double pitched, each ending at a vertical masonry wall. The shallow transepts are almost as wide as the nave, so the ridge of their roofs is only slightly below that of the main roof. The hierarchy of these five distinct roof elements was unique for Gothic Revival. The additional roof of the single story entrance arcade is also hipped so as to cascade from the base of the dormer on the south end. Breaking these elements down this way minimizes the heights of walls and reduces the scale of the whole. This may be further evidence of influence of the work of Jacob Mould in New York City. His Holy Trinity Chapel was built at about the same time Furness returned to Hunt's atelier after the war. Mould similarly used gables and dormers to reduce the perception of the building's size.[51]

The final roof element was that of the corner tower, now reconceived as a porte-cochère as urban mobility was evolving. This unusual structure was in a typical location for the spired bell towers of the Gothic Revival, but its height was only roughly equivalent to the height of the church. Its flattened arches and stumpy round columns were somewhat medieval, but there was certainly nothing Gothic about them. The structure's tall pyramidal roof was supported on four corner piers that framed arched openings. This element has been demolished so it is difficult to judge its effect; in a design sketch, it appears well scaled to the projecting transept end wall. In the few existing photos, it appears to be the most dominant element, and it makes the building less readily identifiable as a church. But the distortions of photography may also be a factor. The character of the porte-

FIGURE 2.8. First Unitarian Church, Philadelphia, nature-themed ornamental details. Photographs by author.

cochère is closest to some of Furness's other designs, particularly those of train stations. He seems to have wanted this most original element with its modern associations to be a primary image of the new church.

By comparison, the main church structure is relatively conventional. However, the shapes of elements such as arches and windows are varied, and other conventions of style were completely invented. Ornamental details, relatively few in number, are primarily nature-themed (fig. 2.8). The front gable is thickened at the top to support a chimney pot (often mistaken for a bellcote) on seven corbels adorned with carved roses whose faces are sequentially rotated from east to west to be lit by the sun throughout the day.[52] Below the corbels, a round rose window is centered in a round arch. While the circular window with a cusped frame was the single most blatantly Gothic element of the church facade, it held a leaded-glass image of a spider's web in place of traditional stained glass motifs. Seen from outside, it spoke of nature along with the flowers above. Seen from inside, it could be contemplated more symbolically. Below the rose window, the rather squat arcade was supported on wide piers that followed no standard architectural form or assembly of parts; a protrusion at the top formed a quasi-capital that was adorned with delicately carved palm fronds. One other ornament that spoke of nature was the rough texture of the masonry walls. Taken together, this ornament was meant to show not only artifacts of nature such as flowers and leaves, but processes of nature—the daily path of the sun, the spinning of the spider's web, and life's path to death. But the web and the rough-textured walls also expressed strength and endurance.

The entry arcade, a common feature for nineteenth-century Unitarians, serves as a narthex, an anteroom to the church (fig. 2.9a). This allows a pause, a chance to make a choice about entering rather than feeling compelled to do so. An unusual feature here was that the last bay was designed to contain a small lending library so that church members (or others) might explore philosophical or theological questions without dependence on a minister. From the narthex, two doors are aligned with the two circulation aisles positioned just as in Germantown—again the individual is forced to choose. The denial of a central axis through doubling the aisles and expanding the space laterally in transepts, like the form of the roof, contravenes expected hierarchies of traditional churches.[53]

Another unusual detail for a church—at least one of this size—is easily overlooked because it is no longer there: a large fireplace centered on the back wall between the two entry doors. While providing for a practical necessity, it was not a common feature in churches of this era. Its capacity to provide heat to the

FIGURE 2.9a. First Unitarian Church, Philadelphia, entry arcade or narthex. Photograph by author.

FIGURE 2.9b. First Unitarian Church, interior view toward the entry taken before the skylight was removed. Library of Congress, Prints & Photographs Division, Historic American Building Survey, HABS PA, 51–PHILA, 296–4.

cavernous space would have been limited; it was meant for sociability, an addition to the narthex for use in the colder weather. Members could gather in conversation and warm their hands and feet before proceeding to the pews.

Inside, the evenly spaced hammer-beam trusses create a high central bay and lower zones on each side (fig. 2.9b). And while it is a lofty space, the flattening of the curved collar braces at the top and the transfer of load at the hammer-beam grounds the space. A lively color scheme was consistent with Victorian practice generally speaking but also can be attributed to Furness's father, who suggested that successful church designs needed to keep the worshipers awake.[54] The most innovative feature of the church was a continuous flat skylight at the apex of the ceiling. Borrowed from banking halls and other commercial or institutional spaces requiring clear and even light devoid of shadows, it was intended by Furness to provide uniform lighting that had no mystical inflection. He "knew the value his father placed on intellectual curiosity and the power of reason; the attitude of ecumenical tolerance; and above all, the sense that divinity was not discrete and separate but was everywhere immanent in the natural world."[55]

Although there have been many alterations, the church is mostly intact today. The biggest losses have been the porte-cochère and the skylight that extended through five bays of the nave. (The parish house still has many features of the original design but has been altered much more substantially.) Michael J. Lewis, the most recent Furness scholar, says that the church was "as close to 'pure' as anything Furness ever did," which I interpret as meaning as effective in synthesizing mass and structure with a spatial idea that suited its use without relying on idiosyncratic compositional irregularities for interest.[56] The proportions of individual elements and the overall massing suggested an earth-bound structure; the material qualities and the ornament also expressed nature as the source of knowledge. Lewis speculates that the clarity of the design was drawn from the Puritan meetinghouse, but this would not have been consistent with Furness's inherited Unitarian progressive spirit and the Emersonian impulse to create always anew. Rather than "squaring the Gothic circle" by taking Gothic forms and fashioning a meetinghouse, as Lewis would have it, he manipulated proportion and light to rationalize Victorian Gothic and to emulate the public spaces of daily life in nineteenth-century Philadelphia. Earlier commentary by James O'Gorman focused mostly on what has been lost, but he nonetheless concluded that "with the original patterns of light filtering down from the ridge, this must have been one of the most impressive small-scale ecclesiastical spaces in Victorian America."[57] Lewis rightfully points out Furness's natural sympathy with his client; it was fitting that Furness's first and perhaps his best designs were both for Unitarian congregations.

AMERICAN ORIGINALITY: RICHARDSON

The other architect of post–Civil War America most often credited with breaking away from stylistic revivals with an original American architecture is Henry Hobson Richardson (1838–1886). O'Gorman has pointed out many interesting parallels and contrasts between Richardson's career and that of Furness.[58] There is no evidence of the two ever meeting, but it is certain that they knew of each other. They both participated in the 1876 Philadelphia Centennial Exhibition, where Furness would have seen on display Richardson's design for the Episcopalian Trinity Church in Boston. Richardson, for his part, would have been likely to see the Pennsylvania Academy of Fine Arts nearing completion on Broad Street.

Like Furness, Richardson was raised Unitarian. An odd connection between the two is the scientist and Unitarian theologian Joseph Priestley, the founder of William Henry Furness's Unitarian congregation, who was also Richardson's great-grandfather. Richardson grew up in Louisiana on the Priestley Plantation and in

New Orleans, where his own father was a cotton merchant. After moving north to attend Harvard College from 1856 to 1859, he never returned to the South. Harvard was still the center of the Unitarian movement, but at some point he rejected his upbringing, choosing instead the Episcopal Church. Upon graduation from Harvard, Richardson went to Paris to study architecture at the École des Beaux-Arts in 1860, and as a result avoided the need to choose sides in the Civil War. Nevertheless, the war did affect his life in Paris. His family's financial situation was quickly and radically changed by the war. Having lost their support, Richardson was forced to find employment, which in turn limited his academic training.

It was his Harvard connection, and perhaps his own Unitarian background, that gained him a first commission when he returned to the United States, determined to start an independent practice. A former classmate was responsible for Richardson's chance to design the Church of the Unity in Springfield, Massachusetts (1869, demolished 1960s). This was another parallel with Furness—being trusted with a first solo project by a Unitarian congregation. Richardson's design was similar to Furness's Germantown church in that it was both straightforward and competent (fig. 2.10a). The Springfield church was a slightly larger basilican Gothic Revival structure, fronted by an entry arcade flanked by a tower. (This arrangement was the same as the contemporary Ware & Van Brunt design for First Boston.) The exterior conformed to basics of the language, although the clerestory windows had round arches rather than pointed. The interior was more idiosyncratic: the arches of the nave arcade were pointed, but their proportion was quite wide, and they landed on smooth round columns rather than Gothic piers (fig. 2.10b). The wide arches allowed the side aisles to remain more spatially continuous with the nave, which was more suitable for Unitarians. Hammerbeam trusses created a sense of the expected Gothic verticality in the nave.

Just a few years later, Richardson had the chance to design another Unitarian church. It was his first building in Boston and just two blocks from the site where he would soon build Trinity Church. In the meantime, he had already designed two other small churches for other denominations. In one, the North Congregational Church in Springfield, Massachusetts, he had dropped pointed arches from his vocabulary completely, using a combination of straight lintels and a few strategically placed round arches. The design for the Boston Unitarians, the Brattle Square Church (1872), departed yet further from the Gothic revival vocabulary (fig. 2.11a).[59] Like Furness's First Unitarian, which it predated by ten years, it is not readily identifiable as a single style, though it does still "feel" medieval.[60] Unlike

FIGURE 2.10a. Church of the Unity, Springfield, Massachusetts, Henry Hobson Richardson, 1869, exterior view. Library of Congress, Prints & Photographs Division, Historic American Building Survey, HABS MASS, 7–SPRIF, 3–1.

FIGURE 2.10b. Church of the Unity, Springfield, Massachusetts, interior view. Library of Congress, Prints & Photographs Division, Historic American Building Survey, HABS MASS, 7–SPRIF, 3–4.

the Furness design, it does not have distinct elements of pure invention. Its originality was developed by an eclectic combination of references, the treatment of materials, articulation of openings, and an unusual amount of plain wall surface. The front elevation on Clarendon Street recalled the entry arcade and flanking tower of his Springfield design. However, the tower is not a Gothic spire but a square campanile, which has been described variously as Norman, Venetian, and

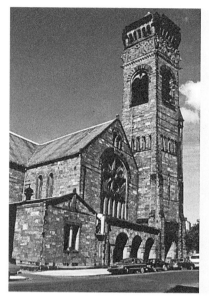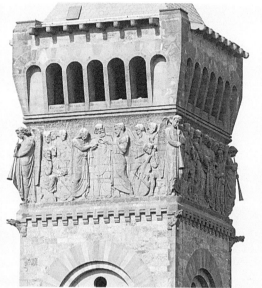

FIGURE 2.11a. Brattle Square Church, Boston, Henry Hobson Richardson, 1872, street view. Photograph by James Barnes, courtesy of Digital Images and Slides Collection, Fine Arts Library, Harvard University, Cambridge, Massachusetts.

FIGURE 2.11b. Brattle Square Church, view of the tower and frieze. Library of Congress, Prints & Photographs Division, LC-DIG-det-4a11377.

Florentine. The church is a Greek cross only slightly longer (116 feet) than it is wide (104 feet), a choice that was described at the time as "realizing the wishes of the Society."[61] The framing of the roof was less elaborate than that of the Gothic interiors: simple rafters and crossbeams reinforced with iron strapping. They spanned between the planar lateral walls, which rose to a height of forty-six feet.

The most remarkable feature of the whole design is the sculptural frieze that wraps around the tower just below the corbel table (fig. 2.11b). Richardson promoted his idea for this public art to his clients, and then he engaged the French sculptor Frédéric Auguste Bartholdi to execute it. The work was completed by John Evans.[62] Each of the four panels that encircle the tower represent a significant passage in Christian life—baptism, communion, marriage, and death—and many contemporary figures are represented in the allegorical compositions.[63] Old Testament angels of judgment blow trumpets from each corner, earning the church its nickname "Church of the Holy Beanblowers." It is ironic that this extravagant feature was agreed to by the congregation, which was bankrupted soon afterward by the construction costs and a dwindling membership. It must be supposed that the prominence of their Commonwealth Avenue site encouraged them to feel responsible for enhancing the city with their building. The church was sold to a Baptist congregation about five years after completion, which saved it from demolition. Many visitors to Trinity Church in Copley Square never realize that there is another church designed by Richardson a mere two blocks away. Although it was the most prominent, the frieze was only one unusual feature of an unorthodox design. Architectural historian Henry Russell Hitchcock was derisive of Richardson's liberties with Romanesque ornament, but he nevertheless concluded that "although Richardson never did anything much like the Brattle Square Church again, here he turned the corner on his career. The rest of his great work could easily follow from this beginning."[64]

Richardson never designed another Unitarian church, but a significant client, Frederick Lothrop Ames, was a Unitarian whose values and beliefs propelled his architectural patronage. His grandfather Oliver Ames Sr. bought a tract of land about twenty-five miles south of Boston along the Queset Brook in 1804 to manufacture the first domestically produced shovels. The town of North Easton, Massachusetts, grew up around the factory buildings of the Ames Tool and Shovel Works. The second generation of Ameses, brothers Oliver Jr. and Oakes, brought a railroad line to North Easton as the country's primary transportation and shipping modes shifted from water to land. Then the Civil War and westward expansion brought spectacular wealth and further opportunities in railroads. Meanwhile, North Easton grew steadily, and "from the beginning North Easton was shaped by Unitarianism."[65] The founder initiated a Unitarian congregation from the start, and one of his sons built its church and a parsonage. For the first fifty years, the scale of the factory buildings and the houses for owners and employees were all relatively similar, which created a sense of unity.

In the mid-nineteenth century, a third generation of the Ames family built larger homes on private estates. Although they failed to maintain the Unitarian values of basic utilitarian pragmatism in this matter, they invested in the common good of the community through the construction of cultural institutions. Oliver Ames Jr. left money for the construction of a public library on his death in 1877. The commission was executed by his son, Frederick L. Ames. Ames was fully involved with the elite culture in Boston and had come to know Richardson while he was working on Trinity Church through mutual involvement in the Horticulture Society and the development of Harvard's Arnold Arboretum. The North Easton library commission was given directly to Richardson without a competition, which was unusual for the time.

The Ames Free Library (1883) was the second in a series of five libraries at the heart of Richardson's creative works. Working at this scale, in a civic rather than residential character, Richardson mastered a clarity of spatial sequence and definition. The necessity of ample daylight drove him to experiment with new ways of treating walls and windows, or openings. His experiments with texture, color, and ornament were both disciplined and expressive. The gift of a free library was in keeping with the Unitarian belief in open access to knowledge and education as a necessity for a democratic society.

Before the library project was finished, Richardson was asked to design the somewhat larger Oakes Ames Memorial Hall (1881) on adjacent land (fig. 2.12). This building provided the town with an auditorium for public functions such as lectures and performances, as well as meeting rooms for civic and cultural clubs. These two cultural landmarks were soon followed by another Richardson building, the Old Colony Railway Station (1884). The two civic buildings at the center of town gave the whole population not only access to knowledge but a call to search for truth, and not only the possibility of community culture but a responsibility for mutual fellowship. Though the railway station was a more practical contribution, the care, thought, and creativity of these significant buildings served the needs and enriched the lives of all citizens.

In Boston, Ames became acquainted with Frederick Law Olmsted (1822–1903) as well, and he engaged Olmsted in the design of the civic landscape of North Easton's center. Olmsted's collaboration was a critical contribution to the success of the Richardson buildings there. In addition to the work in town, Ames was consulting with Olmsted on improvements to his estate, Langwater. As part of that work, Ames identified the need for some sort of structure on its northern boundary. The Gate Lodge (1881) was developed to provide a fitting entry point, which Richardson envisioned as an impressive stone arch across the entry drive springing right from ground level. The building created for the arch to go through was therefore substantial, roughly twice as long on each side of the road. However, the uses for the building were somewhat improvised. There were several rooms adequate to accommodate either guests or servants, and there was one larger space for social use in the main part of the building. A room on the other side of the driveway was for plants and garden equipment. The building remains

FIGURE 2.12. Oakes Ames Memorial Hall and the Ames Free Library, North Easton, Massachusetts, Henry Hobson Richardson, 1877–81. Photograph by Daderot, CC BY-SA 3.0, https://creativecommons.org/licenses/by-sa/3.0/.

an enigma because no defined architectural program compelled its unusual and highly expressive character: rough boulders stacked up over heavy stone lintels give way to a graceful arch over the drive and are roofed by a smooth red shingle roof (fig. 2.13). Historian Margaret Floyd believed it to be Richardson's single most admired building.[66] She examined all of the speculation of previous historians regarding its inspiration and sources and concluded that it was the first of Richardson's designs to show the influence of Japanese architecture that had arisen in American arts from the 1876 Centennial Exhibition.

However, William Pierson's later analysis built on Richardson's knowledge of Unitarian ideas from youth, from his time at Harvard, and from reading Ralph Waldo Emerson "in his search for truth in nature." Pierson understood the rough masonry, animal-themed ornaments, and symbolism of ancient cosmic order

FIGURE 2.13. Ames Gate Lodge, North Easton, Massachusetts, Henry Hobson Richardson, 1881, exterior view. Photograph by Daderot, CC BY-SA 3.0, https://creativecommons.org/licenses/by-sa/3.0/.

embedded in the Gate Lodge to be Richardson's acknowledgment of the life force of the earth itself and an expression of his client's liberal Unitarian vision—"a ringing affirmation of the earth as a living organism and the countless forms of life that are its glory."[67] Ames had intended the social room in the lodge to be used by his three sons; he called it the Bachelor's Hall. While its name and location on the periphery of the estate have been suggestive of parties or other leisure activities of the wealthy class, Pierson explained it as a place for discussion of philosophy and new ideas—a literary club or salon.[68] Pierson further suggested that a deep sympathy between client and architect was itself able to elicit from Richardson one of his most provocative designs.

Furness and Richardson both began their careers with Unitarian churches, and for each a second Unitarian church allowed them the chance for creative invention. For Furness, the church for the congregation he grew up in was a combination of familiar elements and a calibrated degree of invention that was not as "showy" as his banks and other commercial buildings in Philadelphia but nevertheless profound. So, while there is a rose window in a masonry gable, it sits atop an unorthodox arcade and is challenged by the corbelled chimney pot pressing down from above. The corner tower was severely truncated into a modern portecochère. The familiar elements assured that the Unitarian attitudes of welcome and sociability were expressed; the unfamiliar elements remained inviting in scale and openness.

In the case of Richardson, some have seen in the design of Brattle Square Church the first full expression of his personal genius.[69] He had begun to experiment with the North Congregational Church, where the fenestration shapes and other details were freely chosen, but the massing, proportion, and relationship of building elements remained tied to the Gothic Revival norm. At Brattle Square, all of these aspects were liberated from any model. And the cluster of buildings for Frederick L. Ames "provide an exceptional glimpse of Richardson fusing eclectic elements of nineteenth century architectural thought in to the unique, integrated designs" that came to be recognized as the beginnings of an authentically American architecture.[70]

CONCLUSION: "A PLACE . . . TO DO GOOD"

Overall, most nineteenth-century Unitarian churches had a similar variety of form and style as the general architectural milieu in which they were conceived. The adoption of Gothic Revival and other eclectic styles was widespread in American religious architecture, and Unitarians were part of the national trend. While it is impossible to extract any features that defined a church as Unitarian, there were some clear tendencies with respect to use: relatively small scale, relatively restrained in terms of ornament, circulation patterns that invited choice, and spatial patterns that were less hierarchical than other church interiors.

But it is important to note that some trends in Protestant architecture were never appropriate to Unitarian congregations. Among numerous trends in Protestant architecture from the 1830s to the 1890s identified by historian Jeanne Halgren Kilde were the amplification of the church's "martial character" and a conception of it as a "spiritual armory."[71] Although plenty of Unitarian churches adopted the revivals of medieval forms, their smaller scale and ornamental details did not often display this character. The other, central focus of her study was the spatial transformation to a more theater-like arrangement. The typical plan for this type was a square auditorium with a pulpit/stage in one corner and tiered seating arranged radially from it. Unitarian use of this arrangement was extremely limited; though adopted by some mainline denominations, it was most clearly associated with evangelical preaching, which was antithetical to Unitarian intellectualism.

The most important theme for Unitarians was an appetite for innovation. From All Souls, New York, in 1855 to the Brattle Square Church in Boston in 1869 to First Unitarian Church of Philadelphia in 1883, innovation was sought and embraced. This is the best answer to the paradoxes of widespread use of the Gothic Revival. Each congregation had its own character and made choices based on image, cost, and professional advice as well as functional needs and aesthetic ideals. While some congregations either overlooked or were not particularly bothered by Gothic architecture's suggestions of opulence and permanence, these associations are nonetheless counter to the denominational profile. But looking broadly we see the denomination as a whole choosing innovative designers and unique church designs in significant measure. And they were designs that tended to be transformative to architecture as a whole.

Unitarians avoided fixed doctrines and complex theologies set in stone. Much of the change that occurred after the Civil War had to do with establishing a clear identity and a forum in which their array of beliefs could be discussed and exchanged. The variety and innovation that Unitarians sought in church design was a visible reminder of the variety of ways that congregations expressed their beliefs. Nonetheless, as part of affirming a shared identity, it was useful over time to articulate the core principles that united the denomination as James Freeman Clarke did with his 1885 "theology of the future."

Upon returning to Boston in 1841 from Louisville, Clarke taught at Harvard, wrote extensively, and started his Church of the Disciples. After decades of using rented spaces, he was finally able to build his own church. The building was exactly contemporary with the first churches of Richardson and Furness, and it was a more unusual design. The architect was Isaac Samuels, but "in reality the building from top to bottom was an embodiment of James Freeman Clarke's ideas of a church as a place where people go to do good and receive good, a building to use and not to look at."[72] It was "Gothic" only in the pointed arches in low relief on its red brick walls (fig. 2.14). There was no tower or spire, only a large central octagonal lantern with a ring of clerestory windows over the main space. It was the least "church-like" of all the unusual designs of the post–Civil War decades. This large church, nearly eighty-five feet square, could seat 1,500—unusually large for a Unitarian church in any era. Most found it functional but also ugly, and it became nicknamed "The Church of the Holy Gasometer." The exposed iron structure of the lofty clear-span interior, combined with light flooding in through the clerestories, mostly recalled train sheds of the day. Yet it was a magnet and landmark of Unitarianism from 1869 onward. The innovations of a theology that was accepting of techno-logical progress and new scientific theories countering old belief systems were not reflected universally in Unitarian church designs, and yet there were instances that stand out today as extraordinary. And just as Clarke looked to a theology of the future, Unitarians generally looked for an architecture of the future, or at least of their own time, rather than looking back to where they started.

FIGURE 2.14. Church of the Disciples, Boston, Isaac B. Samuels, 1869, exterior view. Photographs of Unitarian Universalist Churches, bMS 15001/2, Andover-Harvard Library, Harvard Divinity School, Cambridge, Massachusetts.

FIGURE 3.1. Unity Chapel, Spring Green, Wisconsin, Joseph L. Silsbee, 1886, exterior view showing the ideal of domestic scale and timeless materials. Photograph by author.

CHAPTER THREE

"... And the Service of Man"

The Almighty had a great mission for this nation. Here the Church was to proclaim the equality of the races. Wherever the oppressed were congregated, there Christ was present, and not on the side of power. Into such a presence . . . I always come with reverence.

—Thomas Starr King, Speech at Pacific Gardens, San Francisco, August 1860

Whoever loves Truth and lives the Good is, in a broad sense, of our religious fellowship; whoever loves the one or lives the other better than ourselves is our teacher, whatever church or age he may belong to. The general faith is hinted well in words which several of our churches have adopted for their covenant: "In the freedom of the Truth and in the spirit of Jesus Christ, we unite for the worship of God and the service of man."

—William Channing Gannett, "Things Commonly Believed among Us"

REIMAGINING THE CHURCH: FRIENDLY DOMESTICITY

Frank Furness's and H. H. Richardson's noteworthy Unitarian church projects did not have any direct impact on other Unitarian church design. Like Jacob Mould's All Souls Church in New York, they were significant as examples of Unitarian congregations' wanting unique architectural expressions and constructing buildings that contributed positively to advancing American culture—fostering an original American architecture. The post–Civil War period of rapid industrialization, urban expansion, population growth, and other major socioeconomic developments that would blossom into the "Gilded Age" saw only moderate growth of Unitarianism: an expansion from about 250 congregations in 1850 to 400 in 1890, peaking at 455 in 1900. While almost doubling seems significant, it was meager in comparison to mainline Protestant denominations.[1] Nevertheless, Unitarian influence on American culture remained substantial. Edwin Gaustad, historian of American religions, notes, "Indeed, crucial dimensions of the entire history of American education, along with the struggle for emancipation and civil rights, women's rights and identity, and ecumenical encounters within and outside Christianity would not be fully coherent without reference to their Unitarian dimensions. Transcendentalism, religious rationalism, modern biblical criticism, a proto-social gospel, and other currents that ran deep into American life first trickled out of and through New England Unitarianism."[2]

Although the largest concentration of Unitarianism continued to be located in New England, another center of gravity was formed in the Midwest. Cincinnati, Louisville, St. Louis, and Chicago all had congregations from the mid- to late 1830s onward. By 1890, Illinois, Iowa, Wisconsin, and Michigan all had ten to twelve counties with one or two Unitarian churches each; Minnesota had five in all.[3] A Western Unitarian Conference (WUC) was started in the early 1850s with about twelve churches represented. However, the group gained more influence after 1875, the year they withdrew from the American Unitarian Association (AUA), the national organization. The westerners were more progressive, and they resented what they saw as eastern conservatism and snobbery. Under the leadership of Jenkin Lloyd Jones (1843–1918), the WUC gained organizational strength and a strong voice through its independent publication, *Unity*. The ideological rift was largely repaired in the early 1890s, but the WUC continued to operate semi-independently throughout much of the twentieth century.[4]

Jones was born in Wales to Unitarian parents; they emigrated to North America when he was just one year old. They eventually settled in southwestern Wisconsin, where their extended family acquired abundant farmland. Jones served in the Civil War and carried thereafter a lifelong devotion to Abraham Lincoln and racial equality. He attended the Meadville Theological Seminary in Pennsylvania, and then spent most of the 1870s as a traveling minister among congregations of the WUC. He maintained an association with a congregation in in Janesville, Wisconsin, just south of Madison, and began work for the WUC in 1875. When he moved to Chicago in 1882 to form a new congregation on the South Side, he quickly built up his Church of All Souls while at the same time continuing his leadership of the WUC. In all of his endeavors, he promoted his expansive, socially progressive views.[5] Social and political historian Wanda A. Hendricks observes that "the church's design and programs in many ways combined Jones's personal, religious, and political beliefs with his professional mission. Ignoring the segregation that was so prevalent during the period, he argued that in his 'ideal church' blacks were equals. From the beginning blacks found a place in the church." All Souls was not only an integrated congregation; Jones invited women and African Americans to lead services from his pulpit. Fannie Barrier Williams, famously the first African American member of the Chicago Woman's Club, was a member of the congregation and also an invited speaker in 1890. Jones achieved wider cultural impact when he was among the top organizers of the World Parliament of Religions at the Chicago World's Columbian Exposition in 1893, bringing representatives of major world religions together for the first time. He promoted Williams as a speaker there as well.[6]

Among the topics of great interest to Jones and his coeditor of *Unity*, William Channing Gannett (1840–1923), was the idea of a new architecture for the Unitarian church. They pursued these ideas in sermons, essays, and the construction of new buildings in the Chicago area. They also mentored and influenced other ministers in the WUC. Jones described the problem with conventional church design, focusing in particular on Gothic Revival, in sermons of the 1880s and offered an alternative. In "The Ideal Church," delivered in 1882, he laid out a set of values and principles for his new congregation and addressed the kind of building he envisioned for it: "A home where its members will gather for the studying of God's laws, for spiritual culture, for mutual comfort, to lay their plans to do better the work of the world, and to worship. It will be a social hall, a workshop, and an oratory for the soul in one."[7] This stirring combination of shared brotherhood, meaningful labor, and spiritual uplift became the heart of Unitarianism at the start of the twentieth century and inspired a quarter-century of alternative designs for churches of the Midwest.

In May 1885, he presented the All Souls congregation with the design he had commissioned for their church, explaining its intentions and soliciting member donations to support its construction. Jones enumerated the principles that had guided the design as "economy, utility, beauty, and a home-like adaptation to the higher needs and deeper life of today." He anticipated skepticism regarding the overall appearance—"it shocks the eye with an unfamiliar look"—and the novelty, at that time, of locating the parsonage under the same roof as the sanctuary.[8] He made his case for both on the same basis—that the building would be used by members and others in the community alike for social support and educational or cultural gatherings throughout the week. For this array of activities, which would far surpass Sunday worship services, it was important for everyone to feel welcome, and for the minister to be present throughout the week. Jones was passionate about his ideas and able to persuade his congregation with a poetic vision. He followed a Unitarian theme of responsibility to the whole community, not in the building's aesthetic or cultural value this time but through its usefulness beyond worship and the church membership.

The church that Jones built was designed for him by architect Joseph L. Silsbee, a Unitarian from Buffalo, New York, recommended to Jones by Gannett.[9] Silsbee countered conventional church designs with a wood-frame building whose semicircular auditorium was masked by a L-shaped layer of rooms, some of which radiated from its center. These rooms had designated functions, such as library, parlor, and office, but they were open to the auditorium and could be used as expansion space for occasions with larger attendance. This part of the building had a second story, providing rooms for a minister's residence. The second story floor was split between the lower spaces that fronted the streets and additional spaces about three feet higher over portions of the auditorium's perimeter. The facades of the two-story wings faced the streets with bays, gables, and dormers as well as window arrangements that were residential in scale. The corner entry to the church was a welcoming porch signaled by large arched openings facing each direction. Jones feared that the residential appearance would be startling, but a residential appearance and scale was quite normal in many smaller cities and towns.

The clearest embodiment of Jones's vision for Unitarian church architecture was Silsbee's design for a smaller rural chapel near the Jones family property in southwest Wisconsin, which was undertaken at about the same time. Unity Chapel's small scale, simple spatial arrangement, and everyday materials all contribute to a lucid statement of the domestic ideal (fig. 3.2a). It not only fulfilled Jones's wishes for the small rural congregation that was made up largely of family members; it seemed to both Jones and Gannett to be an ideal model for rural chapels throughout the Midwest. Silsbee's sketch of the design appeared in the December 1885 issue of *Unity*, along with Jones's praise and recommendation of the architect. Frank Lloyd Wright (1867–1959), Jones's nephew and an employee of Silsbee at the time, probably had some involvement with the Unity Chapel design;

 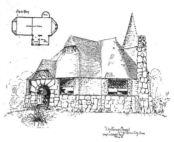

FIGURE 3.2a. Unity Chapel, Spring Green, Wisconsin, Joseph L. Silsbee, 1886, exterior view. Photograph by author.

FIGURE 3.2b. Unitarian Church, Sioux City, Iowa, perspective sketch by Frank Lloyd Wright, 1887. From *Inland Architect and News Record*, June 1887.

his sketch of the chapel was published in the All Souls annual report in 1887, the first Wright drawing to appear in print.[10] Wright then proposed a design for the Unitarian congregation in Sioux City, Iowa, that was almost identical (fig. 3.2b).

Gannett later contributed a lengthy and romantic vision of the values that the ideal church should embody in his 1895 sermon "The House Beautiful." It was published by a congregation member in a limited edition with graphic design by Frank Lloyd Wright—a clear endorsement by Wright of his uncle's ideas ten years before designing Unity Temple (fig. 3.3). Gannett was advocating for simplicity in the face of rising consumer culture and the accepted proprieties of social functions in the typical Victorian middle-class home. He began by recalling the deep natural, and therefore divine, origins of the materials used to build the house, even those materials that had been transformed in factories. For eyes that could see it, "the house in which we live is a building of God, a house not made with hands."[11] He linked much of his advice for the arrangement and furnishing of the house to the familial activities and relationships that they supported with an overarching concern for comfort, nourishment of mind and heart, and natural beauty. The sanctity of the home was a widely accepted American idea in which home and church were ever interconnected. Thus, the harmonies that Gannett elaborated poetically in "The House Beautiful" also expressed his attitudes toward the ideal church.

As with Jones, there were two churches directly attributable to Gannett's vision built in the 1880s. His first congregation upon moving west from Boston in 1877

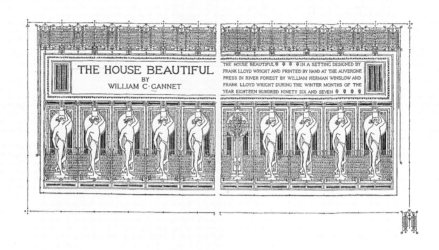

FIGURE 3.3. William Channing Gannett, *The House Beautiful* (River Forest, IL: Auvergne Press, 1896), title page and epigraph, graphic design by Frank Lloyd Wright.

was in St. Paul, Minnesota. By 1880 they had begun to plan for their own church building. Gannett worked with the architect to develop what he called their "church home," completed in 1882.[12] Photographs show that it was somewhat less insistent on being mistaken for a residence than All Souls would turn out to be, though its wood construction and general scale were domestic in character (fig. 3.4a). The facade had a symmetrical arrangement of two entry stairs flanking an open loggia surmounted by a gable. Behind the gable and on the same central axis was a squat square tower rising above the roof and capped with its own pyramidal roof. But the symmetry was countered by the vertical accent of a chimney set farther back on one side and an additional side entry. The effect was not quite residential but not exactly religious either.

FIGURE 3.4a. Unity Church, St. Paul, Minnesota, 1882, exterior view. Photograph courtesy of the Minnesota Historical Society, Minneapolis.

FIGURE 3.4b. Unity Church, Hinsdale, Illinois, 1887, exterior view. Photograph by author.

Gannett left St. Paul in 1884 to serve as a minister-at-large for the WUC. Eventually, he founded a new congregation in Hinsdale, Illinois, just west of Chicago. Although he was only with the congregation for two years, he was remembered for leadership in the construction of a church that was "both a church and a home" (fig. 3.4b). The building is another that would never be mistaken for a house, but it took many cues from Arts and Crafts houses and was not very different in size from residences on surrounding streets. A squat masonry tower element is in the foreground, with a large arched opening to offer entry. The rest of the building is, by contrast, more diminutive. Its hipped roofs and chimneys were familiar domestic forms. The congregation's minister one hundred years later noted that "the very nature of the construction speaks of the human—in the domestic scale and the hand wrought aspects of bead board and beam ceilings, mullioned and colored glass windows."[13] The parlor and auditorium both have fireplaces—the former representing the central importance of the family, the latter the wider kindred of society. Gannett wrote a hymn for the dedication service of the new church that expressed his vision of a welcoming refuge: "Here Be No Man a Stranger."[14] The congregation felt the result was both warm and intimate.

Although Jones formally withdrew from Unitarianism in the mid-1890s and Gannett moved from Hinsdale to Rochester, New York, in 1889, their leadership left a lasting imprint on Unitarians in the Midwest. On the other hand, there were still plenty of conservative views and conventional churches built, even in Chicago. The First Unitarian Church constructed a new building in 1897 that was an unusual version of Gothic Revival. Interestingly, their first church building of 1837 had stood in the spot currently occupied by a Pablo Picasso sculpture in Daley Plaza. The church moved southward twice, in 1861 and 1873, before a final move to a site near the University of Chicago at the end of the century.[15] Their lacey Gothic chapel was constructed just two miles south of Jones's All Souls. It was later incorporated as a transept into a more monumental Gothic Revival church.

WOMEN CHURCH BUILDERS OF THE PROGRESSIVE ERA

Churches built by women ministers and architects were another indication of Unitarian bold thinking. As the leaders of the WUC, Gannett and Jones were not only mentors to the ministers of relatively rural congregations throughout Indiana, Illinois, Iowa, Wisconsin, and beyond; they actively promoted and supported women in the ministry. Their advocacy for women ministers and for the kind of ideal rural church that Unity Chapel represented was complementary. And in return, their vision of the church was wholly embraced by the group of women ministers known as the Iowa Sisterhood. Prominent among the reasons for the domestic attitude of Unitarian church buildings was to further the capacity for and effectiveness of community service. The Iowa Sisterhood ministers embraced this, as they were already fully involved in the family lives of their congregation members and felt an urgent need to be open and available to any farmer's wife whenever she happened to make it to town.[16] They understood the hardships these women faced and knew that they needed some friendly support whenever they could get it.

The sisterhood was responsible for at least twenty new "houses of worship" between 1880 and 1913.[17] Unfortunately, little remains of these outposts. Women were common in these positions because the men in the ministry sought and gained the most prestigious posts; the posts held by women were places unable to attract and retain men as their ministers. The women took on the many challenges that faced them in Iowa and relished their relative freedom to be of service to their communities. In providing new churches, these women ministers worked with architects or builders, as Jones and Gannett had done, but they set the tone and specified the character. They oversaw many of the details as well. Eleanor Gordon (1852–1942) and Mary Safford, working together for a new congregation in Sioux City, adopted the ideal set by Unity Chapel the most literally by engaging Frank Lloyd Wright to provide the design (see fig. 3.2b).

One Iowan example still stands: a church in Iowa City where Eleanor Gordon was the minister from 1896 to 1900 (fig. 3.5). Although she moved on to an organization-level position after that time, she remained involved with the congregation and worked closely with the next minister, Robert Loring, on plans for a new building. They agreed that they wanted a "little church that looked like a house" in order to express a welcoming attitude of personal care and to project a civic presence.[18] They embraced a "down-to-earth workability, the democratic provision of comfort," recognizing too that "a church's responsibility was not confined to its immediate family, but included the whole of society."[19] The building included a good-sized kitchen and parlors with fireplaces in addition to the primary space for worship. It was completed in 1908. The building remained the congregation's home for over one hundred years; in 2017 they moved to their newly completed building in nearby Coralville, designed to be the "greenest church in Iowa."[20]

FIGURE 3.5. Unitarian Society, Iowa City, Iowa, 1908, exterior view. Photograph by author.

The People's Church in Kalamazoo, Michigan, designed in large part by sister-hood minister Caroline Bartlett Crane (1858–1935), offers a clear historical record of how the increased focus on community services could be supported architec-turally. Crane was largely self-taught in ministry, though she had attended col-lege and worked as a teacher and journalist initially. She pursued ministry after meeting William Gannett, who offered his guidance and mentorship in the mid-1880s. In Des Moines in 1887, the Iowa Unitarian Association accepted her as a member. She was soon called to her first congregation in Sioux Falls, then in the Dakota Territory, a congregation that had been organized by sisterhood minis-ter Eliza Wilkes. Crane's arrival consolidated the young congregation, and she focused them on the construction of a proper church of their own. One biogra-pher describes it as "a handsome new building of Sioux quartzite stone, replete with modern furnaces, parlors, and a suite of minister's rooms, was ready for occupancy by year's end."[21] The building appeared to be about the same size as All Souls in Chicago, and it had a similar entrance porch on one corner with arched openings in each direction. While the massing was not as complex, large gable ends facing each direction and a centrally placed chimney were distinctly resi-dential in character. When the congregation faltered after Crane's departure, the building served equally well as a public library.

Crane's short but successful first post was ended by a call to Kalamazoo in 1889. Between the two, she attended some lectures at the University of Chicago, where the sociologists Charles Henderson and George Herbert Mead were leading advocates for social welfare. She met prominent figures in the settlement house movement and visited their facilities, in addition to visiting Jenkin Jones at All Souls.[22] Between her tutelage in the WUC and her exposure in Chicago to social reform movements, she fortified her vocation to social ministry. In Kalamazoo, where she was formally ordained, she rapidly turned a dwindling congregation into a vibrant and growing community. In the summer of 1891 she was able to travel to England where she preached in Unitarian churches and studied the social work of the Salvation Army in the cities.[23]

Within five years of Crane's arrival, the Kalamazoo congregation was outgrowing their modest carpenter Gothic building. An appreciative member donated a substantial sum of money for a new structure; with it, Crane was fully poised to expand the church's programs. She did not make the spaces grand, but she did make a much bigger building than Jones's own All Souls in Chicago by adding more rooms to serve additional civic functions. Her church did not express the idea of domesticity by being diminutive; it did it primarily through simplicity and comfort (fig. 3.6). Not content to simply be available for counsel, she wanted to provide any needed social services not yet publicly available. Additional spaces that served the broader needs of the community, particularly women, included a free community kindergarten, a kitchen and dining room that hosted free lessons in modern home economics and served hot lunches for a low cost to working girls, and a women's gymnasium. The basement contained shops where boys could study metalwork, carpentry, and mechanical drawing instead of spending idle time in the streets. Other groups that used the meeting rooms included a literary club for African Americans, an Audubon Society chapter, a choral union, and an orchestra. The People's Church, a name chosen by the donor, was well used throughout the week, and Crane's preaching continued to keep it full on Sundays as well.

The building was completed in 1895 and succeeded in every way that she planned. Jones and Crane maintained a professional alliance and friendship; he visited her new church himself when he officiated at her marriage to a Kalamazoo physician in 1896. Crane resigned as minister in 1898 due to illness and also apparently some differences with the church's board. But she remained a member of the People's Church for the rest of her life. Ten years after building it, she described the reasoning and the process in some detail for the journal *Charities*.[24] Crane went on to have substantial influence in water, food, and fire safety regulations; urban sanitation; and worker housing.

FIGURE 3.6. The People's Church,
Kalamazoo, MI, 1896, exterior view.
Photograph from the Western
Michigan University Archives and
Regional History Collections.

Among the earliest professional women architects in this country, two were entrusted with designs for small Unitarian churches. Minerva Parker Nichols (1863–1949) was the first woman architect to run her own firm, located in Philadelphia, which she inherited from her employer and teacher.[25] A graduate of MIT in 1890, she maintained a successful practice primarily focused on residences but also designed several institutional buildings. Although a pioneer, she did not find practicing architecture particularly remarkable; she believed women to be as capable as men when given the proper opportunity: "We do not need women as architects, we do not need men, but we do need brains enough to lift the architecture of this country beyond the grasp of unskilled and unqualified practitioners."[26] When she moved with her husband, a Unitarian minister, from Philadelphia to Brooklyn, she gave up full-time practice but continued to do occasional projects for family and acquaintances. Among them were the completion of a renovation for a Unitarian church in Deerfield, Massachusetts, and the design for a new Unitarian church in Gouveneur, New York. This church was a small chapel with a parlor, residential in scale and appearance, though not tied ideologically to the ideas of the Midwest. It was among just five church designs illustrated as models for Unitarian churches in the 1902 publication *Plans for Churches*, produced by the UAU to assist congregations in planning new churches.[27]

Marion Mahony (1871–1961), the second woman to graduate from MIT in 1894, was working in the Oak Park studio of Frank Lloyd Wright at the turn of the century when she was chosen to design a new church for an Evanston, Illinois, Unitarian congregation by the minister, who was a family friend. Mahony later wrote that "he had had experience with my capacity as an artist, and beauty was one of the requirements of his religion; and he knew my qualifications."[28] Her first design proposal was unique: the appearance on the front facade was residential, in keeping with the context and probably influenced by the ideas in the WUC. However, the spaces within were generous: a broad rectangular nave with chamfered corners at the back opened to a shorter octagonal social hall of the same width. Entry to the church was by a vestibule at the juncture of these two spaces with direct access to both. There was really nothing else quite like it in 1900. However, due to "excessive interference," this design was rejected by a board of directors, and Mahony subsequently provided a more conventional plan for a simple rectangular chapel with a social hall in the basement.[29] The minister did not intervene but, according to Mahony, "realized later it was a pity. . . . From that time on he stood absolutely by me, and the board had to accept those [later] decisions."[30] Although the plan as built was not as compelling, the abstract severity of the facade, softened by the textured masonry, was notable (fig. 3.7). A raised platform for the pulpit was set in a chancel, separated from the nave by a wall with three arched openings. The ceiling beyond was lowered in two steps and filled with art glass lit from above. The farthest one dramatically lit a mural in the upper portion of the end wall—a masterful handling of space and light. This church was completed in 1904, two years before Wright began work on Unity Temple in the Oak Park studio.

Unitarians and Universalists were the first Protestant denominations to admit women into ministry in the 1860s and 1870s. The WUC was far more supportive than the AUA in this matter. Jenkin Lloyd Jones and William C. Gannett were critical in providing important mentorship to women. In Iowa, the ministers provided support to farm families that were spread across substantial distances. The church-parsonages that they built in Sioux City, Des Moines, Davenport, Cedar Falls, and other towns followed the ideal of home. There was a practical dimension

FIGURE 3.7. Unitarian Church, Evanston, Illinois, Marion Mahony, 1904, exterior view. Photographs of Unitarian Universalist Churches, bMS 15001/4, Andover-Harvard Library, Harvard Divinity School, Cambridge, Massachusetts.

to it: "Their total involvement in a practical, seven-day ministry blurred the divisions between its public and its private areas, so that the church and home were no longer just similar but were one and the same." But there was also an ideological one: "The clergywomen were just as convinced as the rest of society that a family's residence had a profound bearing on its religious development. As the guardians of their congregations, they therefore took great pains to see that their buildings expressed the ennobling principles that were embraced by the popular ideal of home."[31] Accepting women as architects might have been somewhat easier than as ministers, but entrusting them with a more permanent expression of a congregation's place in the community was not a small matter. Regardless, women's equality was a central belief of Unitarians, so it is not surprising that perhaps the earliest American churches designed by professional women were Unitarian.

AMERICAN ORIGINALITY: A REVERIE OF NATURE

Another context in which a uniquely American rendering of architectural form emerged was the San Francisco Bay area. A Unitarian congregation of San Francisco was started in 1850; it is the oldest congregation west of St. Louis, and its most famous nineteenth-century minister was Thomas Starr King (1824–1864), who served from 1860 to 1864. He was a minister but also a public intellectual of the Emerson type, well-known in Boston and New York before he accepted the challenge of going to the West. His successful antislavery advocacy was noted in the previous chapter. Not only did he preach Unitarian values and political positions to the pioneering Californians but he was important for transmitting back to the East Coast an introduction to and aesthetic appreciation for the natural wonders of California, especially the Yosemite Valley. Historian John Sears notes that his descriptions were widely appreciated: "King's account of Yosemite had a major impact in establishing Yosemite's reputation as a national treasure, not only because he had a gift for nature description, but because his fame as a minister, lecturer, and travel writer gave him authority with his readership."[32] His early death on March 4, 1864, was mourned by the whole population, not only his congregation. State flags were flown at half-mast, and the state legislature adjourned for three days.[33]

King's church was replaced by the congregation in 1891 with a Gothic Revival building. The fairly conventional San Francisco church and a similar Romanesque Revival one in Oakland were built at a point when the local architectural profession was just starting to coalesce. Some new arrivals from the East Coast began to develop an aesthetic response to the local context that would eventually be seen as a regional style. Bernard Maybeck (1862–1957) is the most well-known of this group; he arrived in San Francisco from New York by way of the École des Beaux-Arts in early 1891.[34] He was preceded by A. Page Brown and Albert C. Schweinfurth (1864–1900). Schweinfurth had worked both as an employee of Brown and also as an independent architect in New York, and that continued to be the case in San Francisco. Maybeck worked with them for about two years before accepting a teaching position at the University of California in Berkeley and starting an independent practice.

Charles William Wendte, a disciple of King, successfully advocated for the establishment of a Unitarian church in Berkeley in 1890. The fledgling congregation began by meeting in existing buildings while raising money for a church. They hired an architect in 1894, but his design was too costly, and in any case, the congregation continued to struggle financially. They were finally ready to proceed once again in 1898, commissioning Schweinfurth at this time. (Maybeck was a member of the congregation, but he was deeply involved in planning for the University of California campus and was traveling in Europe in 1897–98.) Schweinfurth's church design broke new ground with a relatively simple Arts and Crafts approach.

Schweinfurth, who died young in 1900, was described in a 1902 article as being "among the earliest architects to appreciate the charm and adaptability to surroundings" of the remains of the early Spanish colonial missions. He was not captivated by particular formal attributes but by a "peculiar air of rich poverty" in materials and assemblies.[35] The same "peculiar air" might be ascribed to his Unitarian church. It is dominated by a strikingly long and low double pitched roof that projects far enough past the width of the church to form an entry porch on both ends (fig. 3.8a). The west-facing front facade is somewhat stark: a large circular window centered in the gable is the only feature in the wall. Porches on each end are formed by an exposed wood beam reaching out to land on a three-foot-diameter redwood log at the corner. The interior is a plain, large open space (about sixty by seventy-five feet) with exposed trusses carried by wood posts set in a plaster wall. Each bay has a single large round-headed opening filled with industrial metal sash, an early use of this modern element. The loft-like space ends in a wall with a plain arched opening to a semi-circular skylit apse flanked by two doors.

The local paper praised the architecture when construction was completed—a unique, progressive design. Its "rustic idea" was considered to be a "radical departure" from the norms of church architecture.[36] Architectural historian Leland Roth described it as "the essence of architecture . . . primal and pure."[37] Its horizontality and rough materials were associated by some, however, with utilitarian buildings; one observer evidently criticized it for looking like a powerhouse. But the church was among the earliest structures to express values held among a number of local residents, artists, and intellectuals, codified in the founding of Berkeley's Hillside Club. The club was established by neighbors interested in preserving the beauty of their environment; they saw a simple life and closeness to nature as essential virtues. These were seen in the church design in the use of raw redwood logs and rough beams and in the simplicity of the barn-like interior. The building seems tied to the site by the reach of the roof and by the curved "buttresses" along the exterior of the nave walls (fig. 3.8b). While they make a whimsical gesture toward traditional masonry church architecture, they also strengthen a visual connection to the ground, seeming to suggest that the building grew naturally. Handcrafted furnishings complemented the simplicity of the interior.

Local historian Betty Marvin noted that the building hosted many cultural events: "Early members of First Unitarian included many of Berkeley's prominent

FIGURE 3.8a.
First Unitarian
Church, Berkeley,
California, Albert C.
Schweinfurth, 1898,
view of the front.
Photograph by Bret
Morgan.

FIGURE 3.8b. First
Unitarian Church,
view of one side look-
ing toward the front.
Photograph by Bret
Morgan.

artists and intellectuals, and the congregation has remained notable for liberal and humanitarian and cultural activities."[38] The congregation called on Maybeck when it added a parish house, Unity Hall, in 1907. He added an arcade outside the north wall of the church to connect the two. It was a simple structure to meet the social needs of the congregation, repeating the dark exposed structure and white wall surfaces of the church interior. The fireplace and chimney best captured the character of the Schweinfurth building. Unfortunately, this addition was demolished when the University of California purchased the property in 1965. Luckily, the church building was preserved and repurposed as a dance studio.

At about the same time, Maybeck designed a Unitarian church in Palo Alto (fig. 3.9). The design may only be known now from a few photographs. (The Palo Alto congregation that built this church disbanded in 1929. A new congregation made a fresh start in 1949 and commissioned Joseph Esherick for a building completed in 1958.)[39] His design displayed a richness of ideas and material effects though it lacked overall unity: a crenellated masonry block was joined to a timber frame shed with shingle siding. The masonry block was slightly taller and wider than the shingled auditorium. The front elevation had a central doorway sheltered by a roof set against the gable end of the auditorium. The roof overhung the first bay of the lateral wall; the remaining bays were planar, but the structural frame was evident. The masonry block was finished with smooth stucco. The same sharp contrast was repeated on the interior. The auditorium, which appears to have been quite dark, was a dense space, and exposed wood framing was somewhat overpowering for the scale of the space. It has been described as Gothic for the way the exposed structure recalled a forest.[40] A contemporary news article regarded it as noteworthy for using "rough, less expensive forms of material for a permanent building . . . redwood boards and battens, common redwood shakes, rough heavy timbers . . . left unplaned . . . [and] stained with an old-fashioned logwood dye . . . almost black. . . . The surfaced redwood of the walls and pews is being finished by a Japanese painter who understands the treatment of this fickle wood."[41] The pews filled the center of the space while aisles were at the sides. The auditorium was terminated by a sharply chiseled deep round arch. Beyond was an indeterminate space finished in glass tile and rich velvets lit by a skylight. The rich materiality and air of mystery was atypical for Unitarian church space. Historian Kenneth H. Cardwell described the effect of the interior as "primitive." Each of the two contrasting motifs was executed with a powerful intensity—the forest and the cave—but they remained independent and unconnected.[42] Although the designs

FIGURE 3.9. Unitarian Church, Palo Alto, California, Bernard Maybeck, 1907, exterior and interior views. Photographs of Unitarian Universalist Churches, bMS 15001/, Andover-Harvard Library, Harvard Divinity School, Cambridge, Massachusetts.

for Berkeley and Palo Alto were quite different, both clearly participated in the "building with nature" movement, both were experimental and innovative, and both could be seen as a conscious search for an original architectural expression. The influence of these designs can be seen in Maybeck's more famous church, the First Church of Christ, Scientist (1910), also in Berkeley.

AMERICAN ORIGINALITY: WRIGHT'S UNITY TEMPLE

By 1892 Jenkin Lloyd Jones realized that he had made a mistake and that his building for All Souls in South Chicago was too small. He wished to provide social services on the scale of a settlement house at his church, which required meeting rooms and workshops, not just a library and parlor. Although he had formed this vision by 1892, it would be another ten years before he could implement it. Design work started in the late 1890s, but fundraising delayed construction, and the design continued to evolve. His nephew Frank Lloyd Wright was heavily involved in the early stages but backed away from the project and a forced partnership with Dwight Perkins, a member of All Souls, before the final designs were completed.[43]

By the time Jones was getting close to a final design, he and the All Souls board of directors had formally withdrawn from Unitarian affiliation. After his experiences in organizing the 1893 World Parliament of Religions in conjunction with the World Columbia Exposition, Jones continued to be a champion of universal religious principles over sectarian differences. Finding his Unitarian affiliation too confining at this point, he conceived of his project as a new typology—a settlement-like social services institution anchored by a spiritual core, "a clearing house of applied religion."[44] However, he did not want to use the word "settlement" because it carried a clear signal that one class was helping another; he resisted a model that heightened awareness of class distinctions. He also did not want to call his new hybrid an "institution." It was intended to provide a "center" for the whole community, with an auditorium to allow for religious services and civic meetings.[45] Consequently, he might have used the term "meetinghouse." He referred to it in his sermons as "a new cathedral" that could bring unity to the modern city not through religious uniformity but through communal activities of all kinds. Still, he felt that a place for prayer at its center would give it a necessary ethical bearing. The fulfillment of Jones's vision was a seven-story rectangular block on a lot across the street from the 1886 All Souls building. The Abraham Lincoln Center, completed in 1905, went substantially further in its social and community mission than All Souls had while retaining a room for worship at its core. Although its architectural design essentially fit the Chicago settlement type, Jones's center would initially serve a middle-class community, not a population in need of a means to escape poverty, illness, and hunger.

Historian Joseph Siry demonstrated with great clarity how Frank Lloyd Wright's involvement in the Abraham Lincoln Center project from the mid-1890s to 1903 was influential in his design for Unity Temple in Oak Park, Illinois, undertaken in 1905. Most importantly, Wright's own development of the centrally placed auditorium of the Lincoln Center as a two-story cubic volume with galleries on three sides prefigured the auditorium of Unity Temple. Other previous works of Wright, such as the Hillside Home School, his Oak Park Home Studio, and the Larkin Building, were also clearly related.[46] But the auditorium of Jones's "cathedral" was almost a rehearsal for Unity Temple.

In terms of Unitarian design, of course, Wright had knowledge of Joseph

Silsbee's designs for All Souls and Unity Chapel. But Wright clearly rejected the domestic ideal that Jones had pursued in those projects and one of its basic premises: that the auditorium be subsumed within a larger structure. Among Wright's clearest statements on the design of Unity Temple was the desire to make the auditorium not only visible but fully legible as a distinct and independent spatial volume—a room—on the exterior (fig. 3.10). Ancillary spaces made a wrapper

FIGURE 3.10a. Unity Temple, Oak Park, Illinois, Frank Lloyd Wright, 1909, exterior view. Library of Congress, Prints & Photographs Division, Historic American Building Survey, HABS ILL, 16–OAKPA, 3–1.

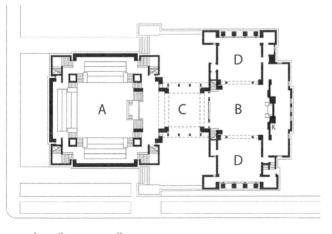

FIGURE 3.10b. Unity Temple, composite plan: A—auditorium, B—social hall, C—entry/narthex, D—classrooms/meeting rooms. Drawing by Alissa Tucker.

for the auditorium at All Souls, creating the domestic camouflage that Jones had wanted, and at the Abraham Lincoln Center, the auditorium was integrated into a much larger, prismatic rectangular block. It was completely invisible on the exterior. Wright chose to put the auditorium of Unity Temple forward on the site so that it was the face of the building; the entrance hall and the social rooms were placed in a subordinate position behind. Where Jones had rejected monumental expressions of the church functions, Wright chose a modestly scaled but deliberate monumentality.

While Unity Chapel's domestic scale and materiality were not adopted, the idea of unity in the conjoined but separable worship space and social space stayed with Wright. Even though the two spaces in the chapel were just a subdivision of one large volume, the entry vestibule had two interior doors that were equal options: left to the auditorium, right to the parlor. At Unity Temple, Wright pulled the two rooms apart, put them under separate roofs, and then linked them with a lower entrance hall, or narthex. This vestibule gave equal opportunity to choose either direction—an arrangement that expressed two separate but equally important functions of the congregational community. Wright later confessed to the difficulty of getting their similarity into balance with their distinctions: they were a unity, born of the same family of forms, but there was a clear hierarchy.[47]

Although Wright did not adhere to Jones and Gannett's domestic ideal for church architecture, their core ideas on the concept of unity were inherent to Wright's own philosophies. When Wright wrote about the design in his *Autobiography* in the mid-1920s, the continuity with Jones was clear.[48] His words have been parsed for two reasons—the obvious one being to better understand the genesis of such a remarkable building, the other that this is the only instance in which Wright offered explicit insight to his design development. His words, however, must be read in the light of Jones and Gannett's ideas to be fully understood. Wright did not have a significant amount of formal education, so the influence of his family's worldview was all the stronger and internalized. The nineteenth-century rhetoric of the Unitarian worldview that Wright grew up with was as integral to his creative imagination as his Froebel blocks were to his compositional sensibilities.[49]

Jones and Gannett's style of writing included using words poetically rather than literally. For instance, the word "temple" was used loosely when Jones called the Gothic cathedrals of Europe "the greatest of temples" in his critique of American Gothic Revival churches.[50] Years later, he described his vision for his next building, more like a Louis Sullivan office block than a church, as a "cathedral." These words used in unusual applications were meant to draw attention and spark imagination.

Wright was doing the same when he promised the building committee of Unity Temple a "modern meeting-house" and a "temple to man." He was intentionally switching and conflating diverse terms to divert his listeners from their conventional mental image of a "church." He described his vision in the same sentence as a "meeting place, in which to study man himself."[51] Reading Jones is the necessary key to understanding Wright's more enigmatic suggestion that Unity Temple would be "a good time place." Jones had told his own congregation that he aspired to create a church that "in some way . . . [will] have something to do in bringing about this good time."[52] The "good time" he aspired to was a time of greater brotherhood and what we would now call social equity; it would be "the Kingdom of Heaven" that was promised by Jesus to Galilee. Just as the Ames Gate Lodge "bachelor's room" was meant as a place of intellectual engagement and exchange, so Wright's "good time place" signaled meaningful discourse and social progress.

Additional concepts that are particularly pertinent to Unity Temple can be found in an 1882 sermon "The Ideal Church" in which Jones made a case for a new church building to his congregation, and an 1886 document presenting the design proposal. After a full critique of the typical Victorian Protestant church, he implored, "Build us instead, O architect, a building whose walls will be instinct with human fellowship and human needs. *Flood it with sunlight* and fill it with pure air."[53] This plea repeated his earlier declaration that "Goethe's dying request is the demand of this church: 'Light, more light, let in the light.'"[54] The auditorium of the All Souls building resulting from Jones's campaign was lit by a large central skylight in addition to its windows. Wright followed this example but with superior artistry and effect. The combination of baffled skylight and sheltered clerestory kept the light indirect but nevertheless abundant and consistent. Wright promised that it would be light even on a cloudy day. No matter the condition outdoors, his forced entry through the dark cloister automatically made the light of the sanctuary fresh and surprising.

Also among the words Wright used in describing his design objectives were "simplicity" and "repose." These are not as dominant in his description of Unity Temple, but they are first among six principles of design listed in the essay "In the Cause of Architecture," written while Unity Temple was nearing completion.[55] These two words were of great importance in Gannett's published sermon "The House Beautiful," for which Wright created the graphics. Gannett borrowed them from the German art historian Herman Grimm, declaring that "the ideal of beauty is simplicity and repose' . . . it applies to everything—to wallpapers and curtains and carpets. . . . The ideal of beauty is simplicity and repose—not flash, not sensation, not show."[56] Gannett also recommended that the only ornaments of the ideal house be books and bits of nature collected and brought indoors— flowers, mosses, feathers, and more. Wright found the sentiments expressed by Gannett so attractive that he was the one to suggest publishing the text. He revisited Gannett's ideas while considering the design of Unity Temple: his very first sketch for the design was made on the end page of his copy of the book.[57] The ideal beauty of nature extolled by Gannett went hand in hand with the importance of daylight in Wright's final design (fig. 3.11).

Although the use of concrete for the structure and envelope was an innovation adopted for the sake of economy, its strangeness for a church was in keeping with the unfamiliar nature of the architectural forms. A few churches and one synagogue had been built by then with exposed concrete in the East, but they were not widely known. In those cases, the architect had used concrete but mimicked classical styles of masonry construction.[58] Unity Temple was the first one to really let the concrete be seen as concrete. The congregation's minister, Reverend Rodney Johonnot, found virtue in the use of concrete in supporting the design; he thought it brought a wholly different kind of monumentality to the town and so would not be seen as wanting when compared with other, more expensive heavy masonry churches.

Numerous historians have found many possible influences for Wright's design, but the overall plan arrangement was completely unique for a Unitarian church.[59]

FIGURE 3.11a. Unity Temple, view of the entry with the inscription. Photograph by Dell Upton.

FIGURE 3.11b. Unity Temple, exterior view, auditorium clerestory pier and windows. Photograph by Dell Upton.

Often described as a bi-nuclear plan, the two main elements of conventional churches were, in Wright's design, pulled apart and then linked by a generous entrance hall. Prior to Unity Temple, there were three main ways that the worship and social spaces were related. They might be stacked one atop the other, as in some of the old New England meetinghouses and in many masonry buildings, utilizing the necessary foundations. The more widespread pattern in the later nineteenth century was to place the social hall adjacent to the auditorium so that the two could be joined together when needed for larger crowds, often in an L-shaped form. A different pattern, less widely used, placed the social spaces in separate nearby or attached parish houses that were architecturally distinct from their churches. This would provide a residence for the minister and would contain some social rooms in which church business and pastoral duties could take place. Although the social space of Unity Temple was labeled Unity House on Wright's drawing, it was not a residence for the minister. Instead, the social hall was a double-height space in the center flanked by double-story blocks on either side. These wings provided an expansion of the central space or could be used as educational and meeting spaces. All of the elements of the design were unified by axes and repeated geometries as well as color and surface treatments.

An unusual circulation sequence is fundamental to the spatial experience of Unity Temple. An entry vestibule or narthex that offers a choice between the worship and the social spaces is not unusual. However, one with an additional choice to pass right through was unique. Of course, that is a byproduct of the building being equally accessible from different directions and not having a front door on the main street. But the experience of entering in and seeing back out the opposing door was a whole different kind of arrival at church—presumably one is also face to face with people entering from the other side, foreshadowing the galleries that face each other in the sanctuary. Entry to the sanctuary is somewhat hidden, while the doors to the social hall are directly available. This difference in ease was also new to this design. The "hidden entry" to the auditorium and the "cloister" contrast the openness of the vestibule; in combination, they hint at something vaguely ritualistic before climbing up to the main floor level and entering fully into the space, which returns the experience to light and clarity. The path to the main floor is essentially a long, looping U-turn that allows the pulpit to be set on an interior wall rather than on the street wall. An advantage of this unusual arrangement is that exiting back to the vestibule by direct stairs flanking the pulpit allows the flow of people to move toward the minister rather than turning away. The novel and engaging experience of this circulation pattern has long been appreciated, and it fits the Unitarian idea of community extremely well. Skewed views of the main church space from corner entries or an extended loggia were much more common than axial arrangements; this is a further elaboration of that practice. Wright's unusually extended sequence was not adopted or explored much in later Unitarian churches. Only one other used the key idea of placing the pulpit closer to the entry and forcing circulation to pass it and then turn around: the First Unitarian Church of Schenectady by Edward Durrell Stone, built sixty years later.

Seating at Unity Temple is arranged in two tiers of balconies set into the depth of three arms of a Greek cross plan. Some believe them to be inspired by the early New England meetinghouse, but a particular source to explain how Wright came to think of this method for achieving the requisite number of seats with an economical footprint is unnecessary. Galleries were common in all kinds of churches and also in theaters. Furthermore, they were just as common in the steepled New England churches that Wright despised as they were in the earlier meetinghouse types that preceded them. There is also a crucial spatial difference to the galleries of Unity Temple. Their front edges, the balcony rails, form the perimeter of the square main floor rather than projecting over part of it, as is usually the case. The lower one is just four feet above the auditorium floor, and the other is directly above it. The resulting isolation of the central main floor creates a fundamentally different spatial experience than galleries in meetinghouses and churches. Perception of the space and of the other people in it from these galleries is almost uncanny—there is a simultaneous awareness of position and space itself, and the shared experience of the space, that lends it vibrancy. Wright almost certainly agreed with Jones's judgment that "a nineteenth century gospel cannot fully utter itself in a sixteenth century pulpit."[60] The isolation of the main floor, along with the choreographed circulation path, is one of the unique features making Unity Temple a pulpit for the twentieth century.

Wright later claimed in his autobiography that he had to convince the minister and building committee in Oak Park to deviate from the conventional sort of church they had lost to fire; he particularly railed against the spire. But the spire as a symbol of traditional church architecture was a red herring; there were few churches being built with spires by that time.[61] Not only was there an absence of spires, there was professional hand-wringing about so many churches that were indistinguishable from other buildings.[62] And Chicago itself was already home to several Unitarian churches that did not adhere to traditional models, including Jones's All Souls and Marion Mahony's church in Evanston. Furthermore, the

Oak Park congregation was more inclined toward progress than tradition. They had already begun a building fund before their church burned down. In a letter to the congregation soliciting donations for the fund, the minister wrote that the current church, at thirty years old, was no longer adequate, and that it was not representative of "present ideas of church architecture."[63] He may not have been looking for the degree of innovation that would ultimately be proposed and adopted, but he was certainly advocating for something up to date in its time. From a social and cultural point of view, the meetinghouse of the Old Ship type would not have been an inspiration to Oak Park Unitarians at the beginning of a new century. And Wright himself was interested in conjuring something unique and even more fundamental to the human condition. Historian Vincent Scully believed that Wright succeeded in initiating a new idea "wholly at the beginning."[64]

As an icon of American architecture, Unity Temple has been admired and interpreted by many scholars with a variety of perspectives. It is not my purpose to add another interpretation so much as to expand on Siry's work and further situate it in the context of Unitarian architecture. It was unlike any Unitarian church that came before it, but it was not the sole experimental church of its time. It is also important to note that it did not become a widely adopted model for Unitarian churches to follow. There were just three churches in the next six decades that showed a clear relationship to Unity Temple as an architectural precedent. Churches in Arlington, Virginia, and Rockford, Illinois, share a rather muscular exposed precast concrete structural system, once again pressing against conventions of what a church is expected to look like. A hilltop church in Berkeley, California, also a concrete structure, is the most literal restatement of the axial alignment of Unity Temple's three primary spaces. They each capture one of the essential elements of Wright's design—the noble room; the familial relationship between auditorium and social hall; and the axial alignment of the auditorium, social hall, and narthex/vestibule.

The design of a new building for the Unitarian Church of Arlington (1961) consists of a square auditorium of similar exterior dimensions to Unity Temple. There was also a continuous clerestory window separating an overhanging flat roof from the enclosing walls on all four sides (fig. 3.12). As at Unity Temple, the auditorium is clearly visible on the exterior, and in this case the external form and interior volume are even more closely equivalent. The concrete exterior is just as dramatic, if not quite as exotic. The flat roof with sculptural scuppers extends outward emphatically in order to shade the tall clerestory windows. Precast concrete panels that form the walls are textured with vertical channels, which lightens their appearance. As designed by Charles Goodman (1906–1992), there was

FIGURE 3.12a. Unitarian Church, Arlington, Virginia, Charles Goodman, 1961, exterior view. Photograph by author.

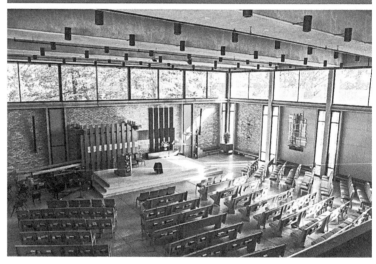

FIGURE 3.12b. Unitarian Church, interior view. Photograph by author.

to be a contiguous social space extending from the south wall of the auditorium. The shorter appendage would have been tied to the main structure by the use of the same precast concrete wall panel system: a continuous treatment but a clearly subordinate element. Due to budget and schedule overruns, the social hall was put on hold when the auditorium was built. (When finally undertaken thirty years later, a new design was commissioned.) Goodman's "noble room," to borrow Wright's phrase, therefore ended up as a freestanding pavilion. Its overall design shared with Unity Temple a certain purity of elements and directness. Interestingly, the architect's statement about the ideas that drove his design made no mention of Unity Temple.[65] But it appears that Goodman was being coy. He had studied architecture at the Armour Institute in Chicago and was taken with the works of Sullivan and Wright. And in his description of the building's design concepts, Goodman referred to the sanctuary as "the great room," which is how Wright described Unity Temple in his autobiography.

The similarity between Wright's design and the Unitarian Church of Rockford (1966) by Pietro Belluschi (1899–1994) is somewhat more subtle. In each case, the auditorium and the social space can be seen as independent elements of similar design linked by lower subordinate spaces. At Rockford, the two are formed by similar (but not identical) exposed concrete structural frames set in equal bays and supporting an overhanging flat roof. While the Rockford complex was larger than Oak Park and included a greater variety of functions, the spatial relationship from auditorium to social hall is direct: doors are aligned across a subordinate narthex. They are also spatially distinct: the auditorium is a clearly directional series of structural bays, while in the social hall the bay rhythm is less dominant (see fig. 6.5). Yet, the familial relationship between two independent spatial volumes can be discerned easily (fig. 3.13). While these parallels to Unity Temple can be drawn, they are not quite as immediately obvious as those of the church in Arlington. In her analysis, architectural historian Meredith Clausen makes no mention of Unity Temple as a precedent; rather, she points to the influence of Le Corbusier, Louis Kahn, and Brutalism in general.[66]

The debt that the First Unitarian Church of Berkeley (1962) owes to Unity Temple, if any, is one of plan arrangement (fig. 3.14). This was a new church that the Berkeley congregation built when they sold their Albert Schweinfurth building to the expanding University of California Berkeley campus. A hilltop site with engaging views had been donated by congregation member Bernard Maybeck. William Wurster (1895–1973) designed this building with landscape-based themes of the Bay Area tradition as his foremost inspiration. The main social hall shares a central axis with the auditorium and the large entry atrium that links them. However, these distinct spaces are not visible in the massing—they are unified by a single, extended double-pitched roof. The atrium is more of an ordering or centering element than a subordinate link, and there are additional subordinate meeting spaces off-axis. The atrium's spacious quality and its doors opposite the entry to an outdoor terrace have a clear connection to Unity Temple's vestibule. However, in this instance, the size of the space is closer in proportion and volume to the main spaces it connects. There are generously scaled skylights and four trees bringing nature straight through the building. In contrast, the sanctuary and the social hall are darker and more enclosed.

Many have noted that Wright used his explanation of the design of Unity Temple

FIGURE 3.13a. First
Unitarian Church,
Rockford, Illinois, Pietro
Belluschi, 1966, view
of the entry with the
auditorium visible to
the right and social
hall on the left. ©
Massachusetts Institute
of Technology,
photograph by G. E.
Kidder Smith.

FIGURE 3.13b. First
Unitarian Church,
plan: A—auditorium,
B—social hall and
lounge, C—narthex.
Drawing by Alissa
Tucker.

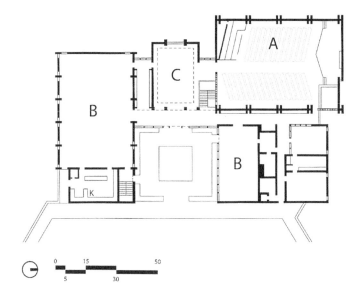

to mythologize his artistic genius, yet at one point he wrote, "*His* [the architect's] message he feels. None the less is it 'theirs,' and rather more. And it is out of love and understanding such as this on the part of an architect that a building is born to bless or curse those it is built to serve."[67] Unity Temple was built in a transitional time. While the Progressive Era would leave its mark on Unitarian values and

FIGURE 3.14a. First Unitarian Church, Berkeley, California, William Wurster, 1962, exterior view. Photograph by HarZim, CC BY-SA 4.0, https://creativecommons.org/licenses/by-sa/4.0/deed.en.

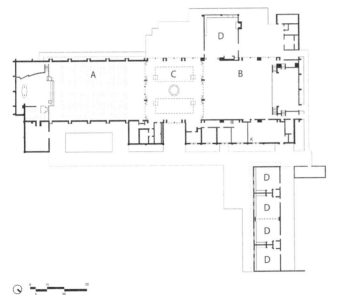

FIGURE 3.14b. First Unitarian Church, plan: A—sanctuary, B—social hall, C—narthex, D—classrooms/meeting room. Drawing by Alissa Tucker.

priorities, few ministers and congregations could sustain the level of social ministry seen in south Chicago and Kalamazoo—the institutional church. Religious education was rising in importance, and social space would continue to be an important element of church designs. Unity Temple expressed the essentials of the

Unitarian congregation: worship and community. The architecture has "blessed" and inspired the congregation that built it and used it continuously for over one hundred years. However, no later design was articulated in as elemental (that is, with such purity of elements) a fashion—two almost freestanding blocks axially aligned and linked by a simple circulation space. And for Wright himself the questions at the heart of Unitarian ideals were analogous to his questions about architecture itself. Historian Sydney Robinson builds on Siry's 1996 analysis with a focus on three stages of the design of the interior; among his conclusions, he suggests that "Unity Temple may be seen as the opening skirmish in Wright's life-long quest to build architecture that maintained the primary virtue of 'plasticity,' but left behind its traditional source in favor of a much more accessible manifestation through the folded plane."[68] The free-thinking congregation allowed him to explore the unity of two and three dimensions in an organic architecture.

CONCLUSION: FREEDOM, FELLOWSHIP, CHARACTER, AND SERVICE

"The conventional church is ill adapted to the service of man." Jenkin Lloyd Jones made this statement in his explanatory sermon on the design of All Souls Church in 1885.[69] Jones continued to expand his own notion of the "service of man" by conceiving, constructing, and directing the Abraham Lincoln Center. Under the leadership of Caroline Bartlett Crane, the People's Church in Kalamazoo had already moved beyond pastoral care and community support services to initiating social programs for the whole city. There were some others of similar institutional scale, such as the First Unitarian Society of Minneapolis, but the Abraham Lincoln Center was the most ambitious, initially planned to include rental space for doctors' and dentists' offices, artists' studios, and apartments in addition to meeting rooms and workshops in order to maintain its own operations. That level of economic obligation remained beyond the scope and capacity of most congregations. However, involvement with causes of social inequity and social justice has been a prominent focus of the denomination ever since. While the Abraham Lincoln Center shared with the New England meetinghouse the idea of a single structure serving religious along with other community functions, the nineteenth-century institution and the city it served were socially as well as architecturally far more complex than the meeting place of a New England village with a theocratic social basis.

The Progressive Era was a dynamic time for the country in general, and for its civic and religious institutions. Women made more and more visible contributions to public life. As Unitarian ministers, the women of the Iowa Sisterhood provided broad support for their congregations and communities, including the construction of church-homes in accordance with their vision. As architects, two women were given the opportunity to design churches by Unitarian congregations at a time when women professionals were generally chosen only for residential projects or institutions that served women. Unfortunately, neither one remains standing today. However, women in the professions of ministry and architecture would not continue to be acceptable. The social transformations of the World War I Era resulted in the loss of these opportunities despite other gains, such as the passage of the Nineteenth Amendment in 1919.

Unitarianism itself continued to transform as well in the Progressive Era. Although there were differences in styles and beliefs between regions of the country and between congregations, a coherent middle seemed to hold. In the 1880s and into the 1890s, questions of belief in God and a Christian identity caused wide debate. In 1887 William C. Gannett provided a statement that both sides of the controversy could accept. At the heart of "Things Commonly Believed among Us" were ten statements of an ethical nature; these were subsequently condensed and promoted by the establishment of the American Unitarian Association:

> Freedom, the method in religion in place of Authority;
> Fellowship, the spirit in religion, in place of Sectarianism;
> Character, the test of religion, in place of Ritual or Creed;
> Service or Salvation of Others, in place of Salvation of Self.[70]

Gannett's words were also used by Wright, who memorialized them as an inscription over the doors to Unity Temple: FOR THE WORSHIP OF GOD | AND THE SERVICE OF MAN (see fig. 3.11a). Words, rather than symbols such as a cross or spire, communicated the spiritual and ethical intentions of a congregation that succeeded in building a church more suited to the present and the future than the past.

The new congregations of Berkeley and Palo Alto, California, wanted a church architecture that was true to its place. It was a new kind of church, and a new kind of American architecture. Schweinfurth was the first since Frank Furness to imagine a church that was something altogether new—"character" in place of tradition. This was not a humble house-like form; it was a grand gesture with an arresting presence. Bernard Maybeck may have responded to the ubiquitous architectural context of Stanford University with a language of arcades with repetitive round-headed arches and whose over-scaled entrance arch—a tall masonry block—was destroyed in the 1906 earthquake. The interior was his first use of the heavy timbers that make the First Church of Christ, Scientist (1910) seem to be a work of nature itself. These two California churches and Unity Temple were all unconventional and innovative designs that marked the end of the era of Theodore Parker, Thomas Starr King, Ralph Waldo Emerson, and James Freeman Clarke and looked ahead to the new century.

PART II
UNITARIANISM ON THE EDGE

FIGURE 4.1. First Unitarian Church, Des Moines, Iowa, Amos Emery, 1957, view of the entry showing the integration of the church into the natural beauty of its site. Photograph by author.

CHAPTER FOUR

From Commons to Campus

My father was a Unitarian, my mother was a Unitarian; my grandmother was a Unitarian, and it has always been a wonder to me that all the world has not become Unitarian. But I think we are verging in that direction.

—William Howard Taft, 1913

The time has come for widespread recognition of the radical changes in religious beliefs throughout the modern world. . . . Science and economic change have disrupted the old beliefs. Religions the world over are under the necessity of coming to terms with new conditions created by a vastly increased knowledge and experience. In every field of human activity, the vital movement is now in the direction of a candid and explicit humanism.

—Raymond B. Bragg, "A Humanist Manifesto," 1933

CHURCHES AS "DURABLE WITNESS" (1900-1930)

Unitarianism evolved continuously in the nineteenth century with its development sometimes described as rationalistic, romantic, and finally scientific stages. A persistently strong emphasis on the value of individual freedom continued to disincline Unitarians from maintaining a meaningful national organization. This lack of a central voice to define the denomination weakened its identity and its internal coherence during a time of continued religious diversification in America. Although the American Unitarian Association (AUA) was founded as early as 1825, it remained quite small and largely irrelevant to the course of Unitarianism for the first forty years. In fact, it was just one among many organizations established by individual Unitarians to serve a variety of causes. After the Civil War, New

York Unitarian minister and civic reformer Henry Bellows (1814–1882) initiated a campaign to make the organization more participatory, deliberative, and morale-boosting. He was aware that the geographic scale of the expanding country created an ever-greater need for a central organizing body to establish an identity, support congregations, and foster growth. He raised money for it and built a system of local conferences by which Unitarian churches could join in fellowship. However, after his death the organization soon lost vitality and relevance.[1]

In 1894 Samuel Atkins Eliot (1862–1950), son of Charles William Eliot, president of Harvard University from 1869 to 1909, and a grandson of one of the founders of the AUA, joined its board of directors. He brought a new outlook and set of expectations to the board's operations and influence, along with a more modern sense of management.[2] He was committed to updating and strengthening the organization so that Unitarianism could expand and thrive in the twentieth century. He implemented modern accounting and business practices and proposed a reorganization with executive management positions. As a result of these innovations, he became the first president of the AUA in 1900, a position he held for twenty-seven years. In addition to increasing revenue and imposing fiscal order, he also toured the country frequently to strengthen existing congregations and to prospect for the need and means for starting new ones. He brought an optimistic vision for a stronger denomination, and he pursued it through a variety of programs and initiatives.

Among Samuel Eliot's accomplishments as president of the AUA was the substantial growth of a church building loan fund and its systematic management. Some loans had been made previously, but the fund was small and there was no regularity in their administration. Eliot was a champion of financial clarity and transparency as well; he initiated a regular column in the *Christian Register*, the journal of the AUA, to report on capital projects throughout the country, including construction costs and funding.[3] He placed a high priority on loan repayment as a cornerstone of congregational independence and integrity. Most new congregations started out with meetings in houses or rented spaces and naturally aimed to eventually build their own churches. Eliot understood that the denomination would prosper if nascent congregations were assisted in moving more quickly to the construction of their own buildings. He knew that the presence of an admirable church building in cities and towns across the country was the best possible means for Unitarianism to be known and counted among America's religions, and perhaps to even attract new members.

Eliot also held strong opinions on church architecture. Biographers have noted that while he was forward-thinking in a variety of ways, he also maintained certain common attitudes of his time. He can be applauded for his views on the importance of architecture and a high level of appreciation for its potential effects, but he remained conservative in his idea of architectural beauty, which he connected to well-known styles. He preferred Federal and Greek Revival meetinghouses of New England (popularly called the Colonial style) and Gothic Revival church buildings, preferably with a spire or tower. In praising two recently dedicated new churches in a column in the *Christian Register* in 1911, Eliot made it clear that he wanted a church to be easily identified as a church, and he warned against "passing fashions." This was possibly a reference to Unity Temple, which was completed in 1909. He valued dignity, beauty, and sincerity; he expected church architecture to "suggest the unseen" through what is present and seen. He believed that beautiful church buildings could have a "spiritualizing influence" even on passersby, and that such churches were the "durable witnesses to the presence and reality of things of the spirit."[4] Eliot influenced new church construction from the turn of the century up to the Great Depression to a degree that was never seen before or after in the Unitarian denomination. This was the last era in which churches were uniformly integral to the fabric of towns and cities, where they were part of a shared public realm along with other religious and civic buildings. Eliot acted in part on a sense of duty to contribute positively to American cities.

During Eliot's AUA presidency, most new church construction continued with nineteenth-century idioms, and although some Gothic Revival churches continued to be built in the early twentieth century, a return to neoclassical models was seen as the more up-to-date choice. Among congregations that chose the columns, pediment, and portico, for instance, were those in Brookline, Massachusetts (Second Unitarian, now Temple Sinai), in 1916; Omaha, Nebraska (First Unitarian), in 1917; and Washington, DC (All Souls), in 1924—all of which are now listed on the National Register of Historic Places. First Unitarian of Omaha is described in its nomination as "exemplary in illustrating the heritage of Unitarianism in America."[5] More idiosyncratic designs appeared occasionally where a strong regional tradition was being referenced, and smaller churches still followed a variety of more domestic images. Good examples of the latter include those in Indianapolis, Indiana (1911); Quincy, Illinois (1914); and Sacramento, California (1915).[6] The main changes that took place in the first three decades of the 1900s were not stylistic and did not affect the space for worship in any discernible way.

Instead, the main development was in the number and sizes of secondary spaces that were desirable, especially in larger cities.

The more complex church campuses of the larger urban centers can be seen clearly in the third building for All Souls, the Unitarian congregation of Washington, DC.[7] Founded as First Unitarian by John Adams and Charles Bulfinch, among others, the All Souls congregation had moved twice since its beginnings in the Bulfinch-designed church on the corner of Sixth and D Streets NW. That 1821 building was transformed into a hospital during the Civil War, after which it was judged to be too derelict to restore. The congregation decided to sell it and build elsewhere. It took ten years to resolve all of the issues, but in 1877 the congregation voted to change its name to All Souls and construct a new church at the corner of Fourteenth and L Streets NW. Their conventional Gothic Revival church had a tower on the corner and an open arcade forming a porch on Fourteenth Street, much like those built in Boston after the end of the Civil War. However, the growing congregation started contemplating yet another move by 1913. Delayed by World War I, their new church on a prominent hilltop site facing Sixteenth Street NW was dedicated in 1924.

This was the sole congregation representing the Unitarian denomination in the nation's capital, so there was a strong desire to build something noteworthy. Not surprisingly, Samuel Eliot took a strong interest in the architecture of what some referred to as "the national church." The design was chosen by means of a competition with an independent jury of three prominent New York architects.[8] Still, it is easy to imagine some influence from Eliot. Their choice of a neoclassical design that replicated so faithfully the model from which Bulfinch had derived the New England churches of the post-revolutionary period (as well as their own first church) was a conspicuously conservative selection for a liberal church. The building, designed by Boston architect Henry R. Shepley, is a close copy of James Gibbs's St. Martin in the Fields in central London (fig. 4.2). Contradicting Unitarian philosophies that usually favored innovation, both interior and exterior follow a pattern that was two hundred years old at the time.

To be fair, there were several factors that might have supported this decision. The most compelling was the context of the still-young federal city. All prominent government buildings were in the neoclassical style, including more recent ones such as the Library of Congress and the Lincoln Memorial. Urbanistically, the classical columns were the mark of civic responsibility and cultural importance. Furthermore, these monuments were expressive of values in tune with Unitarian

FIGURE 4.2. All Souls Church, Washington, DC, Henry R. Shepley, 1924. Library of Congress,Prints & Photographs Division, LC-F82-702.

ones, so adherence to the same architectural code would connote an important association. Finally, the church in Boston that many Unitarians at the time considered the "cathedral of Unitarianism," based on its historic prestige, was the Arlington Street Church of 1860, also a fairly direct copy of St. Martin-in-the-Fields, at least on the exterior.[9] At the dedication service of All Souls in October 1924, Eliot expressed his approval fully: "We rejoice in the skill and taste of the architect and builder and in the unwearied devotion of successive building committees. . . . We rejoice in this achievement, more beautiful and commodious than we dared to expect."[10] When Samuel Eliot resigned his AUA presidency three years later, he resumed his long-suspended ministry at the Arlington Street Church.

All Souls was fortunate to obtain a through-block site facing west onto Sixteenth Street NW at the top of Meridian Hill. The church was placed in the middle of the site, allowing the mass of the traditional church body to stand forward and appear freestanding like the church it was modeled after. The additional spaces now required—a substantial social hall, classrooms, and offices—were placed in two symmetrical two-story wings that connected to the northeast and southeast corners of the church building. Together with the east facade they formed a court-yard along Fifteenth Street NW. Eventually the area underneath the church was finished for use as a gymnasium to serve the neighborhood.[11] Although the neo-classical language of the architecture was a conservative choice, the modern need for more differentiated spaces was fulfilled.

The regionally inflected revival style of the First Unitarian Church of Los Angeles, completed just two years later by the firm of Allison & Allison in 1926, shows greater flexibility.[12] The poured concrete building derived loosely from neo-Renaissance classicism but without the academic correctness of All Souls (fig. 4.3). The relatively plain structure benefits from an influence of the California mis-sions in both the character of the facades and in the arrangement of its various spaces around a courtyard.[13] Its open arcade along West Eighth Street links the church building to a secondary structure and gives a view into a welcoming space from the street. The church building is taller; its smooth wall is topped by a thinly traced pediment and pierced by a central grand arched doorframe. The classical ornament is both sparse and thin. Strip pilasters mark the corners and frame the entry arch. Above the entry a broken segmental arch contains a panel with the inscribed name of the church. The axial entry and central aisle create a focus on the chancel in the traditional church manner. The entry is under a balcony, but the space then opens upward, with flat lateral walls rising approximately thirty feet to a shallow vault. The bottom half of the walls are finished in wood wainscot-ing, while the top half are exposed concrete. The vault is supported by a series of curved wood beams and purlins whose dark stain contrasts with the honey color of the upper half of the space. Square windows in the upper half of the wall, one per bay, may be a reference to mission churches such as the one in Santa Cruz.[14]

The wing containing the social hall in the Los Angeles complex presents the same simple outline to the street as the church, though much shorter. It is visually balanced with the church by the higher relief of four engaged columns forming a central figure with two stories of windows set between the columns. The three vertical spaces between the columns echo the three arched openings in the arcade joining the parish house to the church. A two-story assembly hall occupies the front half of the rectangular footprint; a dining room and kitchen abut it on the

FIGURE 4.3. First Unitarian Church, Los Angeles, Alison & Alison, 1926. Photograph by Carol D. Elkind.

first floor, with one large room and two smaller classrooms above. A link between the two primary structures at the rear of the courtyard contains a parlor on the first floor and a kindergarten above it. The courtyard is a source of light and air for all major rooms. It is also a welcoming shady spot with a small fountain and a few trees. Rising above everything at its rear is a tall square bell tower, furthering the clear reference to the early mission churches of California. And yet the character of this church remains indeterminate; there is something easy and familiar but not explicitly associated with a particular tradition.[15]

These 1920s churches for existing congregations in Washington and Los Angeles are two large urban examples that show the general architectural conservativism of many Unitarian congregations during the tenure of Samuel A. Eliot as president of the AUA. They are evidence of their congregations' aspiration to express a stability, and perhaps even an influence, in their respective cities. The historian that chronicled the Washington congregation observed that "the desire was for a building that expressed the simple and open theology of Unitarianism and facilities that made possible more involvement in their surrounding communities."[16] Although these two churches were stylistically conservative, they both achieved the modern ideal of a complex that served social and educational functions for the congregation and the community. They represented a modernization of the kind of institution Jenkin Lloyd Jones and Caroline Bartlett Crane had pioneered, which emphasized the educational mission and community outreach.

Another indication of Eliot's attempt to increase denominational identity through architecture is the publication under his oversight of a picture book ambitiously titled *Types of Unitarian Churches.*[17] The publication date is uncertain, but the latest date among the examples illustrated is 1907. The book contains illustrations of about ninety Unitarian churches, which would have been roughly 20 percent of the churches in the United States at that time.[18] It is a compilation of single photographs of Unitarian churches ordered alphabetically by location. Each church is identified by name and location, and the majority include the date that the congregation was founded and the year that the building was completed. For some, brief notes on additional historical information are provided. But an indication of the so-called type of architecture is included for less than half of the entries. Moreover, these notes on type contain a variety of information. A few name a recognized style of architecture, a few deal with context (urban, suburban, country, village), some identify the primary material, and in three cases the architect's name appears. Only about one-fifth of the illustrations are of churches built before 1860, so the author does not appear to have been promoting nostalgia or suggesting that architectural identity might lie in denominational roots. In fact, about the same number were built in last seven year period represented, 1900 to 1907. Most of the remainder were from the 1880s and 1890s. The combined effect of the images seems to have supported the quality of revival styles and their continued relevance into the twentieth century. Of the innovative designs in Chicago and the Bay Area, only the Albert C. Schweinfurth design for First Unitarian of Berkeley, California, was included.

Of much greater influence, Eliot also convened a committee, led by Boston architect Edwin J. Lewis Jr. (1859–1937), to consult with congregations on denominational architecture. To aid that work, Lewis and colleagues created a small handbook for congregations to follow in the construction of a new church building. The 1902 publication of *Plans for Churches* provided ten brief pages of practical advice followed by illustrations (one plan and one perspective or photograph of each) for eight designs.[19] Topics covered include the choice of a building site and an architect, the building committee, fundraising, building materials, interior finishes, and furniture. There is no overt mention of a particular style or character; economy was the chief concern throughout. As the authors were well aware, no Unitarian congregation wanted too much interference. This fact was reflected in the erratic history of the AUA, as well as in self-reflections such as Edward Everett Hale's nearly contemporary observation that "in this communion every separate church or society is absolutely independent and would resent any instructions given from a central body."[20] Only in discussing the interior does the *Plans for Churches* text stray toward aesthetic advice: "The interior of the new church should be beautiful, church-like, and an aid to worship. . . . It is our duty to give [our young people] . . . so far as is in keeping with our faith, that which appeals to the sense of the beautiful. We aim to make the true, the beautiful, and the good, one."[21]

The pamphlet first offers three variations on a generic plan—three versions (basic, enhanced, and premium) of a simple longitudinal auditorium plan. Each one is designed to seat one hundred; the differences are in the provision of a social space (parish parlor) and its size, the exterior materials, and the inclusion of a tower. The cost for each is noted so that a congregation might gauge the level of amenities they could afford. These model designs are followed by five actual church projects presented in the same manner. Surprisingly, only two of the five are similar to the generic plan, and all five have different stylistic allusions. Three of the five would fit well with the residential ideals of the Western Unitarians, though for Lewis and his committee, such a result was more pragmatic than ideological. The last two are larger; one has a steeple, of sorts, and the other a tower. But each also has domestic elements such as dormers and chimneys, and a relatively modest scale. The book was produced for use by building committees to illustrate variations on modest churches—it gave them a clear sense of relative costs for three structures with different features for serving the same size of congregation. It could provide a shortcut to a first conversation with an architect, offering clarity on the congregation's means and intentions. Unitarian pragmatism was at least as strong a factor as Unitarian interest in the arts, so many smaller churches of the subsequent decades would follow Lewis's approach.

If there was any basis for what a Unitarian church of the early twentieth century should be, it is this document. The three generic plans for cost comparison are all longitudinal spaces with central aisles that lead straight to a platform for the minister contained between fin walls for an organ on one side and a stairwell on the other. The larger two have a roughly square social space that opens off of the front half of the auditorium and a fireplace centered on the outer wall. Two of the plans place the entry through a vestibule that is on the side of the church rather than at the end. This arrangement seems to have been the norm, bringing people into the space on the diagonal. The third generic plan is the exception—it has a tower added to the end wall, which then serves as the entry vestibule. Four of the five built churches illustrated were longitudinal as well, with just one being more square in proportion. The off-center entry, easy access from the entry to either the social space or the auditorium, and the importance of a fireplace and books or a library are the common themes of the additional five building plans.

The publication's purpose remained ambiguous despite statement by the authors that the "illustrations of inexpensive churches are offered, not as perfect models to be reproduced throughout the country, but rather as suggestions showing what has been and what may be accomplished with very little means."[22] This suggests that there may have been congregations that had gone into debt and perhaps even folded after ill-planned construction projects, as did the Brattle Street Church in Boston in the post–Civil War era. While this might have been the publishers' primary motive, a book of plans was bound to be seen and used to some extent as a pattern book. The establishment of some basic norms to facilitate the design process inherently promoted more convention than would otherwise naturally occur. Like the Asher Benjamin pattern books that made new professional knowledge accessible to craftsmen, the Lewis and company plan book empowered congregations to be in control of a process that was an important defining moment for them. It may have been intended to resist professional architects' predisposition toward monumentality, and its inherent costs and cultural superiority, for church buildings. In any case, it promoted a tradition of relatively humble structures with common, everyday stylistic accents at a time when urban building construction was increasing in scale and complexity.

Between the adoption of the generic plans and his own commissions, Edwin Lewis had a major influence on Unitarian church design of the early twentieth century. Lewis designed some thirty-five Unitarian or Universalist churches between 1890 and 1925, including the somewhat monumental Second Unitarian Church in Brookline. Of the five more modest designs illustrated in *Plans for Churches*, two were his own. One was described as a suburban Boston congregation and is very close in character to a Lewis church in the Wollaston neighborhood of Quincy, Massachusetts (fig. 4.4). The other was in Ottawa. The two had distinctly different materials and characters, but both were modest variations on his generic plans. His eclecticism suggests that plan was of little concern; the unique character lay in the material selection and the shapes of roofs and openings. His overall sensibility was to favor churches that blended into the ordinary and everyday fabric of towns. In addition to Edwin Lewis, at least one other Boston firm was engaged by the national organization under Eliot's leadership to provide designs for new churches that received building loans from the AUA.[23] Smith & Walker were involved in several renovations of important older Boston-area buildings (Harrison's King's Chapel in Boston, Old Ship in Hingham, and the Old Meeting House in Lynnfield) as well as the design of new ones: straightforward neoclassical designs for All Souls, Tulsa, Oklahoma (1921); First Unitarian, Oklahoma City (1929); Unitarian Church, Salt Lake City (1945); and a mission-style building for United Liberal, St. Petersburg, Florida (1930).[24]

Samuel Eliot's interest in influencing church design and construction was unprecedented in the AUA. Eliot's contradictory legacy was to modernize the national organization of democratically governed congregations with increased

FIGURE 4.4. Wollaston Unitarian Church, Quincy, Massachusetts, Edwin J. Lewis Jr., 1888. Photograph by author.

centralization and efficiencies—he achieved his aims by imposing a greater degree of control than Unitarian principles would suggest. His strategic investment in church building as the means to legitimize and expand the denomination, to use the church building as a "durable witness," was among his contradictions. Despite his support of the Lewis committee and publication, he eventually favored monumentality and a spiritual expression over more humble, essentially vernacular structures. It is possible that he was influenced by (or felt provoked to compete with) the institutional image and civic presence of a much newer denomination, the First Church of Christ, Scientist. Eliot's tenure was synchronous with a national building campaign they undertook in order to be accepted as a mainstream.[25] Their original church opened in the South End of Boston in the same year that Eliot joined the board of the Boston-based AUA. With all of the traveling he did and his interest in architecture, Eliot must have been aware of their building program and its rapid expansion to major American cities. Eliot similarly supported a large urban presence and overlooked smaller or rural congregations and their building needs.[26] His architectural conservatism opposed the Progressive ideas that Chicago and Bay Area Unitarians had pursued in the first decade of the twentieth century. However, in architectural terms, those innovative designs have served as a more truthful witness of Unitarian spirit.

FROM CHRISTIAN CHURCH TO HUMANIST HUT

Various historians have described the state of the Unitarian denomination in the first three decades of the twentieth century in different ways. David B. Parke surmised that "the turn of the twentieth century found Unitarianism in a contented slumber."[27] He believed that the trauma of the First World War finally shook the foundations of a late nineteenth-century liberal worldview and Progressive Era assumptions regarding the potential for global fellowship. There was no clear replacement; theism and humanism, both still simultaneously supported by the majority of Unitarians, had to confront the new realities of science and technology. However, there was still optimism, trust in the future, and a firm sense of a moral imperative to champion the cause of good over evil.[28] David Robinson described the primary interests of the time as "the humanist debate" and the gradual impact of Eliot's administrative agendas.[29] The humanist debate was led by ministers ready to abandon theism altogether, a debate that would continue up to the next war. Eliot avoided the debate entirely and focused his leadership on building the institution rather than considering the moral and spiritual dimensions of the denomination. While the humanist debate and some relatively ineffective international missionary efforts characterized the denomination's attempts to modernize along with a changing world, the reality of Unitarian life at the congregational level was apparently unaffected: "The predominant theological position within Unitarianism in the early years of the century was what Eliot called 'lyrical theism'"—belief in a benign deity, present in nature, and present in human capacity for creativity and moral goodness.[30]

Many sentiments and values that could be described as humanistic were promoted as part of Unitarian belief in the late nineteenth and early twentieth centuries, exemplified by William C. Gannett's "Things Commonly Believed among Us." But after World War I, ministers more directly questioning the concept of God began to provoke denominational uncertainty.[31] Central to this debate was the question of what a religion can be without belief in a God, in this case the American Christian God. Humanism's response was, essentially, the promotion of the good in humankind, both individually and collectively. The debates of the 1920s sharpened the position of the humanists and led them to propose a major philosophical statement, the "Humanist Manifesto" of 1933. Like Transcendentalism before it, the humanist philosophy was created outside the official context of the denomination, but it represented the views of a significant group within, and ultimately came to represent unofficially the denomination as a whole. One of the two main authors of the manifesto, Raymond Bragg, was a Unitarian minister, and of the thirty-four philosophers and theologians that signed the document, thirteen others were as well. The signers professed "confidence in our capability to achieve moral perfection and happiness along the lines and within the limits of our earthly nature."[32] While it was not representative of the whole of Unitarianism at that time, the debate made an impact, and the beliefs stated in the manifesto would become ever more widely held after World War II.

Meanwhile, mainstream Unitarians recognized by the mid-1930s that their sense of a coherent denominational definition was faltering. The Depression brought both instability and pessimism. Samuel Eliot had retired as president of the AUA in 1927 at the height of prosperity and was succeeded by Louis Craig Cornish (1870–1950). Cornish was a less effective leader, and the onset of the Depression brought new challenges. Eventually, the AUA board undertook a formal self-assessment to address a sense of lost unity and direction. Their 1936 report, *Unitarians Face a New Age*, was an effective analysis with meaningful ideas for new initiatives at the national level.[33] Quite naturally, the lead author of the study was asked to spearhead the changes, and so Frederick May Eliot (1889–1958), a fourth cousin of Samuel A. Eliot, took over the presidency of AUA in 1937. Some immediate goals included the compilation and distribution of a new up-to-date hymnal, renewed emphasis on religious scholarship, and a modernized curriculum for religious education.[34] Another important priority that Frederick Eliot pursued was a refreshed call to social action, which had lagged in the general prosperity of the 1920s and the deprivations of the Depression. Eliot started a quasi-independent organization, the Unitarian Service Committee, to prioritize and manage humanitarian initiatives and social activism. Most dramatically, in the face of the Nazi threat in Europe, Eliot sent Reverend Waitstill Sharp and his wife, Martha Sharp, to distribute relief and aid Jewish flight.[35] All of these initiatives served Unitarians well throughout the war years and in meeting the changing conditions of postwar America.

There was one architectural reflection of continued Progressive thinking in the malaise of the 1930s, which was unusual because the Depression naturally discouraged much new construction. The Third Unitarian Church of Chicago had been founded in 1868. Located on the West Side, this congregation had occupied several locations over time. When their church at the corner of Lake and Pine Streets burned down in 1934, they purchased a new lot just a few blocks to the west. However, they were denied a loan from the AUA when they refused a mandate to build "in the Colonial-Revival style."[36] Evidently, Samuel Eliot's policies regarding church architecture were still in effect in the national organization. The congregation refused and instead commissioned Paul Schweikher (1903–1997), a young architect whose work had been exhibited in the Museum of Modern Art in New York the previous year. Schweikher accepted the economic constraints of a small congregation in the midst of the Depression. Echoing the novelty of materials used by Frank Lloyd Wright at Unity Temple just over a mile away, he chose materials that were both economical and distinctly modern. He acknowledged the necessity for simplicity of form and construction, and so he adapted one of the generic Lewis plans. However, he put the entry on the main axis of the auditorium, and he inserted a narthex, a vestibule with a stair and coatroom, and a balcony above. A wing extending from the main building block at the east end was for the minister's office and a study rather than a parlor as in the Lewis plan (fig. 4.5). The social space was then placed in a daylit basement under the auditorium, along with a kitchen and conference room.

FIGURE 4.5a. Third Unitarian Church, Chicago, Paul Schweikher, 1936. HB-04585-C, Chicago History Museum, Hedrich-Blessing Collection.

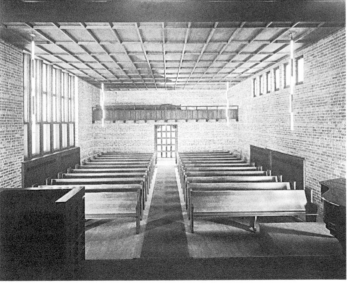

FIGURE 4.5b. Third Unitarian Church, interior view. HB-04585-A, Chicago History Museum, Hedrich-Blessing Collection.

Although the plan was conventional, the materials and treatment of the openings were not. Schweikher allowed the plain brick bearing walls to provide finishes for both exterior and interior, and used common brick rather than the more expensive—and expected—face brick. In addition to saving money normally spent on finishes, the choice of brick walls also allowed the use of unskilled labor of congregation members in order to reduce construction costs. Rather than evenly spaced openings marking the length of the auditorium, the windows were arranged in gridded fields of differing scales. The ceiling of the auditorium and the chancel wall were finished with a grid of painted plywood panels, still considered an industrial material at that time. Wood details such as railings and trim were plain sawn lumber, sanded and oiled rather than turned or painted. And though the roof was double-pitched, its profile was extremely low—not creating any sense of gable or pediment on the facade. The subtle modernism arising from these details was recognized by *Architectural Record*, where an article about it appeared in the December 1936 issue.[37] The building was praised for its simplicity, functionalism, lack of ornament, and economic use of materials. When the congregation could afford an addition in 1956, Schweikher was not available to do the design, but he recommended William Fyfe, who had worked with him on the original structure. Fyfe's addition reoriented the auditorium and provided a new entry vestibule and additional meeting space. The addition successfully balanced an intention to maintain the general material qualities and respect the massing and scale of the original elements while at the same time easily recognizing the new space as an addition. This church building documents through its defiance the AUA's policy requiring traditional styles as a condition for financial support. It does not signify a new direction, only that there was, even in the context of general architectural conservatism produced by coercive policy, continued architectural innovation. While a quiet and humble building, it was a clearly a progressive architectural expression of the Unitarian ethos.

As the president of the AUA, Frederick Eliot believed that growth was necessary for revitalization, but he sensed that Unitarianism was misunderstood, mysterious, or completely unknown to many Americans. He undertook a campaign to make Unitarianism more widely accessible that included a series of radio addresses. In them, he explained that Unitarians had "faith in the truth as we discover it by the use of our own human powers of observation and reason . . . faith in the universe of which we are a part, of which our ideals are a part."[38] After World War II ended, numerous ministers contributed to broadcasting what Unitarianism could mean to a wider public. One minister who was active in trying to start congregations in new places would publish an invitation to an open meeting in a local paper. His advertisement described Unitarian beliefs this way:

Unitarians believe that striving to live nobly and constructively is more important than the accepting of religious creeds. Unitarians are convinced that religious truth cannot be contrary to truth from any other source. Unitarians offer a religious program for children and adults of all cultures, with reason as our guide, and service as our aim. Unitarians believe that the great end in religious instruction is not to stamp our minds irresistibly on the young, but to stir up their own.[39]

Reverend A. Powell Davies (1902–1957) of All Souls Church in Washington, DC, proposed a simple and clear statement of five principles of belief that were later adopted by the AUA as definitive: "individual freedom of belief, discipleship to advancing truth, the democratic process in human relations, universal brotherhood, undivided by nation, race, or creed; and allegiance to the cause of a united world community."[40] It was Davies's statement that first made "democratic process" explicit in Unitarian tenets. While the philosophies of democracy had always been central to Unitarians, this overt statement reflected the consciousness of the Cold War Era.

While Eliot achieved the desired growth, the denomination could still be difficult to characterize. Postwar Unitarians represented an ever wider spectrum of beliefs but were connected by their desire to have a spiritual home and community. Each congregation continued to have its own personality within broad commonalities. Congregations experiencing growth usually looked for ways to renovate their existing buildings as a first measure. However, the need for a new building often arose from more than just an increase in membership. The expanded religious education program now needed separate classrooms for various age groups. Community kitchens needed modernization, and perhaps most significantly, more substantial parking lots were also required. All of these factors contributed to a construction boom in the 1950s and 1960s. Central denominational control over design had ceased, and each architect commissioned needed to work with a congregation that was self-defining within a broad denominational framework.

While the twentieth century up to World War II had seen an eclectic mix of mostly traditional church designs, the postwar building boom brought forth an array of modern church buildings almost exclusively.[41] Modern architecture offered the variety needed for each congregation to express its individual identity with a distinctive architectural design. The dozens of Unitarian churches built between 1948 and 1970 exhibited this variety while all being undeniably modern. The idea that their church needed to "look like a church," the philosophy on which Samuel Eliot based his efforts, was no longer relevant to a denomination that did not ground itself in belief in God. Each congregation that needed a new church had to solve for themselves, along with an architect's help, what the shape and character of their place of worship would be. Postwar modernism was evolving from its early adherence to a narrow set of themes; architects were asking new questions and admitting new values to their design intentions. The situation for postwar architects was somewhat analogous to Unitarianism: a recognizable set of commonalities but varied enough in its themes and vocabularies to provide individuality to each church. The uniformities of the revival styles were replaced with churches that were fully modern but not as stylistically homogeneous.

Architectural modernism seemed practically tailor-made for a progressive, liberal religion. Formal conventions of early modernism such as bright interiors, large areas of glass, a vocabulary of planes and flat roofs, and asymmetrical compositions would be antithetical to the image, atmosphere, and liturgical needs of most Christian congregations. But they were all quite acceptable to Unitarians, and these features can be found in a number of different postwar examples. The International Style's vocabulary of exposed structure and "truthful" use of materials were still widely employed, and these themes fit Unitarian rationalism and pragmatism quite well. However, the architectural vocabularies of 1950s diversified as designers explored interests in history, monumentality, and psychological or emotional effects. Some of the change in the character of 1950s modernism arose from interest in challenging the elite cultural associations of the International Style by making architectural forms that were accessible or appealing to a broader audience. A renewed interest in historical elements such as arcades and domes, and typologies such as hut and pavilion, expanded the vocabulary and was useful in creating a modern religious architecture with an emotional appeal.[42] The range of architectural possibilities of the era allowed congregations to imagine that they could create unique places for their spiritual homes; on the other hand, it also allowed architects of the era to define their practices in accordance with personal artistic visions more so than as a matter of disciplinary knowledge. Since their Unitarian clients were seeking innovation, it was a fruitful correspondence.

The First Unitarian Church of Houston (1953) by Thomas E. Greacen II (1907–1994) provides an early example that can be viewed in contrast to the interwar conservatism of the First Unitarian Church of Los Angeles.[43] Perhaps attributable to similar climate conditions, Houston's church and its additional spaces are arranged around a courtyard in almost exactly the same way as that of the Los Angeles church that preceded it by some twenty-five years (fig. 4.6). Its urban lot faces south onto Fannin Street between Southmore Boulevard and Oakdale Street. Just as in the case of the earlier church, parallel structures serving the worship and social spaces extend perpendicular to the main street and are joined at the other end by a wing with classrooms and offices. The courtyard formed by the three structures is partially visible but screened from the street by a semi-open colonnade and gate. This covered walkway connects the entry doors of the two main building blocks. In both cases, the courtyard orders the elements of the building complex and also gives all of them a connection to light and air and views of trees and sky. Both courtyards offer the possibility to linger outdoors, weather permitting, as a welcoming prelude to attending services or other events. The Houston courtyard could likewise be used as an extension of the social hall by means of three overhead doors. The complex achieved a modest "calm, logical" character that was both "inviting and protective"—there was an open attitude despite the wall to the street and the withdrawal of the building entries from view.[44] The simplicity and relatively small scale of the Houston buildings' elevations is somewhat amplified by the planar minimalism of the wall and gate, and softened by the courtyard vegetation visible from the street. Its modernism arose from a simplicity of materials, an overall horizontal character, a lack of ornament, and the articulation of each element within the whole. The contrast between the 1926 Los Angeles church and the 1952 Houston church was expressive of the new clarity and denominational identity that Frederick Eliot achieved.

FIGURE 4.6. First Unitarian Church, Houston, Thomas E. Greacen II, 1953. Photograph from *Architectural Forum* 99 (December 1953): 95.

SITE MATTERS: MODERN CHURCHES IN THE AUTOMOTIVE CITY

A large number of congregations needed new churches in the 1950s, partly because of the growth that Eliot had generated. Once the decision to undertake the construction of a new church was made, two tasks generally occupied congregation members first: finding a site and fundraising. Architect selection and a discussion of desirable architectural qualities would usually follow these sometimes lengthy processes. The attributes sought in a site were generally less well-documented than those desired for the building in church records. However, discussion of the need to relocate often included consideration of some of the things the congregation wanted: room for a larger building, space for more parking, and better proximity to where current members lived were the dominant motivations. Once possible sites were being reviewed, the general sense of an adequate lot size for the growth they were managing, availability, and affordability were paramount. The fact that the eventual architectural expression of congregational identity would be strongly influenced by the site was mostly overlooked, at least in explicit meeting notes. Due to suburbanization and increased automobile dependency, there was a much wider range of possible site conditions in the postwar era. However, I have found only two cases in which the choice of a new site was explicitly related to the identity of the congregation. For one, it was to maintain a highly valued existing identity, while for the other it was a chance to invest in a site that would recenter their identity.

A Unitarian congregation was originally founded in Richmond, Virginia, in the 1830s, but it did not survive the Civil War.[45] The congregation made a fresh start in the 1890s and gained enough strength to build a church on the west edge of the downtown area in 1906. The little church was expanded once in 1926, but by the time more space was needed in the 1960s, there was no possibility of an addition on its small lot. Growth of the surrounding state colleges, eventually combined into Virginia Commonwealth University, was engulfing it. So the congregation began to search for a new site. They inquired first about several sites relatively close to their existing location. However, it quickly became clear to building committee members that they were being denied the opportunity to make offers because the congregation was racially integrated. Their determination to stay in the city rather than move to a less restrictive suburb inspired them to become a bit more devious in the purchase of land. When they found several adjacent house lots available for purchase, congregation members individually purchased each of the lots and then sold them to the church, bypassing exclusionary real estate practices. This combined site was framed by three streets, the busiest of which was a boulevard serving a major city park on the opposite side. The others were secondary residential streets. Securing this property allowed the church to maintain a vital presence in the city near a familiar landmark in the park; such visibility was important for activities such as hosting public lectures, often on political topics; sponsoring film screenings; and maintaining an art gallery for local artists.

Once they had raised sufficient funds, the congregation engaged architect Ulrich Franzen (1921–2012), who was working in Richmond for Philip Morris at the time, to design their church. (The land was purchased in 1965, construction began in 1969, and the church was dedicated in 1972.) Franzen was at the height of his career, and this was his first church (fig. 4.7). Facing Blanton Avenue, a paved open court with a circular pool was framed on one side by the sanctuary and by an L-shaped arrangement of social and educational spaces on the other two edges.[46] The building spanned most of the full width of the block, hiding the parking lot behind. An all-glass sanctuary wall with a continuous series of doors allowed a direct connection to the fountain court, making it a twin space of the sanctuary, only open to the sky. The court was defined on the street edge by a low concrete wall that angled outward in one direction, inviting passersby to enter. However, the main building entry was not located in the courtyard—the space was intended for congregational activities spilling out from the sanctuary and other surrounding spaces, not for circulation or entry. The rest of the building consisted of a series of linked modular spaces lit by clerestories and skylights that could be furnished and used for social purposes, meetings, or religious education as needed. Each module was formed by low concrete block "towers" on the corners, giving the building a Brutalist character; it was described as "cubist-Romanesque" by one favorable review at the time. The only fully defined rooms were the sanctuary, a library, and the minister's office on the west half of the site. The provisional nature of the relationships of spaces and functions suited the congregation well.[47] Franzen remarked, "It is not just another imposing edifice, but a house of life."[48]

The Richmond congregation felt strongly that their leadership role in important social issues of the 1950s and 1960s required them to maintain a visible presence in the city and to be identified with other civic institutions. The location was fortuitous with proximity to a well-known landmark, the Carillon in William Byrd Park, and a neighborhood to the west that was integrated evenly at the time.

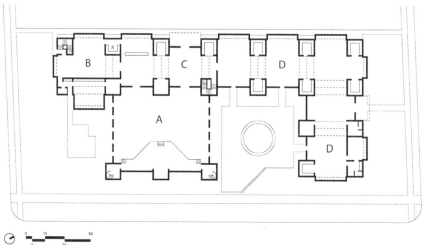

FIGURE. 4.7a. First Unitarian Church, Richmond, Virginia, Ulrich Franzen, 1968–1972. Photograph by author.

FIGURE 4.7b. First Unitarian Church, plan: A—auditorium; B—library; C, D—flexible modules serving arrival, social, and meeting and classroom functions. Drawing by Alissa Tucker.

But it was also practical. Their service mission was less about providing social services for citizens in need and more about providing a venue for liberal views and education. They clearly felt that activities such as the Richmond Forum, a public speaker series focused on major national and international issues, would not attract significant audiences if the church were located on the periphery of the city. For them, location mattered a great deal.

A congregation in Memphis had quite a different motive for selecting their site: the chance for a vital connection to their city's image and sense of place. This congregation also dated back to 1893 but had needed a significant restart in 1908. It occupied a number of different existing buildings and venues until finally purchasing land and building a community house with an auditorium and class-rooms in 1923. The original plan for a sanctuary on the site as well was never real-ized. However, the congregation remained in that location through World War II and the following decade. Upon the arrival of a new minister in 1962, the congre-gation was inspired to organize a campaign to relocate and build a new church.[49] The committee that was charged with the search located what they thought was a suitable site in the suburbs of Memphis. When a vote was put to the congrega-tion, a new and relatively young congregation member, Kathryn Boyd Rice, was dismayed by this lackluster proposal—she had the strong sense that it would be a mistake and suggested what she later described as a "more exalted location."[50] She persuaded the congregation to seek a site on the Mississippi River. By chance, there was a parcel of land on the bluffs that had been cleared by postwar highway construction and urban renewal projects being auctioned by the city.[51] The min-ister, James Madison Barr, made a successful bid, and Roy Harrover (1928–2016), the leading modern architect of Memphis at that time and a member of the con-gregation, provided the award-winning design and drawings.

Such was the impact of this site that the First Unitarian Church of Memphis was rechristened the Church of the River (fig. 4.8). The church is entered from the parking lot through a small laterally extended courtyard; this restricted space increases the drama of entering the building. The sanctuary space expands in all dimensions from the entry point toward the opposite wall. There, a fully glazed wall seventeen feet tall and thirty-six feet wide provides a sweeping vista of the river as it flows by. As the architect explained, his design "emphasizes a cardinal principle of Unitarian belief: the reason, logic, simplicity, and order of the universe as revealed in nature." The minister at the time of the building's fiftieth anniver-sary, Reverend Eric Posa, noted that the river's prominence in the experience of the congregation's worship "encourages us to embrace that life is in motion."[52] As much as the river and its bridges and traffic impacts the experience of worship from within, the site also provides the congregation with great visibility as an integral part of the image of Memphis as seen from the Mississippi. Their church building is considered an icon of the city. Rice's vision for the new church started with the river; in later remarks, she explained her intuition in spiritual terms:

FIGURE. 4.8a. Church
of the River, Memphis,
Tennessee, Roy Harrover,
1966, exterior view.
Photograph by Rod
Starns.

FIGURE. 4.8a. Church
of the River, Memphis,
Tennessee, Roy Harrover,
1966, exterior view.
Photograph by Rod
Starns.

FIGURE 4.8b. Church of
the River, view of the
sanctuary with a view
of the Mississippi River.
Photograph by Rod
Starns.

"DeSoto called this river Rio Espíritu Santo (River of the Holy Spirit). No matter what your interpretation of 'holy' is, we are endowed with a capacity for reverence, a sense of beauty, a respect for life, and onto that we build man-made stories that evolve into our rituals. And what better place to enjoy this talent for feeling awe than our bluff on the wonderful river, the Mississippi."[53]

While the Memphis congregation chose an explicit connection to the most important manifestation of place for their city, and the Richmond Unitarians understood their particular contribution to the political and intellectual life of their city as a matter of physical presence, the selection of site was not widely viewed as a matter of congregational identity elsewhere. The need to leave the congestion of a downtown was generally more critical than the question of exactly where to go. And for many, the distance was not that great—a matter of two to four miles. But the context was profoundly different. Along with the necessity of more space for parking, there was a vague expectation that there would be some outdoor space with grass and trees. There may have even been a hope for substantial natural beauty. The location and sizes of the sites from that period varied from affording a small garden or a residentially scaled lawn to multiple acres with lawns, woods, and gardens. This came not as an expectation or requirement but with hindsight, in histories that express gratitude for some lucky circumstance that led to the acquisition of substantial plots of land. One of the greatest factors that differentiated the resultant character of new churches in this variety of contexts was not necessarily the extent of their suburban site but the placement of the building and its consequent relationship to the street, and the visibility of the church to the public way. There was a range of attitudes from designing the building as part of an urban/suburban order to creating an insular condition with no relationship to anything beyond the site boundaries, and often not particularly visible from adjacent roads.

Several church sites of the time were enmeshed in first-tier "suburban" neighborhoods—residential neighborhoods with older single-family housing developed in the early decades of the twentieth century. While the modern architecture of these churches was foreign to its context, the buildings were designed in relation to the street. Two examples used a single element, a striking facade, to address the public realm, where the front wall presented a singular unqualified statement of the building's modern character. The more dramatic example is the First Unitarian Society of Schenectady, New York (1958), designed by Edward Durrell Stone (1902–1978).[54] The austere design faces the street with a simple gleaming white plane overhung by a flat roof, stretching two hundred feet and only broken once—for the entry doors (fig. 4.9). The wall is enlivened by the texture of its precast concrete blocks, which were molded with a custom decorative pattern forming interlocking circles. It is fronted by a long pool with several jets that also give life to the severe quiet of the composition. A bridge crosses over the pool from the sidewalk to the asymmetrically placed entry doors. The stark minimalist formality of this composition is alien to the environment, a planned residential neighborhood of 1900, but the site is somewhat screened by topography and vegetation from adjacent properties—only the street edge is exposed. The pools are lined with planters and beds, lending the public street and sidewalk the sensuous qualities of a contemplative scholar's garden. For the congregation and visitors, it provides the forecourt—this is the narthex where churchgoers can linger in conversation or contemplation. The wall fronts a simple rectangular structure with a large central room, an almost square void, serving as the social hall and containing a sunken amphitheater as the sanctuary. The rear wall opposite the entry is fully glazed, overlooking a grassy slope edged by a fringe of trees—a contrasting view of natural beauty. No neighboring structures are visible, allowing the main space of the church to visually engage the natural open space and the trees beyond.

St. John's Unitarian Church in Cincinnati (1960) was built around the same time and in a neighborhood of similar character as that in Schenectady. It was designed by local architect John Garber (1916–1988). This church also presents a startlingly white wall parallel to the street, and it too is the only visible element (fig. 4.10). However, this church was set back about seventy-five feet, in general agreement with the neighboring houses on the block. The church was also a good neighbor by placing its parking area at the rear of the lot, completely out of sight from the street. A level green lawn stretches from the sidewalk to the church facade, relieved only by a single tree. The lawn is bordered on both sides by entry and exit driveways that define the site's edges, and originally by a slightly

FIGURE. 4.9. First Unitarian Society, Schenectady, New York, Edward Durrell Stone, 1958. Photograph by Jwilson855, CC BY-SA 4.0, https://creativecommons.org/licenses/by-sa/4.0/deed.en.

elevated concrete walk on each side. (One walk has recently been removed and a planted area has been created on that side of the lawn.) Although the church is only about forty-five feet tall, its height is amplified by twenty-one exposed steel columns on four-foot centers that extend another eight feet past the roof line. The architect felt that doing so would give the exterior columns "the glory" he felt they deserved.[55] He thought they produced an interesting sense of spatial volume, presumably with the outstretched lawn. The facade might easily be described by some as spikey (or even aggressive), but the simplicity of the flat lawn is a serenely familiar foil for its strange expression. This was a congregation that certainly wanted to be unique, to be clearly modern, and to be noticed.

A site in the midst of a residential neighborhood with an urban sense of a street grid seemed to demand a building that addressed the street. Some sites located on arterials that had broken out of the downtown grid patterns in terms of access or adjacent structures allowed a building design that could be perceived more three-dimensionally. The buildings that were visible in their entirety from some distance tended to express their character through a clear formal order rather than a facade.

FIGURE 4.10. St. John's Unitarian Church, Cincinnati, John Garber, 1959. Photograph by Anton Harfmann.

An example of a strong, unique formal expression is the essentially round building of the Unitarian Society of Hartford, Connecticut, designed by Victor Lundy (b. 1923) in 1964 (fig. 4.11). The building was placed over two hundred feet from the road in an open grassy expanse that slopes slightly downward. Like a Renaissance centrally planned ideal church, it can be seen and comprehended as a whole. Although there was plenty of space on the site, Lundy gathered all of the required functions together within a single defining architectural form. Concrete walls radiate outward from the center of the plan creating wedges of space around a central round void for the sanctuary. Lundy's innovative roof is a particularly distinctive element of the design: roof segments were supported by cables suspended between the radial walls. While the building has architecturally grand gestures in the focused certainty of a singular form and in the simultaneously outstretching and upsweeping concrete walls, there is also an attitude of openness and of casual happenstance that counters its formal certainties. The drape of the roof forms gives the impression of a tent set up in a meadow. The scale of the open space allows the unusual building form to blend into the site almost as if it were a natural feature.

Other designs that were governed by a chosen formal order were also forced to organize the variety of functions and spatial needs into a single, legible building form. Joseph Amisano (1917–2008), like Lundy, used the definition of a centrally

FIGURE 4.11. Unitarian Society, Hartford, Connecticut, Victor Lundy, 1964. © Massachusetts Institute of Technology, photograph by G. E. Kidder Smith.

located sanctuary to order the whole design for the Unitarian congregation of Atlanta. However, Amisano used the pure geometries of circle and square, and gathered all of the functional elements under a single bilaterally symmetrical roof. This had the value of being highly legible; the site was tightly defined by streets on two edges, but it was also adjacent to an interstate highway under construction, which was a whole new order of visibility. Unitarian churches with a single formal order were among those that came closest to a monumental expression usually expected of a church, even one that was relatively small in scale. They show that Unitarian congregations were open to the range of exploration current in architectural modernism around 1960.[56] While most congregations would be drawn to images that gestured toward religious sentiment through intimacy and a sense of value in everyday experience, some were touched by the suggestive qualities of poetic form with a promise of physical and psychological engagement. Still, Lundy's striking roof forms—for Hartford and another for a Westport, Connecticut, congregation—were among the very few fully celebrating the vertical dimension that became so common for other denominations.[57] A dominant sculptural roof form was widely used as a means to make modern architecture church-like and therefore acceptable for other denominations.

SITE MATTERS: GARDENS AND PARKS

Most American cities of the mid-twentieth century had a distinct downtown, or central business district, with a concentration of tall commercial buildings often in close proximity to major industry. New highways were added to the existing transportation networks of street and rail. Increased car travel in an era of leaded gasoline quickly exacerbated industrial pollution. Urban renewal sought remedies to some of these problems in addition to addressing housing needs, but it also brought uncertainty and rapid change to many cities. Negative political and environmental factors drove some congregations to favor sites that were removed from these adverse urban conditions. No church in the 1950s or 1960s could actually escape the city for a truly rural site and hope to maintain its membership. But many congregations chose sites that were either large enough or wooded enough to feel secluded and therefore away, or at least apart, from the city. Some of these were conceived as a clearing, where articulated elements of the building complex were arranged in an open space with lawns and parking lots placed around them, and with the whole encircled by trees, providing a buffer from roads or other properties. Others were treated more as a wooded landscape with the church buildings integrated into the topography and vegetation. These sites allowed the congregations the greatest breadth to develop a variety of indoor and outdoor spaces to serve their needs. Both types afforded the chance for the development of one or more gardens, and some included walking paths as well. And both allowed the building design to find order in the site itself, rather than in accordance with roadways or adjacent structures. They were able to establish an independent sense of place.

While seeking a contrast to urban degradation may have been a motive for an impulse toward park-like settings, Unitarians had philosophical reasons as well to value a more natural setting. For many, nature itself was the focus or source of a spiritual dimension in life. Twentieth-century mainstream Unitarianism had finally merged the rationalist and romantic streams of the nineteenth century. Ralph Waldo Emerson's views of nature—as a catalyst for individual self-knowledge and a "symbol for spirit"—were probably widely held American values, not just Unitarian ones.[58] However, other religions would have placed knowledge of God on a higher plane of importance. For Unitarians, the Transcendentalist view of nature as the key to knowledge of the divine and the cosmic order remained a central truth. This view of nature had been expanded later in the nineteenth century by the grandeur of American western landscapes. Thomas Starr King wrote sermons and letters with extensive praise for the sacred nature of the California landscape. For twentieth-century Unitarians, the spiritual and aesthetic qualities of nature was one certain shared value. Architectural theorist Bart Verschaffel, in his effort to find a new understanding of the sacred in our time, calls nature "a new—and at the same time very old—source of sacredness," one of only three sources of the sacred in modern society.[59] It is a universally sought source of beauty and renewal, and it can raise religious sentiment. Specific associations with certain landscape types even figure in the development of some American religions, but nature in general is widely embraced by religious communities as a reminder of the interconnection of all things.[60]

In addition to the promise of nature, larger sites allowed congregations to imagine that construction could be phased, and that continued growth in the future could be accommodated as well. Two congregations that took a similar approach to their extensive sites were those in Princeton, New Jersey, and Rockford, Illinois. In each case, a driveway was pulled deep into the site from the road; there, the church buildings provided an edge between a large, paved parking area and a sloping green lawn ringed by trees. The congregation of Princeton, founded as a fellowship in 1949, met in a variety of spaces around Princeton while finding land and raising money for the construction of a church.[61] A three-acre lot was purchased in 1955, and the architectural firm of Warner, Burns, Toan & Lunde was selected. The site appeared much larger than it was because its southeast border adjoined Princeton's Community Park North, where the woods that buffer the site to the southeast from the heavy traffic of State Road 206 continued. The Rockford congregation purchased ten and a half acres in 1960, the same year that a new minister arrived, but did not undertake design and construction for another five years.[62]

The Princeton congregation proceeded with initial construction in 1957–58. In considering what they wanted in their church, an important quality was "a quiet spot in a confusing world, a haven for people who will always love the unending search for their own certainties about God, Man, and the Universe."[63] This sense of needing a haven from the everyday world of concerns was most clearly manifested by churches set deep onto large sites, not even visible from public roads, as was the case in Princeton (fig. 4.12). The first round of construction consisted of two separate buildings for church and school. The church was a singular example of an A-frame shape for a Unitarian church; this shape was often selected by other denominations for its expressive upward dynamism and possible association with Gothic architecture. The glue-laminated wood structure and decking of the pitched roofs created a warm interior lit by central skylights and continuous glazing at the ground level on three sides. The school building was a small rectangular structure with a flat roof set at some distance from the church. Ten years later, an addition that linked the buildings was constructed to provide an entry courtyard and vestibule, meeting space, and offices; further additions have extended the classroom space. The original buildings were quite modest, but the site was developed with stone walls, plants, and trees to create borders; a small entry garden; and other accents across the site, all of which were catalogued with care.[64] A memorial garden, now known as the Garden of Remembrance, was begun in 1971, and a memory wall was added in 1996, followed by a wood pergola. The meaning these features may hold for a congregation are well expressed by a similarly extensive garden plan at a Unitarian Universalist church in Blacksburg, Virginia. Their five acres include a winding meditation path, a labyrinth, "two picnic areas with firepits, a water feature, a butterfly garden, a small animal habitat area, a wildflower garden, a crescent garden, a peace pole, a pet memorial pole, and many beautiful views of the surrounding area."[65] This congregation regards its collection of gardens and natural features as "a spiritual venue," with value for contact with natural beauty, for meditation or prayer, and for social renewal. It is not reserved for congregation members or church events only; community members are invited to benefit as well.

In 1962 the Rockford congregation engaged Pietro Belluschi to design their new

FIGURE 4.12a. Unitarian Church, Princeton, New Jersey, Warner, Burns, Toan & Lunde, 1958, view of the church, entry court, and classroom wing. Photograph by author.

FIGURE 4.12b. Unitarian Church, view of the pathway and pergola of the memorial garden. Photograph by author.

building. This is an instance in which the architect's own response to the site was recorded. He felt that "it needed a strong symbolic expression, a form removed from the old ecclesiastical tradition, yet possessing convincing qualities particularly relevant to the Unitarian commitments."[66] The "strong symbolic" character was achieved with a hierarchy of massing in which the main spaces were articulated by their separate but related exposed concrete structural systems (fig. 4.13). Its Brutalist demeanor was unusually monumental for Unitarians but is more readily understood as Belluschi's response to what was at the time an open landscape. Also, the early exploration of Brutalism was understood to be a humanistic modernism, more expressive and emotionally evocative than the International Style.[67] The sloped site allowed for windows to the lawn for the spaces on the lower level, but the overall character of the interiors was tuned toward controlled and focused views of nature to make it visible. In this way the building becomes a different kind of lens for seeing nature.

Scholar of religion Susan Power Bratton identifies the "church in the wildwood"

FIGURE 4.13. Unitarian Church, Rockford, Illinois, Pietro Belluschi, 1966, view from the lawn behind the building. Photograph by author.

as an idealized American archetype, one most memorably fulfilled by the Thorncrown Chapel in Eureka Springs, Arkansas (1980), designed by Fay Jones.[68] The mutual identities of the church and the woods recall their shared capacity to evoke a spiritual presence and the memory of buildings that achieve a spiritual sense by a formal reference to the structure of trees. The result creates a strongly evocative sense that "going to church" is something separate and distinct from everyday life—in this case, from the busy suburban roadways with commercial developments not too far away. It is an idealized view in which the site is almost enough on its own. Three Unitarian churches that illustrate this condition in slightly different ways are among those that were offshoots from All Souls in Washington, DC, in the 1950s: Cedar Lane Unitarian and River Road Unitarian in Bethesda, Maryland, and Fairfax Unitarian Church in Virginia.[69]

These buildings were all carefully integrated into the landscape, but each has a different approach and resultant character. Cedar Lane was built in 1955 on a six-acre wooded lot that slopes toward the southwest, along the Rock Creek Park greenway. Its church building, also designed by Pietro Belluschi, is approached on the uphill side of the campus, where the building elements are arranged around a small garden court. This courtyard was originally the only planted area, contrasting with the surrounding woods. "Instead of having us enter the building directly from the parking lot, the courtyard gives us a transition space," according to Reverend Roger Fritts, minister in 2008. "Belluschi intended the courtyard to prepare us for the religious experience both emotionally and psychologically."[70] The pitched roofs of the various structures are low and spreading, giving a distinctly domestic scale to the whole and allowing the surrounding trees to dominate the scene (fig. 4.14). The larger volume of the social hall was placed to the rear on the slope and is therefore less imposing on approach. (The congregation chose to build the social hall first and use it for worship as well until they were able to add the church. But in the end, they decided that they were satisfied with their auditorium-as-church.[71]) The grays and browns of the walls and roofs further tune the buildings to the site. The woods surround the building on the other three sides, and every space in the complex has a view to the outdoors.

When the Cedar Lane congregation continued to grow, it was clear that another church was needed. A group of members envisioned a new congregation, purchasing their four-and-a-half-acre site located on River Road in 1960, and building their church in 1964–65. The architectural firm selected, Keyes Condon & Lethbridge, was the local architect that had worked with Belluschi on the Cedar Lane church. The River Road building achieved a different kind of harmony with

FIGURE 4.14a. Cedar Lane Unitarian Church, Bethesda, Maryland, Pietro Belluschi, 1958, view from the entry drive. Photograph by author.

FIGURE 4.14b. Cedar Lane Unitarian Church, view of the auditorium from the rear of the site. Photograph by author.

its site. It is located centrally on the upward slope of a wooded knoll facing Whittier Boulevard and is the opposite to Cedar Lane in terms of color, material, and proportions: white brick walls and more steeply pitched shed roofs were not meant to blend in. Yet, the buildings fit into the wooded site by verticality, by precision of location, and also due to a strategic sectional offset (fig. 4.15). Sensitively terraced parking levels preserve the natural character of the hillside to a surprising degree. A much-debated "bell-less" tower guides visitors toward the entry, which is not directly visible from most of the parking area. Direct and generous access to the outdoors is a feature of all major spaces.

The Fairfax congregation chose a design concept that was distributed throughout the site as a series of smaller pavilions set in the woods—a village. The highest part of the site is along the road from which an entry drive passes a level parking lot on the way to a turnaround at a slightly lower elevation. This arrival point gives

FIGURE 4.15a. River Road Unitarian Church, Bethesda, Maryland, Keyes, Condon & Lethbridge, 1965, view of the main entry. Photograph by author.

FIGURE 4.15b. River Road Unitarian Church, view toward the rear porch and lawn from the sanctuary. Photograph by author.

access to what is now three buildings—sanctuary, administration, and program. However, the original Anshen & Allen plan anticipated three linked round structures to the south of the circle and five petal-shaped classroom structures, all connected by a covered walkway. Only the first phase of the original plan was ever completed: two of the three slightly larger round buildings and three of the classroom structures. The two round structures were replaced in the mid-1980s by a new sanctuary building, and two of the classroom buildings were joined by a new program building. Although the original plan had a lighter footprint on the wooded site, it may not have been as flexible in use if it had been completed. The modifications of the phased construction are less architecturally coherent, but they still leave a substantial portion of the site unbuilt. In addition to a children's playground, site features now include a large picnic area, a performance stage, a memorial grove, native plant gardens, and hiking trails. In the notes for the original building program, there was a call for natural materials and plenty of glass to "open to the natural beauty of the property."[72] The resulting character today is not unified to a coherent image, but the elements remaining from the initial design show a modest approach to small pod-like structures that allow the natural beauty of the site to dominate.

Two Iowa churches illustrate a slight variation on the wooded landscape. Their sites are both sloped, and an entry drive traverses a stretch of lawn before approaching the building set higher up among the trees. The Unitarian Church of Davenport completed a new home in 1959.[73] The congregation had determined that its existing church was in need of too much repair, and a curved stair to the main sanctuary posed accessibility problems. Quite judiciously, they bought ten acres of farmland that was just a few miles from the downtown area and sold one-third of it for two-thirds of what they paid. The firm of Lundeen & Toline was asked to design a modern building; the result was clearly influenced by Frank Lloyd Wright's Prairie Style (fig. 4.16). The structure was placed well off the road, becoming known as "the building on the hill." Parking was placed to the rear, allowing the driveway approach to traverse open green space and to present a view of the building from a dramatic angle. A few large trees punctuate the lawn on the western portion of the site; they become denser in the area of the building. Over time the site has been developed into a series of distinct gardens: a welcoming garden (which also serves as a rain garden in the low spot on the site), a butterfly garden, a dragon garden for children, a meditation garden, a giving garden, a pollinator garden, and a prairie garden. The site was recognized for its capacity to serve contemplative practices such as walking, sitting, and gardening. It also

FIGURE 4.16a. Unitarian
Church, Davenport,
Iowa, Lundeen & Toline,
1959, view from the lawn.
Photograph by author.

FIGURE 4.16b. Unitarian
Church, view out to the
lawn from the sanctuary.
Photograph by author.

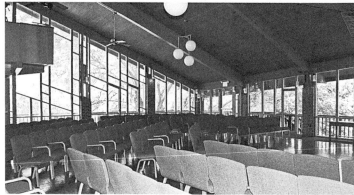

serves one of the congregation's service commitments—the giving garden provides produce to a local nonprofit serving daily free lunches.

The new site for the First Unitarian Church of Des Moines was donated by a local architect, Amos Emery (1895–1973), in memory of his parents, who were longtime congregation members. Emery designed the building himself, placing it on the east-facing slope with a generous setback from the road to the north, Bell Avenue (fig. 4.17). This left both a large area downhill for a parking lot and the entire southern half of the site unbuilt. A landscape plan from 1964 indicates two distinct grassy areas, each surrounded by trees. The steeper slope is designated as a "theater area," and a more gentle slope at the southern end was labeled "manse area," suggesting the eventual construction of a house for the minister. It is not clear how much of this planting plan was executed; an additional parking lot was later added close to the church building, and the rest of the southern portion of the site is now dense with trees. However, the area between the original parking lot (still in use) and the church building forms a transitional space from denser trees to a garden court in the crotch of the L-shaped building. While the Davenport and Des Moines congregations made effective and sensitive use of their sites, neither building was designed to "blend in" to the degree that River Road and Cedar Lane were. Each one makes good use of the topography to merge the larger spatial volumes with the other building elements. But both also present dramatic moments, establishing unique self-identities with an unusual architectural gesture as the first impression on arrival.

A final example, the Church of the Unity in Springfield, Massachusetts, recedes into its site such that the whole complex is somewhat hidden. This congregation

FIGURE 4.17a. First Unitarian Church, Des Moines, Iowa, Amos Emery, 1957, view from the entry drive. Photograph by author.

FIGURE 4.17b. First Unitarian Church, view of the rear garden. Photograph by author.

voted in 1959 to vacate their H. H. Richardson church in the downtown area and secured a site located on the southern edge of an extensive park that preserves the impressive natural topography formed by the Pecousic Brook where it flows into the Connecticut River. The site features the same wooded character as the park that surrounds it. The building was placed in the middle of the site, where it was encircled by mature trees. From the entry driveway and parking lot, only the entry area and a hint of the administrative wing stretching to the west are visible. The entry is formed by a two-story open structure that is set a half-flight of steps down from the parking lot (fig. 4.18). The main material is red brick, accented by

FIGURE 4.18a. Church of the Unity, Springfield, Massachusetts, Roy D. Murphy, 1961, view of the entry porch with the roof terrace above. Photograph by author.

FIGURE 4.18b. Church of the Unity, view of the sanctuary looking out to the woods. Photograph by author.

some dark wood elements. The sanctuary is in a wing extending at a right angle to the main north-south block; connected only at the east, it has windows open to the natural beauty along both edges of the rectangular space. While there is a strip of lawn alongside the classrooms in the main block, the primary impression is that the building is completely enveloped by the woods.

Unitarians were completely content with the fact that their modern buildings would not look like churches to most people. But they did want their buildings to express their values—values that are not easily codified by architecture in a fully recognizable way. The move to larger sites with lawns and woods added greater scope for expression in their environment—buildings and landscapes together said something about the values of place and of nature, and of human responsibility to them. As the report on the building program in Fairfax states, "A church must represent the thoughts, feelings, and beliefs of the congregation while . . . adapting well to site topography and orientation. A successful church design should contain beauty with delight, and suggest the highest standards while recognizing the human qualities of man."[74] Gardens are not meant to merely "prettify" the place; they are more intentional, more meaningful. Giving gardens, butterfly gardens, and memorial gardens express human participation and natural processes as well as the interconnection of all living things.

Two trends have appeared more recently, and congregations with more generous sites have been able to make space for them. Memorial gardens have reconstituted the colonial church graveyard, bringing it full circle (fig. 4.19a). Nineteenth- and twentieth-century developments in social attitudes toward death and burial practices pushed graves out of town and into ever-larger cemeteries: "Death and the commemoration of death had insensibly become a private, family matter, and the graveyard accordingly was relegated to an out-of-the-way spot."[75] Many churches have created contemplative gardens serving congregation members as a place of beauty to experience grief, loss, and remembering. With the rise of cremation in America in the late twentieth century, some churches also include personal markers, with or without interment of ashes. This brings a more personal sense of community back to the process not only of mourning but also of long-term honoring and remembering.

Another common feature nowadays is a labyrinth (fig. 4.19b). Labyrinths in medieval churches celebrated complexity brought into order with artistry by human ingenuity or represented an intellectual and moral challenge that requires divine aid, such as the chaos of life's journey and the perfect order that only God can see.[76]

FIGURE 4.19a. Unitarian Church, Annapolis, Maryland, George Van Fossen Schwab, 1965, view of a more recently constructed memorial garden. Photograph by author.

FIGURE 4.19b. Unitarian Universalist Church, Elgin, Illinois, view of the labyrinth, dedicated in 1997. Photograph by author.

In modern times the labyrinth has come to be associated with pilgrimage, a symbol of persistence in pursuit of a goal, or the inevitability of human life as a natural journey. Most Unitarian labyrinths are outdoors, although the First Unitarian Universalist Church of New Orleans followed the medieval practice of embedding it in the sanctuary floor. The labyrinth is not just a symbol; it is also a tool for contemplative practices. As one of the church websites explains, "At its most basic level the labyrinth is a metaphor for the journey to the center of your deepest self and back out into the world with a broadened understanding of who you are."[77] Labyrinths have many meanings, and that may be why some symbol-resistant Unitarians embrace them: everyone has to decide for themselves what they mean.

CONCLUSION: THE CHURCH, CONGREGATION, AND COMMUNITY

Samuel A. Eliot may have been the leader that enabled nineteenth-century American Unitarianism, a decentralized network of congregations spread across the breadth of the continent, to survive the vast social and economic changes of the early twentieth century. He was strategic, shoring up congregations and starting some new ones even as many evangelical churches were being shuttered.[78] But his conservative taste in church architecture seems to have halted Unitarian architectural innovation for at least two decades. In its place, Eliot imposed a limited set of acceptable forms for congregations seeking loans to assist with construction.

Renewal of the denomination in the mid-1930s came in several areas: there was new leadership and a new focus for the future. Frederick May Eliot initiated processes to develop a robust social service focus, a comprehensive religious education curriculum, and a new hymn book. There was also an independent voice for church architecture to express the progressive agenda of a liberal church—the Third Unitarian Church of Chicago. That is not to say that a single congregation changed the status quo, but their decision to build a modern building was one among many signals suggesting changes were underway. Frederick Eliot's focus on growth of the denomination and his programs for service and education were started in the 1930s, but the wider social changes of the country were sparked by the tumult of World War II. The whole country took up church-building after the war in a whole new way.

The New England meetinghouse on the commons and the mid-twentieth-century church in the woods are arresting images of their time and place. Between these historical extremes of the earliest and latest paradigms there were many urban churches without the green, small-town churches without much lawn, and churches that were various hybrids of these site dispositions. However, before the 1950s, Unitarian churches were consistently woven into the fabric of social centers—villages, towns, and cities. After World War II, Frank Lloyd Wright revived his early idea of a rural church when he received a commission for a Unitarian church in Madison, Wisconsin. He maintained his vision of the Jones family's Unity Chapel as an ideal character—a small church in a rural location, expressing a certain harmony with natural features of the landscape. He labeled the design drawings for the Madison congregation "a country church," even though the congregation rejected his encouragement to build even further out from the city. Their site was only about three miles from the statehouse in the center of Madison, just beyond the University of Wisconsin campus. Wright's vision, even with ever-wider use of the automobile, was impractical for any congregation-based church.

Availability and affordability of land within the congregation members' geographic reach was always a serious factor in locating a new site. The needs of most congregations that relocated were quite similar: room for flexibility in the arrangement of buildings, allowance for future expansion, connection to outdoors space, and plenty of space for parking. These factors naturally led to suburban options, and since car culture was by that time the norm for most Americans, the move was not seen as problematic. Midcentury churches were built in the first wave of near-full car ownership in the United States, and no one yet considered there to be a negative impact. If anything, it seemed to go hand in hand with acceptance of modern architecture.

One well-known exception to the general embrace of suburban relocation occurred when the First Unitarian Church of Rochester, New York, was forced to relocate by the city's urban renewal plan. The congregation struggled with the choice of a new site, pitting practicality against ethical objections. On the practical side, the choice was to move to a site on the edge of the city. Many congregation members wanted proximity to their neighborhoods and some open space for parking and gardens. However, the minister had a similar view as the Richmond congregation, seeing the congregation's social mission as tied to its downtown location, visible in the public sphere, and serving inner-city populations.[79] The issue was ultimately settled in favor of the suburban option by a vote. The site purchased was, in fact, not that distant geographically, but it was psychologically removed from the urban core. Time has caught up in a certain way with that critical decision. The downtown area of Rochester is dominated by commercial and business uses, and the poor neighborhoods that the minister wanted to continue to serve have moved outward too. The chosen thirteen-acre site on Winton Road has, along with its ample parking, a network of small contemplative gardens and a labyrinth. Midcentury Unitarian churches were no longer serving as witness of the presence of spiritual life in the midst of the urban cacophony; instead, they were able to extend the sense of spiritual repose beyond the walls of the buildings and to enjoy the spiritual renewal of natural beauties.

Some of the same debate must have also occurred in the nearby Syracuse congregation of May Memorial because the minister, John C. Fuller (1921–1974), offered some assurance to the congregation that they had chosen wisely in his inaugural, or "housewarming," sermon in their new building on October 4, 1964. He cast the architect as being responsible to "subtle values" to which modern societies had become desensitized, and the design of a church as the closest architectural task to pure art. A major portion of the text was devoted to equating modern architects' rejection of tradition with Unitarian rejection of religious tradition. Having fully validated and praised the design of the new structure, he went on to justify its new location:

> I do not think we have built this house—complete with cedar walls and cedar ceilings—for our own comfortable, affluent flourishing. . . . We have built our house, I insist, for that religion which invites us to the fountain-heads of love and justice, or morality and right. We have built our beautiful house the better to inspire ourselves to serve our fellowman and our community.
>
> I hope we shall always stand in fear of being irrelevant to and unconcerned with the despairs and joys, the sufferings and struggles of our fellowmen. Beauty must ever be of a piece with truth and goodness, lest it be shameful. . . . Creativeness, freedom, universality, beauty, and justice—it is for the religion which stresses these that we have built our new church.[80]

The minister did not shy away from the concern that the new church expressed a certain affluence, relatively speaking. In fact, it was only expensive in the way that any new building was a major undertaking; it was relatively unpretentious in design and construction (fig. 4.20). So the minister rejected that particular polarity. While it was undeniably costly, it had modesty with no sense of display. Its aim was beauty, and the nurturing of the human spirit, and the capacity to create a community of care. And he was not going to apologize for that.

Most congregations probably did not equate a move out of the urban core with abandoning their service, or social activism. The expansion of car culture made visibility less critical than in the past. Unitarian congregational activities to benefit

FIGURE 4.20. May
Memorial Unitarian
Church, Syracuse, New
York, Pietro Belluschi, 1964.
Photograph by author.

their communities and fulfill their core beliefs naturally fluctuate over time, as does the size and vibrancy of the congregation itself. But it does not appear, from church histories, that social missions were forgotten during the decades following such a move. For instance, at the North Shore Unitarian congregation in Danvers, Massachusetts, this happened naturally due to a longstanding relationship with a community of former patients of the Danvers State Hospital.[81] Their move in no way affected the ways they supported those individuals. The River Road Unitarian congregation was still able to confront new needs in the community. In the era of school desegregation, they ran a multiyear tutoring program for bussed African American students who were having academic difficulties in their new classrooms.[82] Other congregations were active in national movements for civil rights and for ending the Vietnam War, for which their locations were irrelevant.

However, without traditions of architecture and context, it was no longer clear that these suburban congregations communicated through their buildings their open attitude toward visitors, new members, or hosting civic events or other active engagement in their communities. Their architecture mostly communicated through scale and character. The scale of Unitarian churches is often quasi-residential, a result of modest building budgets and less interest in the monumentality of grand vertical volumes. Rather than reaching for the heavens, most Unitarian churches tend to be noticeably grounded. Belluschi's designs for both Cedar Lane in Bethesda and for May Memorial in Syracuse are good representatives of Unitarian character—"simple, quiet, functional . . . [and] unpretentious."[83] May Memorial in particular is a relatively compact, even efficient building. The walls are smooth and largely featureless. The whole has a quiet, somewhat timeless character.[84] Locals described it as Japanese teahouse when it was completed—a diminutive structure set in a garden. One may or may not regard it as inviting, but it is entirely approachable.

Modern Unitarian churches in the mid-twentieth century did not look like churches, so their lack of a central location or even visibility from suburban streets may not have seemed to midcentury congregations to pose a problem—they were not depending on easy recognition to be relevant. Many went further, accepting withdrawal into a larger site without visibility from a public roadway. The character of the exterior of the building did not need to communicate values to the broader community—it only needed to represent the values of the congregation to themselves. These churches were set into a dialogue with a natural landscape purposefully, and most designs were driven by site-oriented concerns: integration with topography and vegetation, establishing correspondence between indoor and outdoor spaces, and generous views from interiors, including the sanctuary. A common design for a sloped site presents a one-story structure on the approach side and allows the lower story to access daylight on the other side. This is consistent with an everyday, if not strictly residential sense of scale, even when the forms are not. Whether by choice or by factors of site availability and cost, many of the congregations of the postwar era effectively withdrew from the larger community in the physical sense. Their secluded churches in the woods or in a protected clearing offered a retreat from daily life that made their attendance worthwhile. While other religions offered this distance from the ordinary through ritual and enclosure, Unitarians welcomed each other and the outdoors into their worship in an everyday manner. Thus, they needed beauty, silence, and nature to escape daily concerns and to connect with something more, something of greater value and meaning.

FIGURE 5.1. University Unitarian Church, Seattle, Paul Kirk, 1959, view of the clerestory and exterior shading screen showing the porosity of a sanctuary open to nature. Photograph by author.

CHAPTER FIVE

Church without Cross or Creed

Religious buildings arise as human creations, but they persist as transforming, life-altering environments. They are expressions of and sources of religious experience. . . . In the metaphorical language of Wassily Kandinsky, every work of architecture is both "the child of its time" and "the mother of our emotions."

—Lindsay Jones, *The Hermeneutics of Sacred Architecture*

Our new meeting house—expressing our contemporary faith in contemporary material and design—will be a symbol of the inspiration of our faith and, more practically, a home for the diverse activities in which we embody our religion: worship, religious education in both child and adult form, social action, social service and fellowship, to say nothing of a myriad of community endeavors.

—Rudolph W. Nemser, Fairfax Unitarian Church, 1960

CHURCHES AS "WITNESS TO OUR OWN TIME"

The fact that modernism was nearly universally accepted by Unitarian congregations for new construction after World War II is not particularly remarkable; it was the period in which American acceptance of modernism moved from elite or avant-garde patronage to a more commonplace idiom for institutional and commercial buildings. This wider adoption of modernism suited the American lifestyle of the 1950s, especially visible in rapid suburban growth. It was so pervasive that even conservative religious groups experimented with modern church forms. However, for most religious congregations, modern *versus* traditional styles for their church was a matter of debate. Those who wanted to adopt modern design needed to overcome a widely held view that modernism "represented the triumph of secularization over many aspects of culture and scholarship."[1] The abstraction and minimalism of modern architecture seemed incapable of expressing or inspiring an emotional or spiritual feeling. Even architects were debating whether modern architecture was inherently antithetical to monumentality. For Unitarians however, there was no sense of struggle with modern architecture's rationality and basis in an empirical worldview—these characteristics were particularly suited to their values. Reverend John C. Fuller of the Unitarian congregation in Syracuse, New York, claimed that Unitarians were in fact compelled to build a new church in order to have a spiritual home that would be a proper reflection of their times. In his "housewarming" sermon, he said, "We were not forced to build a new church. We had a house. It held us. It served us. There was elegance and inspiration in it. And yet, there moved within us, as there moves in all free men, a desire, an urge, a restlessness *to bear witness to our own time*, to modern man, and to the vision of what we seek to be and to become."[2]

American modernism entered a new phase of experimentation after the war, but certain formal themes continued to be central to the idea of modern architecture, if not necessarily to be in the foreground of every project: clarity of construction, truth in materials, a minimalist approach, and transparency are among the most prominent themes. In addition to these basic characteristics, 1950s modernism suited Unitarian interests in a variety of other ways. One important factor was the cost of construction. The simplicity with which midcentury buildings were detailed, and the prevalence of everyday (or even industrial) materials, were compatible with Unitarian values, and of course they cost less than the heavier masonry construction used for traditional religious buildings. Furthermore, architects were exploring a wider variety of themes in the modern architecture of the postwar era, so there was a greater range of expressive form. An interest in architecture suited to everyday life and regional expression in reaction to consumerism and its tendency toward sameness appealed to Unitarian clients. Buildings that seemed more vernacular than monumental, and that inspired communal connection, were regarded as democratic and also, in Cold War terms, American.[3] A question arises then as to how this simplicity of expression could be sufficient to achieve a meaningful space for worship.

Growth of the Unitarian denomination was due in part to the leadership of Frederick May Eliot, but it was also consistent with a general rise in religious activity in America in the postwar decades. Scholars have regarded the social trauma and general anxieties of the war itself and of the Cold War that followed as a national crisis that caused a renewal of church attendance and church building. Church growth also reflected a desire for a meaningful community to balance the cultural unease with dominant trends of careerism and consumerism.[4] A renewed investment in religion on college campuses was a phenomenon that put the general trend into somewhat higher relief.[5] The university was a major locus of twentieth-century secularization and the rise of science over religion as an explanation of the nature of life, our planetary systems, and the cosmos. Religious observance as a requirement of campus life dropped dramatically in the interwar years, even if some nineteenth-century college chapels had remained symbolically potent. At the same time, Gothic Revival libraries on campus were themselves symbols of the displacement of religion by scientific knowledge. However, in the postwar period, many campuses build new chapels as a hedge against the hubris of scientific certainty in the conduct of modern life. Like the chapel that was included in the design of the United Nations complex, campus nondenominational chapels used a modern architectural idiom to avoid association with any one religious tradition over another, and to symbolize the acknowledgment that religious belief was not considered antithetical to the institutions of the modern world. Modern architecture was devoid enough of religious association to be inoffensive to all. Unitarians would strive for a modernism that was neutral to specific religious associations but nevertheless offered spiritual inspiration.

Kresge Chapel (1955) at the Massachusetts Institute of Technology in Cambridge, designed by Eero Saarinen (1910–1960), is the premier example.[6] Although its cylindrical form was derided by some with a pejorative nickname, the "gas tank," the more prevalent view is that Saarinen successfully used universal themes and a minimalist articulation to assure every religion a spiritually inflected space for worship on campus. More importantly, as historian Margaret M. Grubiak notes, "Among the various postwar chapels on the American campus, the MIT Chapel especially represents a sophisticated narrative of a preeminent technological school's response to world events and its administration's desire to include the moral and social education of its scientists."[7] The chapel design avoided both the monumentality of traditional religious buildings and identifiable religious symbolism, and achieved nevertheless a sense of quiet spirituality through form, material, and a play of water, shadow, and light.

Of greater interest, however, and unique to MIT's addition of a campus chapel, is the fact that the chapel was only one half of the project; the nearby auditorium, also designed by Saarinen, was part of the same project developed by a

Unitarian-inspired vision (fig. 5.2). While the chapel provided an intimate space for private spiritual contemplation and small religious services, the auditorium could host larger religious services if needed but was more broadly intended for lectures in philosophy, ethics, and other humanistic disciplines to be attended by all students. The president of MIT, James R. Killian, was committed to promoting the humanities as an integral part of the science and technology curriculum.[8] He commissioned the central auditorium along with the chapel as a forum for philosophical questions as well as spiritual ones within the community of MIT students. Killian, a practicing Unitarian, consulted with Dean of Students Everett Moore Baker, a Unitarian minister, regarding the concept for the two buildings that would occupy a central location on the campus.[9] Baker felt that something essential to the idea of America resided in the "village church and the meeting house."[10] Together, Saarinen's chapel and auditorium allowed MIT to meet its responsibilities to society by acknowledging religion *and* humanities-based philosophical and moral leadership as a part of civic responsibility for all.

FIGURE 5.2. Kresge Auditorium and Chapel at MIT, Cambridge, Massachusetts, Eero Saarinen, 1955. Photograph by Nick Allen, CC BY-SA 4.0, https://creativecommons.org/licenses/by-sa/4.0/deed.en.

In the decade from 1947 to 1957, adult membership in the Unitarian denomination increased by around 50 percent, and the number of congregations rose from 325 to 550.[11] The numbers were small in comparison to Main Line denominational growth, yet proportionally the increase was dramatic. A study of the denomination revealed that most Unitarians had grown up in different religious traditions and chose to become Unitarians as adults.[12] The study suggested that most had "dropped out" of their childhood religion, often as a result of changing views during their university education. At a later point, they found that their independently developed values had resonance with Unitarianism. World War II was also an experience that may have caused some to reject old beliefs. Many scientists and engineers of the massive war machine and its catastrophic potentials were among those Americans fueling the renewal of religion. While there is no proof, many seem to have chosen Unitarianism as a religion that embraced modern science and did not require belief in a deity. A Tennessee Valley congregation, serving Knoxville and Oak Ridge, was founded in 1949; that of Los Alamos, New Mexico, in 1953; and the one in Livermore, California, in 1957. Unitarians were still somewhat split on their personal views of the concept of God, but they overwhelmingly believed that "modern science 'strengthens liberal religion.'"[13] Scientists and engineers that were devoted to the truth of science could individually confront moral and ethical uncertainty within the Unitarian community.

Historically, most Unitarian sanctuaries built in traditional architectural styles would be difficult to distinguish from other Protestant church interiors. Smaller-scale churches might have their entry on the diagonal and perhaps avoid a center aisle so that no single point was emphasized as more important or powerful than another. There would be lots of daylight wherever possible and typically no ornament. This left the modern Unitarian sanctuary without rules or widely accepted means to make it suitable for Unitarian worship. Congregations and their architects confronted the problem of making a meaningful space for nondirected worship, for nonsacred spirituality, for celebrating human truth and goodness. For inspiration, one might have to reach back to the ideas of nontraditional church pioneers—Jenkin Lloyd Jones wanted an "oratory for the soul," Frank Lloyd Wright both "a noble room" and "good-time place." Reverend Ross Weston of the Unitarian Church of Arlington had envisioned a "church of life abundant . . . that carries forever forward a shining vision of the beauty of life."[14] Each congregation, each architect attempted to fashion a space that spoke of their optimistic humanism and was amenable to the particular congregation's patterns of use over time.

The full meaning of the architecture would necessarily evolve with community practices.

The Unitarians of the postwar period not only encouraged diversity of individual belief but defined their religion as one in which individuals of varied beliefs regarding theology, religious texts, and traditions united in common aspirations toward goodness, truth, and unity in shared humanity. Their sense of wonder and awe came not from the supernatural but from the natural world and the interconnectedness of all things. The architecture for this religion was enhanced by a reverence for nature and for human community as a part of nature. The space for worship needed to be both inviting and uplifting, often achieved by a connection to nature. Nature could be invoked through a conscientious use of natural materials, primarily wood, but also masonry, which is of the earth. Nature could be drawn in by interconnecting interior and exterior spaces or by opening to an expansive view, and it could be evident in the natural daylight entering freely. While a few congregations chose to create inwardly focused spaces for worship, the more common approach to the modern Unitarian church was an open sanctuary.

Just as MIT recognized the dual function of worship and civic discourse, most Unitarian churches of the postwar period continued to include an auditorium or sanctuary and a social hall as the two most prominent spaces. In many instances, the classrooms and other meeting spaces also had a primary relationship to the auditorium but this was a more variable element overall. Frequently, a congregation could not afford to build all functional elements at once and so took a staged approach to construction. Some later went on to fulfill their full vision, while others never did. In those instances, the intentionality of these relationships was often compromised. This chapter is focused on places where the original intentions are still clear in order to see how the meaning of the sanctuary is dependent on the social spaces that are its complement.

CONNECTIONS TO NATURE: THE OPEN SANCTUARY

Although most American religious architecture of the twentieth century generally moved away from the freestanding church toward a campus of multifunctional spaces, the sanctuary or auditorium remained its central space for architectural expression as a "church." For most Christian denominations, the worship space, the church, would always be in the foreground, presenting the primary architectural identity. For Unitarians, the visibility on approach of this primary space within the overall building complex was more variable. The auditorium was now almost always designed in relationship to the rest of the congregation's needs. But spatially, it remained the foremost single element in which key values, beliefs, and the nature of communal worship were expressed. And the architectural experience of arrival, entry, and worship in the auditorium remained the most important priority in design. Therefore, this chapter focuses on that space and how it diverged from the traditional church interior of the ubiquitous Gothic Revival and Federal-style spaces of the late nineteenth and early twentieth centuries.

Congregations celebrated nature as a source of spiritual renewal in Unitarian churches during the time when they embraced Transcendentalism in the decades following the Civil War. Nature continued to be an important theme for any nontraditional church design in the twentieth century. Modern architecture had, from the start, challenged the insistence on interior space as completely enclosed and separated from the exterior. In adopting modern architecture for churches, Unitarians had new opportunities to engage with nature as part of their worship space.

Connecting to nature directly with extensive areas of glass is a common theme in Unitarian midcentury sanctuaries. It is sometimes directed to a specific view of a natural feature; otherwise visual openness allowed a sense of spatial extension out into the immediate surrounding landscape. The Church of the River in Memphis is an obvious example in which the end wall behind the minister is almost entirely glazed and provides a dynamic view (see fig. 4.8b). Other examples with a fully glazed end wall such as churches in Bellevue, Washington, and Evanston, Illinois, do not have a view into the distance but into the green groves and gardens surrounding the building (fig. 5.3). The "prow" of Frank Lloyd Wright's First Unitarian Church in Madison, Wisconsin, was originally directed to a view of Lake Mendota, although partially screened to protect from glare behind the minister. The open space has subsequently been filled with buildings, obscuring this important view (fig. 5.15).

More often, extensive glazing was used on lateral walls to avoid visual disharmonies of contrast and glare. Dramatic examples where the full length of both sides in a rectangular space are largely glazed can be seen on two wooded sites. At Cedar Lane in Bethesda, Maryland, the two full-height transparent walls are composed of lightly colored glass in a random pattern that both mimics the colors of the natural setting and softens the effects of direct sunlight (fig. 5.4a). In

FIGURE 5.3. East Shore Unitarian Church, Bellevue, Washington, Jack Morse, 1955, view of the sanctuary. Photograph by author.

Springfield, Massachusetts, the fully glazed lower register of the wall is protected by an overhang at the upper level of the space while the view out to the woods is completely unobstructed (see fig. 4.18b). A similar openness can be seen in Davenport, Iowa, but the auditorium is square, and the glazed walls are adjacent rather than parallel to each other. The auditorium here is at the canopy level of the nearby surrounding trees, adding a sense of wonder, and doors to a perimeter deck further the strong sense of connection between interior and exterior (see fig. 4.16). In all of these spaces, the surrounding trees also provide some screening and modulation of the light. In other cases, a fully glazed wall provides a purposeful connection to a paired outdoor space such as that at Richmond, Virginia, where it was originally connected to a paved courtyard designed as an outdoor sanctuary, and River Road in Bethesda, where continuous doors connect to a porch and defined lawn (fig. 5.4b). Views of surrounding natural features as well as the ever-changing qualities of abundant daylight are positive qualities of an open sanctuary.

FIGURE 5.4a. Cedar Lane Unitarian Church, Bethesda, Maryland, Pietro Belluschi, 1955, view of the lateral auditorium wall. Photograph by author.

FIGURE 5.4b. River Road Unitarian Church, Bethesda, Maryland, Keyes, Condon & Lethbridge, 1965, view of the lateral auditorium wall from the gallery. Photograph by author.

The conscientious presence of daylight was nearly universal to all midcentury modern church designs. In churches for other denominations, light frequently contributed in dramatic ways to the aesthetic effects of space and materials, but its ultimate importance was symbolic. For Unitarians, light was not symbolic of the divine, and it was generally not manipulated to produce mysterious effects or a devout mood. Light in a Unitarian sanctuary was the daylight of life on earth and a direct reminder of the sun in the sky. There were some designs that used daylight as the sole connection to nature—that is, when the site was in an urban or suburban context that had no significant views of natural features, or when the congregation preferred an interior-oriented sanctuary. The University Unitarian Church in Seattle (1959), designed by Paul Kirk (1914–1995), depends on sunlight for its warmth and beauty. The solution in this instance is particularly interesting because the site's steep slope would have allowed direct sunlight from the east without any negative effects from unwelcome views of neighboring houses, which were downhill. But the only openings in the sanctuary's east wall are relatively small and set right at floor level, one per bay—they light the side aisle but allow the east half of the space to remain relatively dark. The most important daylighting comes from a tall east-facing clerestory placed in a gap between two opposing, and unequal, shed roofs (fig. 5.1). The clerestory is composed of a mix of cream and yellow semi-opaque glass; softened morning sunlight from this tall clerestory is then reflected off of a painted white surface, the top half of the western wall. The resulting warm glow fills the western half of the sanctuary, even on cloudy days. Less dramatically, ambient skylight also enters from the glazed lower half of that western wall, which is partially screened for glare and to mute views. The lofty bright space is in contrast to a lower and darker, more protected space on the east side of the sanctuary. This lateral differentiation is a strong counterpoint to the frontward focus upon entry. Rather than harnessing the drama of direct sunlight, Kirk designed for a climate with a high percentage of overcast days. The quality of light produced is remarkably steady throughout the year—perhaps he was familiar with Wright's claim that Unity Temple would be cheerfully sunny even on cloudy days. Kirk created darkness to make the light more visible, to bring it to awareness without mystery or drama. A contemporary review observed that "light gave University Unitarian its form," affirming the primacy of light in the experience of the sanctuary (fig. 5.5a).[15]

In the sanctuary of St. John's Unitarian Church, Cincinnati, sunlight is more active; the architect described the design as heliocentric.[16] This longitudinal wor-

FIGURE 5.5a. University Unitarian Church, Seattle, Paul Kirk, 1959, view of the sanctuary. Photograph by author.

FIGURE 5.5b. University Unitarian Church, view of the exterior with the social hall to the right and sanctuary to the left. Photograph by author.

ship space has its primary exposure to the south, so light had to be admitted with due care. A general presence of light to activate the space comes through continuous glazing at the level of the floor and a clerestory in the tall south wall (fig. 5.6). This sunlight strikes the north wall opposite throughout much of the year; in midwinter it illuminates the sloped metal decking of the ceiling. Two skylights set into the roof and three vertical slot windows in the south wall were designed to throw direct sunlight onto the golden fragments of a Harry Bertoia sculpture, *Joy*, which was commissioned to animate the chancel wall. (The sculpture is quite similar to the one over the altar in Kresge Chapel at MIT.) The vertical slots were shaped and positioned to act as a sundial, each admitting its direct sunlight on

FIGURE 5.6a. St. John's Unitarian Church, Cincinnati, John Garber, 1959, interior view. Photograph by Anton Harfmann.

FIGURE 5.6b. St. John's Unitarian Church, view of the apertures on the south wall and the mark of sunlight on the pavement. Photograph by Anton Harfmann.

the equinoxes and solstices. Brass splines and a lighter color in the concrete floor mark the solar paths from each slot. This dynamic light, with its calendrical significance, is a vibrant reminder of nature and cosmos, and a primary element in creating a sense of the spirituality in the worship space.

Churches with centrally located sanctuaries, such as Victor Lundy's design in Hartford, Connecticut, and Louis Kahn's design in Rochester, New York, required a careful management of top-lighting to avoid heat gain and potential glare. Both used complex sectional arrangements of vertical glazing and reflected light rather than allowing direct sunshine to enter the spaces. The daylight in Lundy's design is diffused by a suspended ceiling of radiating wood slats (fig. 5.7a). Kahn, after much anxiety and experimentation, placed large monitors in the four corners of the roof, with glazing arranged opposite from solid perimeter walls of the room. In this way, he pointed any direct sunlight away from the space. It is thrown onto soft gray surfaces of concrete, creating a bright spot without sharp edges and complemented by ambient skylight (fig. 5.7b). There is change and movement throughout the day, but it is imprecise. The light enters from well above the broad surfaces of the folded plate that forms the ceiling, leaving them in shadow. Thus, though the light is often subtle, its presence is heightened by contrast. In this way, Kahn avoided not only the undesirable physical effects of direct sunlight but also any sense of spiritual mystery that is common to dramatic light emanating from hidden sources. It was therefore more suited to a Unitarian auditorium. The movement of the sun is more noticeable where it strikes a vertical surface with a visible pattern, as happens in May Memorial in Syracuse and First Boston (figs. 5.7c and 5.7d).

The presence of nature is more subtly woven into the experience of some Unitarian sanctuaries through the use of certain materials, most especially unpainted wood. In the case of East Shore Unitarian Church in Bellevue, Washington (1956), designed by Jack Morse (1911–2000), the wood not only referenced the idea of nature but more specifically tied the building to its regional

FIGURE 5.7a. Unitarian Society, Hartford, Connecticut, Victor Lundy, 1964, view of the auditorium ceiling. Photograph by author.

FIGURE 5.7b. First Unitarian Church, Rochester, New York, Louis Kahn, 1959, view of the light monitor. Photograph by author.

FIGURE 5.7c. May Memorial Unitarian Church, Syracuse, New York, Pietro Belluschi, 1964, view of the central lantern. Photograph by author.

FIGURE 5.7d. First Church, Boston, Paul Rudolph, 1972, view of the tower over the organ loft. Photograph by author.

Pacific Northwest context (see fig. 5.3). A regionally inflected modernism featuring exposed wood construction had already emerged in the area by the mid-1950s. This church was conceived in diagrammatic terms as a sheltering roof for a notoriously rainy climate. It is as if a large square surface were literally folded on its diagonal and laid on a single horizontal ridge beam, 140 feet long and 23 feet above the floor. The triangular surfaces extend in a relatively gentle slope almost to the ground where their edge beams are anchored. Three parallel rectangular rooms are arranged well under the overhangs of this "unifying canopy of an elemental roof," and most of the perimeter walls are glazed. The auditorium occupies only sixty feet of the roof's length, leaving room for a narrow narthex and generous overhangs on each end. Its ceiling consists of exposed glulam beams and wood decking; the ridge beam pierces the front wall of glass and is supported by an exterior steel column further out. The fully glazed chancel wall, well shaded by the roof overhangs, provided a clear view to the nearby Cascade Mountains at the time of construction, though a grove of sheltering trees now encircles the east end of the building. In both conditions, the materials and the view are means of making nature's beauty a primary experience in the space. At the time of construction, one architecture critic observed, "On a high site among tall firs this building is peculiarly responsive to its worship purposes [and] its environment. . . . [It is] a space of simple dignity and strong character."[17]

At May Memorial Unitarian Church in Syracuse, Pietro Belluschi also used wood structure and finishes but with a strikingly different effect than its character at East Shore (fig. 5.8). The exterior of the building sets the theme with uniform wood siding in framed panels. The auditorium at May is formed by a wood structural frame and finished with wood vertical surfaces. Four freestanding fir glulam arches arc gracefully as they intersect the upward sloping ceiling planes and reach up to support the edge beams of a lantern at the apex. Structural members are slightly darker than the cedar finish boards of the walls and ceiling. The smooth solid planes that enclose the space are all uniformly finished with vertical boards. The overall effect is so consistent that the room feels something like a cabinet. The unusual insistence of a single material makes this space extraordinary. In addition to the light coming through the baffled central lantern, the wood is warmed by the daylight entering through a ribbon of continuous windows in the upper zone of the east and west walls. Whereas the use of wood in Washington connects the building to the natural environment of the region, the wood in Syracuse expresses a reverence for nature through craft and a strong sensorial evocation, a calm strength through "simplicity and directness of design."[18]

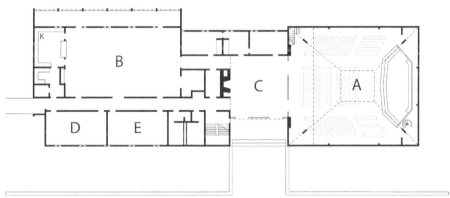

FIGURE 5.8a. May Memorial Unitarian Church, Syracuse, New York, Pietro Belluschi, 1964, view of the auditorium. Photograph by author.

FIGURE 5.8b. May Memorial Unitarian Church, plan: A—sanctuary, B—social hall, C—narthex, D—meeting room, E—library. Drawing by Alissa Tucker.

Material qualities in Unitarian churches were not always referencing nature. Exposed structures and untreated materials of any kind also expressed Unitarian qualities of rationality, pragmatism, and straightforward truth—the laws of nature, if not the direct material quality. The interiors of Belluschi's Unitarian Church in Rockford, Illinois, also feature wood that was expressive of precision and fit, but here it was woven into a more dominant exposed concrete frame (see fig. 6.5). The rectangular space of the sanctuary (approximately forty-four feet by sixty feet) is defined by five concrete column-and-beam frames that are smooth and precise. The frames are spanned above by exposed concrete planks. The wall of each bay is finished with a panel of closely spaced vertical wood slats. This wood provides a color contrast to the smoothly finished concrete columns and also adds some texture to the walls—not wood's inherent textures but as a set of closely spaced vertical slats. In the final bay on one side, the wall panel becomes a backlit screen so that the wood is even more fully appreciated. A bare tree branch added to the space by a congregation member intensifies the quiet stillness of the architecture. The branch was so fitting to the aesthetic that it was retained as a permanent feature.[19] The irregularity contrasts the regularity of the wood grilles, making it visually and materially compelling. This sanctuary derives a spiritual nature from the precision and clarity of each and every element.

Kahn's sanctuary at the First Unitarian Church of Rochester features an unusual exposed concrete vault, but the walls of unpainted concrete block were an even more radical material choice for a church interior. He gave the concrete block walls some visual depth by mixing various shades of grey, simulating a natural color variation found in stone.[20] The result is subtle but profound; it softens a material that would have been otherwise flat, dull, and potentially harsh (fig. 5.9a). Given the brick exterior, the switch to concrete block for the internally focused auditorium heightens an awareness of the layering of spaces. Ulrich Franzen followed Kahn's lead and used concrete block extensively in his design for the First Unitarian Church of Richmond, Virginia. There the concrete block contributes to a feeling of continuity between the exterior and interior of the building. On the interior, the block is complemented by exposed wood framing members on the ceilings, dramatic lighting from clerestories, and panels of bright colors on wall board in overhead monitors. The large space of the auditorium, however, was treated slightly differently. Most of the walls are glass up to an eight-foot-high soffit, which is marked as a datum by a wide wood-trim board. There is smooth painted wallboard above that. The wide soffits and the ceiling were finished with

FIGURE 5.9a. First Unitarian Church, Rochester, New York, Louis Kahn, 1959, view of the principal materials in the auditorium. Photograph by author.

FIGURE 5.9b. First Unitarian Church, first floor plan of the original building: A—sanctuary, B—social hall, C—narthex, D—meeting rooms/class-rooms. Drawing by Alissa Tucker.

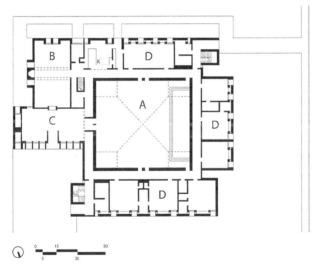

smooth polished wood panels. Clearly these materials were intended to blend with the rest of the building but also make the sanctuary distinctive as the most important space within the whole.

A willingness to use extensive views, a greater amount of natural light, and every-day materials were characteristics that made these spaces unique to Unitarianism. When present, these were also characteristics that often lent informality rather than a sense of formal or even sacred space. In general, there was less insistent focus created by spatial arrangements than was usually found in church spaces, and with some clear exceptions, there was less closure as well.[21] Each congregation established, in dialogue with their architect, their own sense of formality or informality, openness or closure, contemplative or active space, and in what degree the church would be perceived as different, or set apart, from the space of everyday life. In establishing an idea for the design of this most important space, architects needed to avoid arrangements that suggested hierarchy, and they needed to support the creation of a communal feeling among participants. From a functional perspective, Unitarian worship required only an adequate amount of seating for the congregation and a platform for speakers. Most churches at midcentury also had an organ, but not all included a designated area for a choir. And the flexibility of seating (that is, whether or not it was fixed) also varied with each congregation. The lack of rules for the creation of the sanctuary has resulted in such variety that it is nearly impossible to generalize the architectural qualities of Unitarian churches. But there is always some quality that captures attention and engages the imagination. In the more open ones, the connection to the outdoors is the dominant quality. These tend to be slightly more informal interiors, relying on the sensual qualities of the site for their character. In the more closed-in spaces, attention is drawn to the materials and surfaces, with an effect of being slightly more formal. In either case, there is a primary consideration of engagement of the senses, causing attention to the place. Even the most informal spaces cannot be experienced in a distracted way.

ABSTRACTIONS OF NATURE: IDEAL GEOMETRIES

In addressing the question of Unitarian forms of worship, Andrea Greenwood and Mark W. Harris point out that it is not necessarily "oriented to the supernatural." Instead, "Unitarians often focus on the root of the old Anglo-Saxon word 'worship' (*weorthscipe*) or 'worth ship,' which means to reflect upon or celebrate things of worth . . .—an idea, a value, or *a vision of how the world could be*."[22] Without the tradition of a fixed focus (altar, ark, or mihrab, for instance), and without processions or other prescribed rituals, the sense of the spiritual purpose in gathering had to be communicated more abstractly in Unitarian sanctuaries. In general, the architecture was expected to communicate a sense of unity, harmony, and social connection—*this* idea of how the world could be. Congregations worked through building committees to describe their own worship practices and their desires for the space. Although not always as poetic as Jenkin Lloyd Jones's "oratory for the soul," congregations tried to guide their architects with a vision. Some included references to architectural implications, such as materials or light and view, but most were values statements without precise physical correlates.

The following statement created by the building committee members of the River Road Unitarian Church in Bethesda, Maryland, is most explicit in connecting their own identity to an architectural intention:

> Our church shall be designed to contribute to and reflect the warmth of love, the lift of the human spirit in moments of exaltation, and the integrity of the intelligence engaged in the search for truth. Our church shall symbolize the attitudes and aspirations of our congregation. Because we are a unity in diversity, imposing no dogma but believing in the freedom of mind and spirit, our church may incorporate materials and aesthetic qualities which create a unity of effect. Because we are dedicated to the brotherhood of man, our church shall have a universal quality. Because we have concern for people and an openness to the world, our church shall be warm and inviting . . . a place where we can grow as a religious fellowship and as religious persons. . . . Our church shall be creative and artistic, yet honest and simple.[23]

"Unity of effect," "universal quality," and "warm and inviting" provided some guidance without imposing any specific formal or material implication.

Tore Bjornstad, the original architect for the congregation of Ames, Iowa, in 1966, interpreted what he had heard from congregation members this way: "The basic motivation for the fellowship's religious activities seems to be a desire to cement the credibility of man's own integrity of spirit and motivation. In being selected to design the new home for the Ames Unitarians, the challenge became one of expressing that strength of spirit. How can one combine the buoyancy of their spirit and the rationality of their imagination into one building?"[24] Charles Goodman offered his own interpretation of what he had learned in conversation with members of the congregation of Arlington, Virginia, when he wrote a full explication of his design. He understood Unitarian belief as a "doctrine of free and open discourse; . . . directed toward the principle of unity through diversity of beliefs, in which reason displaces dogma and simplicity and warmth enhances the fellowship of men."[25] More famously, Louis Kahn condensed his understanding of the Unitarians of Rochester, New York, into a singular essence: a question mark.

Although each congregation needed to articulate their own version of Unitarianism to their architects, the theme of "unity" was a constant, and the most perfect geometry for expressing unity is the circle. Symbolic of the world or cosmos, the circle has no beginning and no end. A circle is also a basic social unit—circle of friends, sewing circle, and the round table are some of the ways this is evident. The circle is nonhierarchical; a circular auditorium puts people in relatively close proximity and facing each other. It is a natural symbol for the Unitarians, and so it is not surprising to find its adoption in the experimental architectures of the 1950s and 1960s. If anything, it is surprising that it was not more widely deployed. Perhaps difficulty in design and a probable impact on construction costs were too risky despite its symbolic suitability. Several examples of circular auditoria illustrate different ways to utilize the social and symbolic potential of the circle in making a Unitarian space for worship.

The 1965 design for the sole Atlanta Unitarian congregation's new church by local architect Joseph Amisano employs geometry in a most straightforward way. The easy recognition of circle and square by anyone experiencing the building provides a connection to universal religious themes. A pyramidal roof slopes upward to a central lantern from a square perimeter; the circular sanctuary is centered within under dramatic diagonal concrete beams rising from corner piers (fig. 5.10). Tiers of seats rise from the floor with radially placed steps like a Greek theater and can be accessed either from above at the perimeter or from the central circular floor. The seventy-foot-diameter circular sanctuary was bounded

FIGURE 5.10. First Unitarian Church, Atlanta, Joseph Amisano, 1965, view of the sanctuary. Permission of the Georgia Institute of Technology Library and Information Center, Archives and Records Management Department, Georgia Tech, Atlanta.

by a set of concentric square walls that defined a set of classrooms and meeting rooms around the perimeter of the building. The north wing of this outer ring was open for much of its width, forming the social hall connected to an outdoor terrace. The pyramidal roof is low and spreading, and the rise of the sloped seating was also gentle. Still, the space had a clearly defined central vertical axis, which is somewhat antithetical to Unitarian principles but hard to avoid with circular forms. The circle-in-square geometry evokes perfection, human reason, and the human body all at once. The specific reference to Renaissance humanism was no doubt intentional; Amisano had spent a year of study at the American Academy in Rome in 1952, only three years after Rudolf Wittkower's influential *Architectural Principles in the Age of Humanism* was published and the same year that the architectural historian and Palladio scholar James Ackerman was in residence.[26] He would have been primed to give his client's humanistic religion an explicitly humanistic architectural form.

The circular sanctuary of the First Unitarian Church of Schenectady, New York, is a similarly perfect circular amphitheater but set without enclosing walls within a larger open space (fig. 5.11a). The presence of this dramatic circular space is visible on the exterior only by the bulge of its dome, which disappears from view as one approaches the entry. The glazed vestibule is succeeded by a curved screening wall that backs the chancel and forces movement around the perimeter to discover the auditorium's volume. The space was created by sinking the floor plane and correspondingly inflating the hollow of a dome directly above it in the ceiling/roof plane in the center of a large open space. Rows of seats cascade down toward the center on three-quarters of the perimeter, while seats were left off of the carpeted risers of the rest to form a chancel. Six columns mark the perimeter and support the dome, a singular interruption of the otherwise flat ceiling that extends throughout the whole building. The dome is the only feature that was not made of concrete or block. The members of its lamella frame were left exposed, creating a striking geometric pattern of dark strips against a curved white surface—an ornamental feature within an otherwise minimalist context. The remainder of the room in which the auditorium was inscribed is the congregation's social space, called the Great Hall. A minister of the church, Reverend William Gold, described the congregation's relationship this way: "The worship is held together by fellowship; . . . and fellowship also holds the world together."[27] The sanctuary is the heart of the building, a circular space of calm and serenity, a place of contemplation. The sixty-foot-diameter auditorium can seat five hundred for a service. Although the space is focused inward, the surrounding

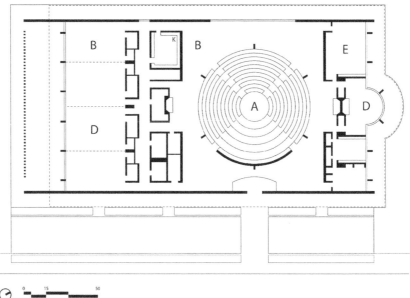

FIGURE 5.11a. First Unitarian Church, Schenectady, New York, Edward Durrell Stone, 1958, two views of the auditorium within the "great room" social hall. Photograph by author.

FIGURE 5.11b. First Unitarian Church, plan: A—sanctuary, B—social hall, C—narthex, D—meeting rooms/classrooms, E—library. Drawing by Alissa Tucker.

fellowship areas temper the sense of inflexibility that concentric circles can suggest. Two lateral walls feature fireplaces and seating areas, while the wall opposite the chancel is glazed, opening onto a green landscape to the rear of the site.

The circular sanctuary of the Unitarian Society of Hartford is, like that of the church in Atlanta, at the geometric center of the whole building (fig. 5.12). The design similarly celebrates the unity of the circular sanctuary, but the geometry is not a pure abstraction perfectly realized in physical form. Rather, the sanctuary is the void between twelve concrete walls on radials that emanate from its center. The spaces surrounding the central sanctuary are defined by the irregularly spaced radials as they expand outward, challenging a circle's static closure. They include rooms for classrooms, offices, and a chapel. Architect Victor Lundy explained that "the concept is that many points of view draw together and become united at the center."[28] The partition walls that enclose the sanctuary form a slightly irregular polygon, but the space is perceived as circular. (An earlier plan with more concrete radials—eighteen—created a more circular sanctuary.) This spatial perception is created by the spectacular configuration of the ceiling: radiating cascades of cedar slats that form a suspended canopy. It originates at the center and extends in two rings of varied slopes to the perimeter walls, where it continues over the walls into the ambulatory surrounding the sanctuary. This dominant feature defines the space more assertively. The roof above the central portion is suspended from the

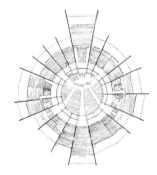

FIGURE 5.12a. Unitarian Meeting House, Hartford, Connecticut, Victor Lundy, 1964, view of the auditorium and plan. © Massachusetts Institute of Technology, photograph by G. E. Kidder Smith.

FIGURE 5.12b. Unitarian Meeting House, schematic plan drawing by Victor Lundy, 1962; the final design has fewer radial walls. Library of Congress, Prints & Photographs Division, LC-DIG-ds-11109.

tops of the concrete radials, allowing light to enter by an arrangement reminiscent of the Golden House of Nero, the Imperial Roman villa where light was admitted to a central domed room through an oculus and to radiating rooms surrounding it through clerestories. The indirect light is diffused as it enters the sanctuary between the slats of the outer ring of the canopy. The convergence of a multitude of individual slats to form a unified effect reiterates the main conceptual theme in which the unity of the circle is the product of the concrete piers surrounding it, each of which is a different height and width. Together they support the singular central space. Lundy described it as a "tapestry of radiating thin wood members" that allowed light from the skylights above to filter through, creating a diffuse glow.[29]

The concrete walls supporting the suspension cables of the roof rise much higher, but Lundy dropped the covering of the void, avoiding an extended vertical axis at the circle's center in favor of an outward flow. The unusual cable-hung roofing shudders in the wind, bringing nature into presence acoustically. This seventy-foot-diameter room lacks the clarity and perfection of the precise circles of the Schenectady and Atlanta sanctuaries. It is not a noble room like a Palladian rotunda, but it is a generous room, humane and graceful. Like the building itself, it can be entered from several places on its perimeter. It embodies the messiness of the Unitarian ideals—individualism contributing to a less than perfect unity.[30]

Lundy's search for form was intuitive, and he was willing to experiment. For instance, he intended for the roofing to be shingles, which would be both visually and texturally consistent. However, shingles applied to a roof supported by suspended cables were subject to too much movement, and the roofing has had to be replaced several times with various rubber membrane solutions. Lundy was a gestural designer; his charcoal sketches were evocative rather than referential. As he commented, "For me, architectural creation is not a consciously intellectual process. . . . I feel my way into problems, and keep working inexorably on them. . . . I think with pencil or brush or charcoal. . . . It is a pushing and pulling to mold the building into its final image."[31] The building's form is striking, but its imagery is elusive. Some see a spaceship, a big tent, or a lotus flower. The plan and section suggest something else yet—the plan geometry is like a spider's web, which is echoed in the cables of the roof structure, and the hauntingly beautiful building section from the construction drawings is strongly suggestive of the body of a spider.[32] No single image can capture this complex and highly animated building.

While the circle is perfect for symbolizing unity, its many meanings include the Christian tradition of representing heaven. This would not be a welcome association for Unitarian space. Square geometries, being earth-bound, seem more appropriate for Unitarian philosophies. Certainly, one of Frank Lloyd Wright's means of making the auditorium at Unity Temple a distinct and "noble" place was to use the perfect geometry of the square, a geometry that is perceptible notwithstanding his layered, or folded, articulation of the central space.[33] Further, he lifted it off the ground, the plane of the everyday, and insulated it from the urban life and noise of the main street it fronted. The circuitous arrival and entry forced visitors to pay attention and to actively choose to go in. In that way, it was a temple in the sense of the Latin root, *templum*, a place for a particular activity cut off from the rest of daily life spaces. Inside, color and light create a somewhat ethereal atmosphere; it is not mystical but it is vibrant enough to be unlike everyday experience. This room has a greater sense of being a "place apart" from everyday life than most of the modern designs of the 1950s and 1960s, and the geometry plays an important part in achieving this effect.

A square geometry offered advantages without the challenges of the circle. It was symbolic of nature and the known order of the world. As noted previously, Charles Goodman's use of the square and the continuous clerestory under a flat roof connect the church in Arlington, Virginia, to Unity Temple (see fig. 3.12). However, Goodman claimed that the square plan and flat roof were suitable to a Unitarian church because they are *temple* forms, rather than *church* forms. In his view, "temple" described a place where reason reigned over dogma and would therefore require greater rationality and simplicity than a church.[34] The perfect geometry of the square plan, simple and rational, made the auditorium a special, extra-mundane place, but one that was demonstrative of human intelligence rather than a place of faith or emotion. The square room in this case is directional, not centralized, as a result of its exposed structural system.[35] The concrete roof beams rest on columns lining the two lateral walls. The southern bay of the sixty-foot-square room is taken up by entry vestibules and stairs to the choir loft; the insertion of the loft creates a lower ceiling that was designed to merge with a social hall beyond. The architect intended for the seating to be arranged by sections in a pinwheel fashion, which would work well with the square geometry to create a non-hierarchical sense of space, and place some people face to face. However, the room was not furnished with fixed seating in the end, and the chairs are now arranged conventionally. The room is slightly elevated from the surrounding ground plane, and a recessed basement level contributes to an impression that it is floating just above the ground in its wooded knoll. Most importantly, a continuous clerestory

connects the space of the sanctuary to the space of the grove of trees that surround it. Goodman described its intention: "The view of dappled sunlight in the
woodland setting will also be captured from within.... The upper ribbon of glass
completely surrounding the Auditorium will seem to extend the interior in all
directions and frame views of the upper fingering of trees as their branches reach
for the sky. The suggestion of serenity and quiet urbanity ... should be conducive
to the thought repose for which you have expressed a desire."[36]

Architect John Toline created a more dynamic square sanctuary by highlighting the diagonal for a Unitarian church in Davenport, Iowa, perhaps inspired by
Wright's design in Madison. The geometry was not accidental; Toline was aware
that a legacy of the Renaissance was to bring fresh creativity to universal forms:

FIGURE 5.13. Unitarian
Church, Davenport, Iowa,
Lundeen & Toline, 1959,
views of the sanctuary
along the diagonal ridge
beam. Photographs by
author.

"The contemporary architecture of this Unitarian church expresses a traditional spirit of ideas, truth, logic, and creativity born as the Renaissance. Traditionally it has been the contemporary approach which has resulted in the revered examples of Classic, Gothic, and Colonial architecture, each of which was the best of its once-contemporary period."[37] This space is ordered by a north-south ridge beam that ascends from the pulpit in one corner to a small choir loft in the one opposite; secondary beams run at forty-five degrees to it out to piers on two perimeter walls (fig. 5.13). The majority of the perimeter walls are fully glazed, allowing expansive views to the trees and lawns surrounding them. On the one fully solid wall that is engaged with other parts of the building, a small lounge is carved out at the back of the auditorium, focused on a fireplace. A sloped site allowed the sanctuary to be placed on the higher elevation and entered on grade from the rear parking lot, while social and religious education rooms could be tucked in beneath and still have access to the outdoors at the lower elevation. While brick and wood detailing were clearly inspired by Wright, the space was not of the Prairie Style. The lofty feeling combines with the craft and detail of a conscientious material palette to elevate the room to a sense of uniqueness.

Other perfect and easily perceived geometries are the hexagon and octagon. Two examples illustrate different ways of utilizing the properties of these shapes. The octagonal sanctuary of the Unitarian Church of Concord, New Hampshire (1961), designed by Hugh Stubbins, is an almost freestanding figural element punctuating a complex organized around an open courtyard (fig. 5.14). The other elements of the campus form a more neutral L-shaped background. The exterior form of the sanctuary reveals the space within, in the same way that Unity Temple's "noble room" is visible to passersby. Although the Concord sanctuary can also be reached from the main internal corridor, its primary entry is direct from the approaching walkway. The entry was indicated by a short, covered walkway that originally held a modern interpretation of a church spire. This symbolic element was highly unusual for modern Unitarians, and when it was damaged in a storm in 1969, it was simply taken down. Inside, the pulpit is directly across from this entry as would be expected. Eight columns carry a higher central roof over the seating area, while an aisle is formed around it by the lower ceiling at the perimeter. The high central roof consists of folded plates that form a ring of triangular clerestory windows. This room has the frankness and clarity of the circular auditorium in Schenectady. The geometry is simple and direct, and the resultant character is even and rational. A congregation member later recalled that "the architect was . . . charged to create a sanctuary that would express freedom in relation to belief and freedom within the democratic

FIGURE 5.14. First Unitarian Church, Concord, New Hampshire, Hugh Stubbins, 1961, view of the sanctuary. Photograph by author.

congregation. . . . Somehow the search for truth should be felt, . . . there should be a feeling of warmth and stillness and aspiration. . . . We do not wish to have just a traditional church *with the essence removed*, but to have a positive creation which expresses our faith."[38] They did not want a "church" stripped of religious feeling, an emptiness; they wanted a room that was not a church but that was inspiring. Its brick walls with white painted trim make the interior feel like New England, though without particular reference. The shape provides a sense of intimate space. Its primary virtue is that the ring of triangular clerestories combines with full-height vertical openings at the vertices of the polygon to allow a generous view of the surrounding trees and sky, thus creating a porosity in what would otherwise perhaps be a too-compact space and static use of geometry.

The hexagonal auditorium of the Unitarian Church of Anne Arundel County in Annapolis, Maryland, is similar in its overall dimension to the Concord sanctuary, but there is no emphasis on the vertical; the space spreads out more laterally from the central high point of the roof.[39] The walls and roof form a straightforward container, so the geometry is experienced in a direct way. The design makes use of the geometry to offset two entries from the lobby and social area in a nonaxial relationship to the speaker's platform. The hexagonal geometry also ordered the secondary support spaces, knitting the primary space together with them. The perimeter walls are just ten feet tall, allowing two long portions on opposite sides of the hexagon to be glazed full-height, giving a view to a garden on one side and to woods on the other. The column-less space is defined most completely by the relatively low spreading ceiling, composed of simple framing along the hexagon's radials and exposed wood decking. The darker wood framing members look like a spiderweb against the lighter decking. The sheltering aspect of the room's covering gives it an almost tent-like effect. It feels like a genial place for stopping a while, but it is not a contemplative space. It is a space for gathering and for the action of community worship. Although it is the same dimension across as the church in Concord, they are spatial opposites.

Lastly, there is the singular case of triangular geometry—Frank Lloyd Wright's design for the First Unitarian Society of Madison, Wisconsin (1949), among the first Unitarian churches completed after World War II. This perfect geometry is not fully perceptible in the experience of the space, though the general idea of the triangle is obvious. The triangle was part of a larger geometric form, so only two sides are formed by the auditorium's walls. The room is open along the triangle's base to a smaller living room beyond with a lower ceiling. The triangle is most easily discerned in the shape of the ceiling: a central ridge line starts low at the vertex of the triangle beyond the pulpit and rises to about thirty-six feet at the rear of the room. The two surfaces that stretch from the ridge line down to the tops of the perimeter walls are gentle hyperbolic curves that suggest "the underside of the wing of a bird."[40] The complex intersections of piers supporting a choir loft over a pulpit and the glazing at the vertex of the triangular room focus attention dramatically (fig. 5.15). The unique qualities of the space derive not from architectural strategies that can be generalized but from the convergence of its unusual shape, the high relief texture of converging stone walls, and the linear patterns of a sculptural endpoint. The design was similar to Unity Temple in the way that the main space can be anticipated by the form of the exterior, but the Madison church was more inscrutable than Unity Temple. It is impossible to make a precise mental translation from mass to space though its triangular nature is clear.

Wright claimed that the symbolism of the triangle in the plan and of the shape of the roof added spiritual meaning. He asserted that the symbolism of the triangle was "unity," or the resolution of the idea of a trinity in a single figure. Wright also described the triangular form as aspirational, symbolic of structural integrity, and "an expression of reverence."[41] The complexity of the whole is at least as prominent as its triangular geometry, but it is still somewhat surprising that Unitarians accepted a shape with long religious association to the concept of the Trinity, which they disavowed. Despite his later rationalization, Wright was not likely to have chosen the shape for a symbolic purpose—his true interest was compositional and spatial. Joseph M. Siry points out that Wright was working with these geometries in other, nonreligious projects at the same time, so his claims on its symbolic value may well have been a matter of persuasion. The first minister to use this building, Reverend Max David Gaebler, found unity in the triangular form because the space narrowed at the place of the speaker and expanded outward, giving the congregation the greater space—space itself was distributed democratically. He also appreciated the diagonal lines as "particularly appropriate to Unitarianism," pointing "both skyward and earthward . . . [creating] an atmosphere of adventure and openness characteristic of our approach to religion."[42] Overall, the building's lyricism was so appealing that explanations seem both awkward and too limiting.

Perceptible geometries in architecture help to prioritize one space over the others, those in the same building or those in the rest of daily life. For a congregational room in which there is no given ritual to dictate an architectural order, geometry is an abstraction that defines the container. It allows the rational brain to comprehend the space, to assess its measure, and to know one's place in the world. Perfect

FIGURE 5.15. First Unitarian Society, Madison, Wisconsin, Frank Lloyd Wright, 1949, view of the chancel. Photograph by author.

geometries are meaningful, even if they are not used for explicit symbolic purposes. They are part of a humanistic tradition of monuments, spiritual practices, and sacred buildings across time and culture. Joseph Amisano was highly likely to have used a circle and square under the influence of Wittkower's *Architectural Principles in the Age of Humanism*. Other architects familiar with Wittkower would have been likely to make the connection, whether they chose to act on it or not, or may have felt its indirect influence on architectural culture of the 1950s, contributing to a general notion that ideal geometries and proportions in themselves can assure beauty and distinction. Several designs were based on the golden section, which had many adherents in the twentieth century.[43] While modern architects were likely to "herald in the new age free of the past and its recourse to localities and traditions that encumber a vision of a unified modern world, they still seek to find the intimacy and sacredness in the facts of everyday experience."[44] The tension between those interests and beliefs can be found in many of the designs for Unitarian churches.

SPATIAL AND SOCIAL RELATIONSHIPS: REFLECTION, EXPRESSION, AND PARTICIPATION

Although the sites of the twentieth-century Unitarian churches were larger and allowed for more dispersed designs, as noted in the previous chapter some instances of a more compact order remained. In these cases—most significantly in Kahn's design for Rochester but with some similarities at Hartford and Richmond—a more distinct spatial hierarchy prevailed in which the auditorium was dominant both by position and size (see fig. 5.9b). Nevertheless, a hierarchy of social importance remained ambiguous. These designs share in the earlier vision of Jenkin Lloyd Jones in the placement of smaller-scaled, potentially more welcoming elements at the perimeter—if not masking, then at least enveloping the primary space within. In Kahn's design, the central auditorium is completely ringed by a corridor on not one but two levels. The individuated spaces for educational and social functions fully envelop the auditorium and follow a less obvious formal order. As Kahn noted, the auditorium was a metaphor for a "question, and the school . . . was that which raised the question."[45] In sections, the surrounding social spaces almost interlock with the double-height auditorium, but the bars of classrooms and meeting rooms are sized according to their own needs. The entry area and the social space are part of the wrapper but are slightly larger and formally differentiated. It is impossible to say which came first—the ring of rooms as a container or the central space that they contain. All of Kahn's preliminary designs express the sense of total interdependence between a central auditorium and a variety of spaces for social interactions.

A somewhat similar relationship occurs on a single level in Lundy's design for the Hartford congregation. In this case, a single geometric order originates from the central space and carries through to the ring of rooms on the perimeter (see fig. 5.12b). The individuated meeting and classroom spaces are less like a wrapper, but they nevertheless contain and support the central void. Although not centralized like the others, the plan of Ulrich Franzen's church in Richmond shares a similar ambiguity. The auditorium is not centrally located, but it is a distinct kind of space, while the supporting spaces form a uniform if incomplete wrapper with a separate architectural order (see fig. 4.7b). They have minimal spatial or functional distinctions. The building entries were placed in this string of connected rooms that are as essential to congregational discourse as the auditorium. Passage through the layer of meeting spaces delays access to the auditorium, suggesting the opportunity to discuss and reflect in advance of communal worship.

In the case of more horizontally extended or dispersed plans, the relationship between the two primary spaces, auditorium and social hall, is primary. It is less a matter of access but how the parts are related architecturally and experientially. A number of modern examples follow the tradition of having the worship space and the social space stacked vertically. This was common on sloped sites for economy, as seen at Davenport. While economical, the social space did not tend to have the spatial importance to match its social role in the congregation. There are also some cases in which the construction took place over time without following an initial design. These may have ended up with more limitations on achieving a preferred relationship. Therefore, it is most instructive to focus on original designs or completed buildings that reflect a single coherent design intention for the architect and congregation.

Some designs allowed for spatial continuity between the sanctuary and the social hall, with differing degrees of definition for the two, and the classrooms would either be under this unified space or organized into a separate wing. Edward Durrell Stone's design for First Unitarian in Schenectady went the furthest to unite all functions in a form established by a single wall plane and a simple rectangular roof plane. A wall-less sanctuary is centered within a larger room that serves as the social hall. The sanctuary and fellowship hall, or great room, occupy the central zone of a rectangular plan divided roughly in thirds and is flanked by the classrooms facing out to a terrace on one side, and the offices and meeting rooms on the other (fig. 5.16). Social spaces with central fireplaces flank the circular auditorium on two sides. There is clarity and logic in this highly integrated solution; there is also ease of circulation (fig. 5.11b).

FIGURE 5.16a. First Unitarian Church, Schenectady, New York, Edward Durrell Stone, 1958, view of the great room surrounding the sanctuary. Photograph by author.

FIGURE 5.16b. First Unitarian Church, view of the classroom and meeting space. Photograph by author.

In his design for a Plandome, New York, congregation, Charles Warner Jr. (1911–2004) placed the entry between two parallel wings—social hall and auditorium to the left, and classrooms to the right of a linking entry area with offices (fig. 5.17). The classrooms stretch out along a corridor, with a split between rooms for the youngest children and those for older age groups. The other wing contains three continuous spaces: the auditorium, a central lounge or living room, and the social hall. The lounge is differentiated from the auditorium by a slightly reduced width and a much lower ceiling height. A fireplace serving both spaces

forms the transition from the lounge to the social hall. While there is a continuous flow among all three spaces, they each have distinctive characters. The minister praised the worship hall as "conducive to spacious and lofty thinking," while
the lounge offered "warmth and intimacy."[46] This was a subtly designed instance
in which the sanctuary and the social hall spaces of the Unitarian program were
unified and intimately connected. It is clear that this congregation valued the
continuity of spaces mildly calibrated to only slightly differentiated social relationships. Social and worship functions formed a continuity.[47]

A more compact variation of the same continuous relationship can be seen
in the Paul Schweikher design for the Unitarian Church of Evanston, Illinois
(1958)—a Miesian design that replaced the building that had been designed by

FIGURE 5.17a. North
Shore Unitarian
Church, Plandome,
New York, Charles
Warner Jr., 1956, view
from the approach.
Photograph from
Progressive Architecture
37 (October 1956): 106.

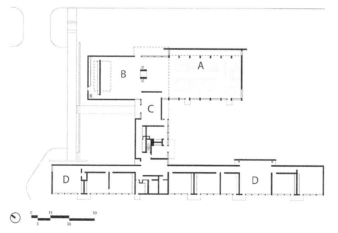

FIGURE 5.17b. North
Shore Unitarian
Church, plan:
A—auditorium,
B—social hall,
C—entry/narthex,
D—classrooms.
Drawing by Alissa
Tucker.

Marion Mahony. Schweikher was seen as an "up-and-coming" local architect.[48] In the resulting design, the classrooms were in a daylit basement rather than a separate wing, allowing the building to be conceived as a single, minimal gesture: a rectangular prism of pure space with solid lateral walls and voided end walls. Five concrete structural frames were pushed to the exterior, making the interior space clean and continuous (fig. 5.18). Two entries, one from the street and one from the parking lot, are opposite one another in the second of the four bays. The larger space to one side forms the sanctuary, and the smaller is the social hall. A stair and a small walled kitchen with a balcony above are the only elements separating the two main spaces. Blending the whole into a single continuous space designed with ideal proportions was intended to express "unity." Architectural critic Peter Blake found numerous problems, such as a lack of intimacy and poor acoustics, and yet he admired the bold simplicity of the concept and found it to be a "strong, poetic statement."[49] The degree of continuity and the shared geometric order of this relationship is similar to Wright's design for Madison.

A contrasting conception of the relationship of these spaces was proposed by Paul Kirk's design for Seattle's University Unitarian Church. In this complex, the two spaces almost appear to be separate buildings and are experienced quite differently. Here worship was set purposefully apart from the social functions, and education

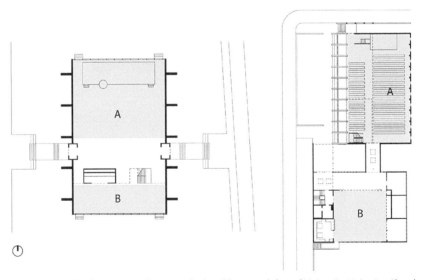

FIGURE 5.18. Unitarian Church, Evanston, Illinois, Paul Schweikher, 1958, left, and University Unitarian Church, Seattle, Paul Kirk, 1959, right, plan comparison highlighting the different spatial relationships of their sanctuaries (A) and social halls (B). Drawing by Alissa Tucker.

was pragmatically placed in the ground level, where the two structures lose their clear architectural distinctions. The entry is in a lower, flat-roofed structure containing the social hall and offices (fig. 5.18). A stair provides direct access from the entry to the classrooms below. More prominently, the entry leads into a narthex—a wide circulation space that is open to the social hall on one side and therefore offering an alternative or a pause. The narthex also connects to a bridge that provides access to the sanctuary. The enclosed bridge is a neutral space with translucent skylights and no windows. Like Wright's cloister at Unity Temple, it is an unusual sensory zone that increases the delight of emerging into the sanctuary. It is a thickened threshold dividing the social hall from the sanctuary and dramatizing their difference. The sanctuary is a taller volume with dramatic structural lines and two distinct spatial zones (see fig. 5.5). Glulam beams rise continuously upward from the east wall to the west, while the space opens above them toward the west. The light works with the wood structure and details to create a sense of warmth and welcome.

Even between two churches for Unitarians designed by the same architect, the relationships of the major spaces may be conceived very differently. At May Memorial in Syracuse, designed by Pietro Belluschi, the auditorium is visible as a distinct element with its own roof and a unique spatial order. The social hall is integrated into a lower wing also containing meeting rooms and classrooms on two levels (fig. 4.20). The use of wood for structure and finishes is a unifying element, but the sanctuary and social hall are different kinds of space. The entry foyer provides direct access to the sanctuary, but it is a square room with a fireplace as an invitation to pause and visit. In Rockford, Illinois, Belluschi expressed the two most important spaces as independent elements, making everything else subordinate. The two were in dialogue, composed of the same materials but with a slightly different articulation, and their structural frames were set perpendicular to each other. Despite the use of similar concrete structural framing for both spaces, the interiors of the sanctuary and social hall have distinctly calibrated characters (see fig. 6.5). And though the narthex gives direct access to these distinct functional elements, it is oriented to a view out into the open landscape rather than to the adjacent spaces.

Many congregations have a library, but there is minimal evidence of its treatment as an architectural "event." One possible exception is First Unitarian of Rochester, New York. The first published plans identify the unique space with a fireplace accessed from the entry area as a library. However, in a sketch plan of Kahn's from a year before, it is called a "lounge library," and Kahn's note about the ceiling height advocates its use as a multipurpose room, so it was never a dedicated library.[50] Where it was not part of another space, the library was generally a designated room within the classrooms or the administrative area, depending on how the congregation defined these needs. Many were probably assigned a library function after the fact. This is regrettable because it is part of the Unitarian identity that could be readily represented in architecture. While these spaces can be perfectly adequate and comfortable for the congregation's needs, the provision of a dedicated library from the start is a further indication of a congregation's self-definition. Another is to see the variety in secondary spaces. A relatively common occurrence was to include two social rooms—a larger one for events or larger numbers of people socializing, and a lounge with comfortable seats for smaller gatherings or casual conversation. Distributed somewhere among these social spaces there is almost always at least one fireplace. And a few congregations include a small chapel for more intimate groups or occasions, children's services, or other spiritual practices.

Perhaps the most distinguishing element of Unitarian spatial disposition is the usual provision of a space for choice. Having entered into the building, one still has a choice about whether to participate in worship or not. Unitarians welcome the pause in which to affirm one's participation and to cross the threshold of the sanctuary, not as a matter of habit or lack of attention but with full awareness of making that choice. Sometimes this space to linger and to choose is an outdoor courtyard or arcade. Bridges accentuate the consciousness of moving forward in a number of designs. But in most modern churches, the experience of arrival involves entering into a larger building of which the sanctuary is a part, rather than entering directly into the sanctuary. The churches of Princeton and Concord are two notable exceptions; each has a visually prominent entry to the sanctuary directly from outdoors. More commonly, the sanctuary is visible by form and position, but entry into it is mediated by a courtyard, lobby, narthex, or a combination of these. The architect of St. John's in Cincinnati explained,

> Several ways of getting into the sanctuary are provided. The principal one, however, is assumed to be from the automobile entrance at the east side. [One enters into a narthex] a neutral spacious area, then through a narrow passageway from which one would walk into the high volume of the sanctuary itself. To get into the church from this direction it is necessary to go single file and we expect that this moment of isolation will help to provide a mental change from life of the exterior to the life of the interior which worship implies.[51]

No other entry sequence was ever quite as circuitous as Wright's design for Unity Temple, but there are echoes of it in some, such as Bethesda's River Road church and Seattle's University Unitarian. In both cases, the door to the sanctuary is not even visible upon entry; one must seek it out. Only in University Unitarian is one forced to reverse direction completely in order to enter the sanctuary. Historian Sarah Williams Goldhagen describes the entry sequence of First Unitarian in Rochester as "jarring."[52] On the other hand, there are often multiple entry points to the sanctuary, continuing to counter any particular, and inevitable, sequence that is customary in ritual-based spaces.

CONCLUSION: "WINDOWS IN THE HOUSE [OF] REASON"

Wright's Unity Temple was unique in its time not for providing an entry with direct access to both the space for worship and the space for fellowship, but for the size and importance given to that space of arrival and choice—and also how the choice between worship and conversation required turning in opposite directions. In churches that came before, the social space was connected to the sanctuary if on the same floor, allowing for occasional expansion of the sanctuary. Often, either could be accessed directly from the entry, and they were equal in importance though not in size. Wright's design inserted a more spacious vestibule directly between the two spaces and slightly offset their floor levels. While his separation of the functions was complete at Unity Temple, his fusion of the same functions was at the opposite extreme forty years later in the design for Madison.

The midcentury Unitarian sanctuaries were generally modest in size and, most particularly, in height, and therefore seem humane rather than monumental. Exposed structure and plenty of daylight were the most common features across all of the churches from this period. The first provided stability and order, the other the presence of constant change. The structure was also an abstract presence of nature, through the materials and physical laws of weight and resistance. The daylight was not abstract or mystical; it was the concrete and real presence of nature penetrating the space, providing the world we know with our daily existence, even in the age of electricity. And we now know more than ever the many ways that sunlight contributes to health and well-being, in addition to appreciating its sensory and aesthetic appeal in the experience of architectural space.

The Unitarian sanctuaries were experimental spaces, built in a time when architects were conscious of their role in the modernization of the American built environment, with cautious optimism for both present and future. The growth of the denomination also brought congregations a sense of confidence. The architects they chose were not given any rules for the creation of a properly

Unitarian spiritual space—no guidelines, no pattern books, and no precedents. Most congregations were eager to encourage innovative and imaginative designs, though many would have insisted on simplicity at the same time. Most were not seeking something exotic in built form, but they did appreciate creativity and innovation, and were ready to accept forms that were unusual for churches. (Examples would be congregations in Ames, Iowa; Wilmington, Delaware; and Rockville, Maryland.) And most were working with highly constrained budgets. Congregational traditions for how they gathered, created community, and worshipped with one another completed the spaces.

In the end, though modernism had a greater variety of formal vocabularies in the postwar period, abstraction and minimalism remained common themes (fig. 5.19). The space of the Unitarian sanctuary was made special not so much by things it had as by what it did not have, such as religious symbols, decorative arts, or grandeur of scale. The architecture was not mediated, or finished, by another layer of elements that supported established patterns of use, such as altar, cross, or communion rail. Some may have had a central aisle, although most did not. And even where a central aisle was used, it did not focus the experience on sacred objects such as an altar or cross. The speaker's area might be constituted by an elevated platform alone; other furnishings tended to be mobile—a pulpit or lectern and several chairs were most common. Often there was a table to hold candles and flowers. The sparse minimalism would have been in strong contrast to the home environments of these decades—an era for most middle-class families of wall-to-wall carpets, the emergence of television and recreation rooms, and furnishings that tended to fill the rooms. The "presence" of the architecture itself—demanding awareness of the shape, surfaces, structure, and light—was a main constituent of the spirituality of the space.

Many churches use their worship spaces for all kinds of secular functions throughout the week or year, and some rely on them for every event needing large spaces. Max Graebel became the minister of the First Unitarian Society of Madison right after its completion. He confessed to apprehension about a central aspect of the design he was inheriting when he first started: the intentional flexibility for use of the auditorium for both Sunday worship and for any social events that required more space than the "Hearth Room"—living room—could accommodate. After some time, he said that "far from regarding this multiple use of the church proper as an unfortunate necessity bordering on sacrilege, I have come to regard it as a wholesome and welcome symbol of the fact that religion is not a special set of activities reserved for a particular time and place, but a quality that

FIGURE 5.19. First Unitarian Fellowship, Ames, Iowa, Bjornstad & Lilly, 1966–1970, view of the chancel in a 1992 addition. Photograph by author.

can infuse all of life."[53] The nature of the space allowed that to happen without any sense of transgression on its spirituality for worship.

As a liberal, progressive denomination, the Unitarians were philosophically disposed toward embracing modern architecture for many reasons: to be forward-facing and in tune with their times, able to accept a modern design even if it would not "look like a church," and interested in some of this style of architecture's general principles, such as the rationality of exposed structure, honesty about materials, and integration of interior and exterior spaces. It is an accident of history that the postwar need to build so many new churches aligned with changing ideas in modernism that made it culturally and financially more accessible to a wider audience. While some congregations were amenable to a certain degree of grandeur, many wanted their buildings to be simple and honest, but not mundane. The International Style modernism that had served a cultural elite in the early twentieth century was being interrogated and extended in ways that made it more broadly accessible—both in terms of its theoretical aims and its construction costs.

Although other denominations also built many notable works of modern architecture in the postwar period, they were concerned with achieving results that would look and feel like churches. The most common elements that would contribute to expressing the religious function would be an upward gesture of the roof and its corollary space inside, a tower or spire, and/or sculptural symbols visible on the exterior such as bells and crosses. For the interior, a familiar configuration of the space, a verticality in at least some part of the space, and a pronounced interiority were common. Unitarian sanctuaries would be different, for the most part, by the lack of strong vertical expressions of space and by more generous provision of light and views to exterior spaces. The lack of religious symbols does not always mean that the space was bare, but the general tendency was in that direction. In some instances there was artwork—paintings and sculptures in some, more frequently colored glass and fiber art installations. Still, the architecture was never in the background; it was in the forefront of the spiritual experience.

Although Unitarians asked for churches that were pragmatic and economical, they also asked for buildings that were evidence of human capacities to create new and beautiful things. They were asking for beauty from the fresh and the unexpected, rather than from old formulas. They wanted something that altered their awareness, either through art, nature, or a purposefully restrained environment. In addressing the possibility of a sense of the sacred in the modern world, architect Juhani Pallasmaa observes that "beauty invokes images of a utopian and spiritualized world," while "human dignity seems to emerge in scarcity." The democratic and ethical basis of midcentury Unitarian congregations was aimed at contributing to making a better world. They sought constant renewal for their optimism in the beauty of their communal homes. Most sanctuaries were somewhat ascetic yet had the power to evoke spirituality through virtuous restraint and through connections to nature and cosmic unity. There was a sacredness not based in religious symbols or theologies but in the architecture itself. Pallasmaa calls this a spiritual focusing that can be brought about through a "dialectics of matter, space, and light."[54] It is experienced individually as a personal response to a certain perception of aura or transcendence from the material and spatial purity, or through the presence of natural beauty (fig. 5.20).

In some cases, such as May Memorial, the whole sanctuary is like a single work of art that can open feelings of richness and connection. In others, certain features, details, or works of art bring forth reflection and interest in something harmonious, and it can invoke a longing for a more perfect world. The presence or awareness of nature within a gathering space touches on a special level. Philosopher Karsten Harries expresses its importance this way: "The beauty of nature, includ-

FIGURE 5.20. Unitarian Church, Arlington, Virginia, Charles Goodman, 1961. Photograph by author.

ing human nature, lets us feel at home in the world as artificial beauty is unable to do. The beauty of art must remain grounded in the beauty of nature. We need art to open windows in the house objectifying reason has built, windows to nature, including our own nature."[55] The art of the architecture in the Unitarian sanctuary is one such window.

FIGURE 6.1. First Church, Boston, Paul Rudolph, 1972, view of the sunken court, entry porch, and organ loft. Photograph by author.

CHAPTER SIX

Architecture of, by, and for the People

He was the true charismatic, and found the actual American religion, which is Protestant without being Christian.

—Harold Bloom, *Ralph Waldo Emerson*

And so we learned that in our art, as well as in our theology and morality, tradition truly meant change, tradition meant honesty and freshness, tradition meant creativity, evolution, search. . . .

We have built a new church to add positive beauty to our truth and our ethic, and thus to make the three one. This, I believe is the necessary historical logic of Unitarianism—to make theology, ethics, and art of a piece. And it is for this that we built this house.

—John C. Fuller, "The Religion We Built It For"

ARCHITECTURE OF . . . : AMERICAN ARCHITECTURE AND DEMOCRACY

The first expressions of the United States' founding democratic ideals in architecture were in formal allusions to Athens and Republican Rome, seen in the earliest neoclassical government buildings and other public works. This political and philosophical expression claimed the dignity of the neoclassical tradition for statehouses such as those of Massachusetts and Virginia. It also gave them a degree of monumentality in spite of their relatively small scale. This style-based expression of democracy was limited in its effectiveness since other buildings, especially religious institutions, were also built in neoclassical styles. However, it continued to be employed in this way for over a hundred years, and the fact that all official government buildings central to the architectural image of America were neoclassical did in fact bind those two ideas together for many citizens.

However, recognizing that the meanings and associations with any style can change dramatically over time, style is not a sufficient indicator of an architecture of democracy. Thomas Jefferson's other works can provide a different starting point. In his designs for Monticello and the University of Virginia, Jefferson demonstrated artistic originality that was derived from absorbing the lessons of a variety of related things and refashioning them to new needs.[1] His private residence is humanistic in its sympathy with its particular place though using the lessons of distant models, and in its resultant expression of human understanding and art. It can be called democratic for its originality, which captures a distinct truth of its time. The architecture of the University of Virginia is humanistic for the same reasons as Monticello; it is more overtly democratic through its "spatial concepts and relationships." It is an "open forum for human development." The Rotunda, the source of knowledge, is paired with the Lawn, the place for discussion and debate. Architectural theorist Sylvain de Bleekere suggests that "for Jefferson the irreplaceable power of democratic thinking lies within a great openness of the human mind. This mind stands in constant dialogue with living nature, source of knowledge and cradle of the open space."[2] The notion of democratic architecture is not fixed but contains various possibilities such as being of its time and place, being in some way original, and serving a purpose that is open, accessible, and moral.

In the second half of the nineteenth century, there was great interest focused on the production of a distinctly American architecture. Visionaries such as Horatio Greenough and Ralph Waldo Emerson called for art forms that were no longer merely derivative of European styles by the 1840s. Emerson, whose ideas were absorbed by Frank Furness from childhood, also expounded values and beliefs that John Dewey characterized as a philosophy of democracy: "That every individual is at once the focus and the channel of mankind's long and wide endeavor, that all nature exists for the education of the human soul— . . . Against creed and system, convention and institution, Emerson stands for restoring to the common man that which in the name of religion, of philosophy, of art and of morality, has been embezzled from the common store and appropriated to sectarian and class use."[3] Emerson's call for originality in American arts was clearly manifested in Furness's architecture. Emerson's philosophy of democracy is less obvious, but Furness's success depended on many relatively new building types serving a changing society. Along with some residences and cultural institutions, there were now philanthropic institutions, banks, and railroad stations. In questions of style, form, and order, he did not look for established ways to solve the architectural problem but used logic and intuition to provide new spaces needed in industrial America.

Louis Sullivan, briefly employed by Furness and impressed by his fresh approach to design, wrote about American artistic originality. He advocated for "democratic form" in architecture, by which he meant an organically unfolding process and an object of symbolic representation that emerges from the collective imagination of a modern, progressive society and is an act of individual poetic genius.[4] Sullivan tied this American originality to a creative process, not a style. For him, it was democratic because the artist was reflecting the new social condition of an industrializing America. His awkwardly titled book *Democracy: A Man-Search* does not address architecture directly; it is a manifesto of his own ideas about man and society, an understanding of which is necessary in his opinion for designing a building in accordance with its social functions, broadly interpreted. Sullivan expressed his deep sympathy and trust in the individual at the same time he recognized social and cultural interrelation and mutual responsibility: "Democracy . . . is but the ancient primordial urge of integrity or oneness. And it is this very urge of nature . . . that is awakening in the heart of modern man the desire to seek a fundamental law of social integrity or oneness, wherein each man shall be truly a law unto himself." He felt strongly that creativity was dependent on this understanding of the reality of democratic man. He claimed that his architecture was democratic because something of the "collective imagination" could be seen in its forms. He was creating designs that suited new socio-economic conditions and felt that the architect, while responsible for a rational provision of space suited to the planned activities, must also provide the design with "expression" to bring it to life. That is, artistic expression is needed to bring out the idea of its beauty and emotional bearing—to the extent that architecture was more religion than art, and part of "a greater religion of Democracy." For Sullivan, democratic architecture had to start with pragmatic realities of the time and the cultural direction but could never stop there. In his view, it had to speak to humanity with emotion and beauty as well.[5] Sullivan was convinced that the United States, with its foundation of democracy, had to expand those ideals in all realms of culture; he envisioned a new approach to design in line with the new ideal of democracy.[6]

Sullivan's views were admired and strongly endorsed by Claude Bragdon (1866–1946). Bragdon's book *Architecture and Democracy* was originally published in 1918. In it, he observed that "we have always been very glib about democracy; we have assumed that this country was a democracy because we named it so." But he asserted that its true expression has been limited: "In the life of Abraham Lincoln, in the poetry of Walt Whitman, in the architecture of Louis Sullivan, the spirit of democracy found utterance, and to the extent that we ourselves partake of that spirit, it will find utterance also in us." In short, democracy is found in new and original forms of human expression and American possibility. Before World War I, he found no evidence of democracy in American buildings and cities, observing, "democracy exists in the secret heart of the people, all the people, but it is a thing so new, so strange, so secret and sacred—the ideal of brotherhood—that it is unmanifest yet in time and space."[7] In his architecture, Bragdon followed Sullivan in the rejection of traditional styles. Like Sullivan, he expressed "the spirit of democracy" by developing his own "organic" system of proportional and geometric order and ornament that represented notions of theosophical cosmology. His system was based on an exploration of universal truths of number, geometry, and the body—it was of his own time and also timeless.

Bragdon's most noteworthy project still standing is the First Universalist Church of Rochester, New York (1907). It was commissioned by the Universalist congregation when their previous church was purchased for development, and since the 1961 merger of Unitarians and Universalists, it is home to a Unitarian Universalist congregation. It is a Greek cross church, visible in the massing: a square crossing is the central element, topped by an octagonal lantern; three arms of the cross are gabled projections slightly shorter than the central mass (fig. 6.2a). The fourth arm of the cross is less obvious as it connects to a rectangular wing to the rear for the fellowship hall. The exterior is red brick, and Bragdon's geometric patterning is woven into the facade. The effect of the exterior of the church is of clearly defined forms cleanly rendered. Minimal references to traditional forms are the round-headed arched openings and a thin corbel table. The church is arresting in overall form and in detail, and it is fortunate that it has survived the twentieth century in good repair. Bragdon deserves more acknowledgment for contributing to the development of distinctive American architecture. However, he was so intrigued by the social dimensions of architecture that his later works were stage sets and festival spaces—democratically open to all but ephemeral and transitory.

Frank Lloyd Wright shared Bragdon's appreciation for Sullivan. Wright acknowledged Sullivan as "my old Master" in the first and third paragraphs of

FIGURE 6.2a. First Universalist Church, Rochester, New York, Claude Bragdon, 1907. Library of Congress, Prints & Photographs Division, Historic American Buildings Survey, HABS NY, 28–ROCH,12–1.

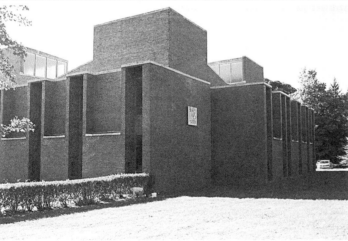

FIGURE 6.2b. First Unitarian Church, Rochester, New York, Louis I. Kahn, 1962. Photograph by author.

a 1939 lecture series that was published as *An Organic Architecture: The Architecture of Democracy.*[8] He also repeated Sullivan's plea for "organic" architecture as the modern and necessary alternative to traditional building styles. He recognized in Sullivan the spirit of creativity that he had absorbed in his youth from his

Unitarian upbringing. His Prairie Style buildings that interpreted the horizontal expanse of the Midwestern landscape—anchored in site but spatially extended—clearly exemplified his sense of a democratic architectural design. While each of these three architects used the same terms—"democratic" and "organic"—in their vision of a more modern and suitable way to build, their meanings were not identical. What they shared was an interest in being responsive to social and cultural changes and an architecture that was expressive in ways meaningful to ordinary people, not only the powerful and educated classes. Although Wright often used it as a slogan, it also held deep meaning for him.[9] "Organic" was how he imagined the building and the landscape, while "democracy" referred to his idea of social and familial forms in American culture. In the same year as Wright's London lectures, John Dewey gave a lecture in which he proposed that "creative democracy implies progressive thinking, which goes beyond the mere opposite of conservatism. Creative democracy is a way of living that adopts democratic thinking in all dimensions of daily and public life. Democracy is more than a state's form, it is a way of living of all civilians, who in an active, or creative way develop their life in the community of their family, the neighborhood, the city, land, the world."[10] Dewey was among the signers of Wright's petition to the National Planning Resources Board to back the development of his utopian democratic vision, Broadacre City, in the early 1940s.[11] Broadacre City was a planning scheme that valorized the "American Dream" of the single family home on its own plot of land as the healthy ideal for all Americans. It is now viewed as a mistaken vision that contributed to the vast suburbanization of American cities and that trend's associated negative consequences, but it also embodied Wright's idea of an organic architecture that promoted individual character, a necessity for participation in American democracy.

In the decade following the end of World War II, as modernism encompassed a widening variety of formal characteristics, architects grappled with intentions and meanings. Vincent Scully, writing in 1957, saw in the quite disparate languages, forms, and materials a new order he called "fundamentally humanistic."[12] He discerned a renewed interest in the building exterior as a means of expression—first in the classicizing rhythms of Ludwig Mies van der Rohe's pavilions and then in the sculptural qualities of Le Corbusier's postwar buildings. The shift of interest from space alone to the solid material defining and enclosing it brought the body of the building back into focus. Scully found a "new humanism" in buildings that surpassed the International Style in serving human functions and actions, as well as in the empathy between the human body and the building elements. He agreed with Geoffrey Scott's 1914 indictment of the architecture arising from the machine and clearly embraced Scott's view that architecture is "a humanized pattern of the world, a scheme of forms on which our life reflects its clarified image."[13]

These qualities are achieved, in part, with the introduction of older forms that echoed neoclassical architecture but were rendered in new materials and construction and transformed by their synthesis. These space-defining elements exceeded the minimalist palette of the continuous forms of early modernism. In response to the optimism of the new world order with a widening embrace of democratic systems, Scully called it the "architecture of democracy." He claimed that "as the impatient nineteenth century discovered the joys of spatial continuity, the beleaguered twentieth century seeks a new image of man."[14] For Vincent Scully, an architecture of democracy inhered the humanistic tendencies of postwar modernism, which he felt ultimately constituted a new definition of a style.

Wright and Bragdon both injected a sense of mysticism into their passion for the idea of democracy in architecture. Louis Kahn's interest in democracy, and in architecture's obligation to provide spaces with dignity, spaces that inspire civic involvement, were integral to his ideas about "institution." Biographer Sarah Williams Goldhagen explains that "Kahn's philosophy of the 'architecture of institutions,' developed while designing the First Unitarian Church in Rochester, stipulated that the architect's first and highest duty was to develop an *idealized vision* of an institution's *'way of life'* and the to give that vision . . . *Form.*"[15] This recalls Sullivan's notion of the "collective will" being discerned by the architect and then given creative expression. Furthermore, Bragdon's Universalist church stands just three miles from the Winton Road site of Kahn's Unitarian church (see fig. 6.2b) The merger of the Unitarians and Universalists was completed in 1961 while Kahn's project was still under construction. Solid red masonry structures, each with a whiff of medieval inspiration, both buildings were conceived by architects intrigued by esoteric religious ideas and inspired to express a civic ideal of social engagement and responsibility in architectural form.

In more recent considerations of democracy and architecture, architectural theorist Joan Ockman and philosopher J. C. Berendzen bring different perspectives but use the same building as one of their illustrations. Ockman recalls a lack of agreement on the meaning of democratic architecture when it was used in the past to describe U.S. embassies during the Cold War acting as cultural representations of American exceptionalism in the 1950s, public spaces serving a populist urban movement in the 1960s, consumer-oriented projects offering a range of choices in the 1980s, and family-friendly developments or destinations in the 1990s.[16] So it is with skepticism that she considers whether the Seattle Public Library (2004), designed by Rem Koolhaas, can be characterized as such. Berendzen pursues the idea of space designed for democracy using Georg Hegel's discussion of Gothic architecture in *Aesthetics* and Jürgen Habermas's theory of democracy. He finds that Koolhaas's library has a "complex, internally differentiated structure that seems to move beyond the constraints put on architecture by gravity" and, following Hegel, proposes that its unusual, gravity-defying forms and complexity provoke awareness. That conscious attention in turn causes users to reflect on their place in the civil community served by the building.[17] Ockman thinks that the building tends toward an idea of democracy by serving the public in a "crowd-pleasing and friendly" manner. However, she sees the complexity of forms as more spectacle than thought-provoking, and ultimately finds that the building fails to embody democracy because it fails to express "what holds us together as citizens and human beings."[18]

For Jan-Werner Mueller, the effectiveness of a democratic architecture is not in representation but facilitation. Democratic architecture is "a space where citizens recognize their polity (and themselves) as subscribing to democratic values."[19] Furthermore it provides space where citizens are free to gather and debate. By this standard, in matters of both process and facilitation, Unitarian churches are explicitly democratic architecture. Within this view, it is also possible to include the "openness" of Jefferson's academy. However, the claims of "originality" that captured a new spirit in the work of Furness, Sullivan, Bragdon, Wright, and Kahn remain more subjective.

ARCHITECTURE BY . . . : WORDS AND BUILDINGS

Religious architecture always held a particular place of importance in the realm of premodern cultures. This architectural form was invested with some of the greatest effort and resources of the whole community, expressing not only a way of under-standing the world but also representing the highest human achievement. In the modern world it remains a special category of architectural design in which the priorities of architecture as an art are more explicitly valued by the client—that is, a community of faith seeking a high form of expression—as much as by the architect. Unitarians of the nineteenth century recognized that their building would be part of a city or town to which they owed a certain civic duty. Urban Unitarian congregations fulfilled this duty by hiring reputable architects or by having competitions. This was felt to assure a worthy building that had cultural value to the entire community. This approach usually brought forth architecture that was either the highest quality design in a current church style or it resulted in something that exhibited creative imagination. Additionally, a few unusual designs from the nineteenth century were the vision of strong-willed ministers, such as Jenkin Lloyd Jones and Caroline Bartlett Crane, who knew just what they needed to fulfill their callings and found architects that would give them what they wanted.

The duty to cultural leadership, while an admirable sentiment, must be recognized as an inheritance from the Boston Brahmin founders. As such, it is part of a defining tension in Unitarianism. The Harvard elite promoted the arts and education for all for complex reasons. They believed the value of human life as a creative and intellectual pursuit should be afforded to a farmer or craftsman just as much as it should to a merchant or professional. But they also believed that American society as a whole was in need of a higher cultural and moral tone, and that education and the arts would bring a more positive social milieu. American culture certainly benefited from public education for all, but the gap between a highly educated elite and popular culture remained wide, and Unitarianism, with its origins in Harvard and its allegiance to ideas and words over rituals and emotion, continued to appeal mostly to the college-educated.

A similar disharmony is found in Unitarian moral commitments to equality and its espoused openness to all, and a critical failure to attract more African American members. Mark D. Morrison-Reed, a Unitarian minister and the leading scholar on Black experience in Unitarian Universalism, chronicled powerful forces of racism that coexisted with liberal humanism. As with the antislavery movement, integration of the ministry and congregations in the twentieth century was championed by some significant thought leaders but not uniformly, and it was not made a reality on the ground. That said, he also acknowledges a wide cultural divide equally at play: the stark contrast between Unitarian rationalism and more emotional, even salvific Black religious practices and their meaning. Furthermore, he concluded that "the main barrier to those who would enter the liberal religious community is class."[20] Lacking a more popular appeal, Unitarianism could not be thought of as a democratic religion. Merger with Universalism, which had always been a liberalism rooted in ordinary, work-a-day people, in a sense offered an automatic fix to Unitarianism's class problem. However, internal tensions persist in Unitarian Universalism.

The aspiration to build something noteworthy for community as well as congregation continued in the twentieth century, but the processes for meeting this goal were more complex and varied. Setting aside the decades in which the national organization, the AUA, took greater control of church design, processes usually involved a mix of congregational committees, conversations and surveys, and votes. In most cases, prior to selecting an architect, the congregation would determine a means for wide participation in the creation of a vision for the building. There would be meetings and surveys in which every member could participate, and there would also be committees for subtopics or areas of concern, such as architect and site selections. Each congregation varied on the extent of full congregational involvement and committee empowerment, but major decisions such as final site selection, architect selection, and final approval of a design were generally subject to full congregational votes. The minister was usually nominally a committee member with one vote like everyone else. Some ministers with particularly strong ideas could exert leadership through influence, but actual authority rested with elected congregational leaders and their duly appointed committee. At some point, the sum of the congregational conversation about the design of a new church would be synthesized into a statement for the architect. In the case of Seattle's University Unitarian congregation, the committee received a lengthy letter in place of a survey response from one member of the congregation, an industrial designer. They found that it expressed most completely the sentiments that had been circulating, so they used Gideon Kramer's letter as their statement. He asserted that the architecture should be

> suggestive, stimulating and awakening. As with all aspects of the problem the aesthetics will be an integrated part of a whole, not considered as something apart or a garish, but will evolve with the conception of the overall design. It will be designed INTO, not ONTO, this structure. It will manifest itself in the space planning, circulation and structure, in the planting, the use of water and light, colored and clear. It will manifest itself in the reflection, the shadows, in the changing surfaces to walk on and things to touch, perhaps even in the orientation of the various components to the sun and the movement of the earth. . . . This building effort should result not in a monument but in . . . a symbol of the summation of man's knowledge, of his attitude and relationship toward his fellowman and the universe.[21]

In short, he was asking for a design that would transcend mere construction to achieve the results of memorable architecture.

The Unitarian values of individual freedom, unity, and democracy were often central to the charges that mid-twentieth-century congregations gave their architects and evident in the ways they viewed and valued the churches they built. At the dedication of a new church in Bellevue, Washington, Reverend Chadbourne Spring said, "And, as we build, let us remember that we do more than build a church. We are by so much strengthening the structure of democracy, which is rooted in the very nature of God. We are by so much assuring our children—and theirs—that they shall have a climate of political and religious freedom."[22] And the congregation of Concord, New Hampshire, stipulated that the sanctuary should express both "freedom in relation to belief and freedom within the democratic congregation. . . . Somehow, the search for truth should be felt." They wanted "a feeling of warmth and stillness and aspiration."[23] And the minister of a Schenectady, New York, congregation recalled in his dedication service that they had begun the process with a desire that their building "would symbolize a free religion nurtured in human fellowship, speak of the democratic process and its respect for the individual, and challenge us never to falter in our search for the good, the true, and the beautiful."[24] The words themselves had weight; the words had heartfelt meaning, and they continued to resonate for those using the building.

Postwar Unitarian congregations sought several things in their architects. They wanted the assurance of an unequivocally modern building, a building that would be unquestionably of its own time.[25] Some wanted a nationally recognized architect in order to achieve not only exemplary modernism in the result but also a building that contributed value to the community. Others embraced a home-grown solution to the design, using in-house expertise (or someone known to a committee member) for a more purposely humble approach to providing for their needs—being pragmatic about cost as well as economical about the relative values of aesthetics and ethics. They did not think that Unitarians should have a church that looked like other denominations' churches. Their distinctive openness to all individuals' beliefs was in the forefront of the character they wished to express. Furthermore, since each congregation had its unique history and general ethos within a liberal perspective, they felt their church should be uniquely tailored to them. So they all wanted an architect who listened to their values and opinions and responded to them in the design, and some additionally wanted to be able to have continued input into the design process. It is clear that fears were expressed about losing control over something that was understood by all to be a matter of congregational self-identity and to involve a deep psychological desire for a feeling of both "fit" and connection.[26] However, after doing their own extensive soul-searching, they generally understood that the architect needed some degree of artistic autonomy. As one committee member in Rochester observed, they would transmit their statement of values to the architect, "whom I fervently hope will perceive all for which we strive. Unfortunately, you can't tell an artist how to paint—only if you like his painting."[27] Congregations approached their architects with varied levels of control and restraint, and varied levels of skepticism and trust, but they all wanted something unique that creatively expressed their own congregational spirit. Most understood that the creative expression had to be left to the architect.

American architects of the postwar period had inherited a model of the professional as an expert authority whose judgement should not be questioned or subjected to revision. Professional certainty in opposition to lay or amateur opinion was common across all areas of expertise. And it was not uncommon for the most confident, and even arrogant, to gain the greatest admiration or fame. The professional system for architects, through awards and journalistic notice, rewarded artistic genius and represented leading designs as the product of a single mind. Paradoxically, while architects were trained to expect complete authority and learned to be demanding in executing their designs, they also needed to experiment in searching for their personal artistic expressions. It seems as if there was an interesting dynamic in which the Unitarians as clients wanted full involvement but at some point released control. At the same time, the architect might be more open and flexible with a client that allowed more latitude for iteration and innovation. The minister of the congregation in Hartford recalled that Victor Lundy had "lived" with them for about a year.[28] In several cases, there is evidence that working interactively with Unitarian clients had a positive and inspiring impact on the architect and the outcome. But even when the architect kept their distance, or the congregation was somewhat less engaged, there was a unique quality to a Unitarian congregation as a client that arose from their condition of polity, or self-governance. Although Unitarians had no creed or liturgy, there was a covenant that had been reached through a process of communal discernment—"a process which exists in a unique space between religious practice, an exercise in democratic process, a cornerstone of developing cultural identity, and the foundation of discerning the mission, vision," and values.[29] It is a statement of why the congregation exists and what its communal aspirations are. The process of covenant binds social, moral, and religious visions into a purposeful common ideal.

The design process of the congregation of Arlington, Virginia, provides a useful illustration. It had been conservative in expending resources when it was first established. Its first church, built in 1949 on a residential street just west of Arlington National Cemetery, was modest in scale and lacking in character. It appears that the auditorium served both worship and social functions; the lower level was divided into meeting rooms. In 1953 an addition was completed that was slightly larger than the church, providing two stories of classrooms. The need for even more space was clear by 1954: two services were needed and classrooms were overflowing. A first committee was formed to consider the likelihood of continued growth and whether it would be better to expand or to spin off another congregation. They delivered their report to the congregation in June 1955. The congregation formed a second committee who delivered a second report in 1956 with the recommendation to increase the size of their site by purchasing an adjacent lot. In 1957 the board of trustees completed the purchase and issued a formal recommendation to build a second addition to their existing building. They began a capital campaign by making the case to the congregation with a visionary brochure, "Building for the Future." The minister, Reverend Ross Allen Weston, used his sermons to promote the idea that the congregation was a leader among Unitarian congregations and should therefore act boldly. This no doubt fueled the momentum and ambitions for a more adequate and perhaps more noteworthy church building. A Physical Planning Committee began meeting in 1958 and concluded that even more land was needed.

In addition to expanding the site once more, this committee also proceeded with the selection of an architect. They considered eight architects; previous church designs that appealed to committee members were an important element in the process. They visited the two Unitarian churches designed by New York architect Charles Warner Jr., in Plandome, New York, and Princeton, New Jersey. Their final selection of Charles Goodman was made based in large part on two churches he had already designed in the Washington area. Their report to the congregation in June 1959 cited Goodman's reputation as well as his design philosophy: they were "confident that his concept of design, his wide experience, and his original and creative genius promise for us a distinctive building which will portray in structural form the spirit and aspiration of this congregation."[30] It is likely they found his work not only suitably modern but also expressive of his commitment to social responsibility, soon after recognized with an award from Rice University.[31] This aspect of his design philosophy must have resonated with the strong social conscience of the congregation.

At the start, the congregation asked the architect to plan their expanded site to accommodate access, circulation, and parking as well as an expanded building footprint with a new auditorium and renovated social and educational spaces. The Board of Religious Education and five different committees submitted their needs and expectations for the new auditorium and for the activities in the renovated spaces. Additionally, the whole congregation was invited to meet with the architect to talk about their hopes for the new church. Goodman tried to understand what Unitarianism meant to them and also did independent research on the denomination's beliefs. He researched further into historical precedents of church design, which was an unusual step for Goodman.

Goodman wrote a report in 1960 on his design for the congregation that accounted for major aspects of the resultant design.[32] The most important considerations were the conditions of the site, historical church paradigms, and the needs and desires of the congregation. He studied the site first and determined that enlarging the existing building with the addition of a new auditorium would force the needed parking lot to extend into the area of the site with the greatest natural beauty and visibility from the bordering streets. Sensitivity to natural features of a site, and the consistent insistence on connections between indoors and outdoors, are design qualities critics have highlighted in his distinctive residential work. In keeping with this sensitivity, he convinced the congregation that to create a building that was inspiring to them as well as the community would require a freestanding structure on the most advantageous spot instead. He knew that he had to demonstrate the negative outcomes of what had been requested. While some in the congregation would be easily persuaded, others would be skeptics. In his report to the congregation, he recalled, "Having done my duty to pragmatism, I no longer resisted the pull of the East site and developed what you see here which your Physical Planning Committee is recommending." He reiterated how his design was responsive to the sentiments of the congregation in "the degree to which the new structure has been integrated with its lovely site . . . out of which the new structure seems to grow—unforced and uncontrived. This seemed singularly appropriate to the Unitarian tradition of honesty and naturalness."[33]

Goodman fulfilled the client's wish to be modern and innovative—it was the first use of precast concrete in the Washington area. The sanctuary is a boxy pavilion set on the wooded knoll at the east end of the site; one writer has described it as an ark. Its modernism is emphatically stated in the exposed regular structural frame, in the flat roof with dramatic overhangs that appears to float above a wraparound clerestory, and a recessed ground level that counters the heavy concrete with a perception of weightlessness. The space of the square sanctuary is pure and symmetrical, and the composition of precast concrete panels set in a grid of exposed structural members is uniform on all four sides. His research led him to believe that the hall-style churches of medieval central Europe were a more appropriate type to the Unitarian needs than a basilica with aisles. The tall clerestory extends the space outward and provides a view of the surrounding trees (see fig. 3.12). The "great meeting room" is a clearing in a grove.

Goodman offered two lengthy quotations from the congregation's minister that were central to his formal design concept. In one, Reverend Weston had called for a sanctuary that would be "a setting for the exploration of new ideas and for stimulus to creative thinking," and "a church proclaiming brotherhood unlimited, . . . a church proclaiming freedom; . . . a church which follows truth with fidelity to science; . . . a church whose god is in the power of conscience, the spirit of compassion . . . a church of life abundant . . . a church that can help people to live their lives" and can remedy a life that is harmed or broken. Goodman took from these aspirations the "ordered discipline guided by the doctrine of free and open discourse and directed toward the principle of unity through diversity of beliefs." For this vision, he felt that the horizontal plane of a flat roof, which he believed to be a "temple form," was more suited than a "traditional pointed church roof." He described his roof as a "great canopy seeming to hover in the woodland setting." He was satisfied that it achieved a "taut design which stands poised elegantly on its knoll, enframed by the stately white oaks and suggesting the dynamics which hold it in equilibrium even as the diverse beliefs of your congregation are held together by your unity of aspiration." The view to the trees through the continuous clerestories would afford the desired sense of serenity and repose. And he assured them that "while the structure has considerable character in form and a sense of integrity . . . it is conceived as a background for the lively discourse to which you are dedicated in your religious quest. And it is hoped that it will reflect the warmth and friendship which is your hallmark."[34]

Goodman's career was long and varied; the experience of working on a Unitarian project did not seem to affect him in any lasting way. However, it did seem to bring forth a slightly different style of working for their project. He had a reputation for being "brilliant, gifted, and egotistical," and even "intense and autocratic."[35] He had always denied a client's right to contribute their ideas to his designs or to make specific requests. However, in this project, he worked cooperatively with the congregation. While he did not want any particular architectural proposal or reference from them, he undertook the responsibility to reflect their beliefs as well as fulfilling his own architectural philosophies, such as using new materials and methods, expressing structural clarity, and creating continuous connections between interior and exterior. The congregation got a lofty space that served their needs and was a noteworthy modern building in the community, now on the National Register of Historic Places. Its openness spoke to the need for discourse, while the view out into the trees connected the congregation with nature's beauty. Something about this client inspired Goodman to conduct research and also consider carefully the words of the congregation and minister in his search for meaningful forms. The congregation members were satisfied that he had "reflected in form and line"—and in his own words as well—their beliefs.[36]

There are echoes in the story of the Arlington congregation's approach to the construction of a new church in the better-known process Louis Kahn undertook with the congregation in Rochester. That process has been described in detail in at least two of the major publications on Kahn in the last thirty years.[37] The visioning was a similarly inclusive process with wide congregational input, with a resulting document that was given to the architect. Both congregations started with a list of eight architects under consideration, and the committee that made the selection wrote a report with their reasoning. In the case of the Rochester committee, they described the awarding of the commission as a "creative assignment" to which Kahn's own ideas and artistic journey were "ideally suited."[38] While they asked for a modern church design, they also sought permanence and true art over fashion.

Kahn believed the architect had the duty to "see past a clients' self-interests" in order to design institutions as "an idealized conception of human interaction."[39] In other words, clients in his experience wanted a project that would answer their needs and desires but failed to think of contributing to a larger context. Kahn thought that they needed an architect to imagine aspirational possibilities rather than merely providing for their own functional necessities. However, in the Unitarians he encountered a group of individuals trained in habits of valuing community for the realization of something grander. A healthy Unitarian congregation "has a clear sense of discernment and purpose, . . . while lifting individuals up into beloved community. This clarity of purpose . . . [is] expressed as a covenant, which addresses an aspiration of transformation along multiple dimensions, of transforming the self, realizing transformational relations with ones' fellows within the church, realizing positive change within the world, all the while inviting the world to share in these covenantal relationships."[40] In the Unitarians, Kahn found a client that was already thinking of their future church building as an embodiment of their conception of human interaction, an embodiment of their covenant.

Conversely, the congregation saw in Kahn what they called a "natural Unitarian." And it is true that his own thoughts about architecture at the time of this commission were uniquely aligned to working with Unitarians. American cultural trends of the 1950s were raising concerns that individual freedom and expression were being lost to corporate environments and mass culture, and that individual fulfillment within a consumer culture was replacing the values of civic responsibility. This cultural critique led architects to renewed interest in problems of the individual and the collective, with a great emphasis on settings for the individual to identify with a larger social context in its positive forms. Kahn's "natural Unitarianism" may have been partly attributable to his own manner of thinking through the values of individuality and of communal forms, and the need to hold both in tension. Maintaining a healthy congregation on a democratic basis requires a foundational alignment, a covenant that is a product of community discernment. It must precede any distribution of authority or control to individuals who are naturally always vigilant for their autonomy.[41] Thus, the partners in the building project, client and architect, had a shared disposition toward a sophisticated conception of the values of individual freedom and responsibility to community as a demanding and dynamic relationship.

The process in Rochester proceeded with several rounds of give and take between Kahn and the building committee, with a substantial change of the design from the first submission to the final approved design. This degree of change is not unique to the development of this particular design. There are, for instance, drawings of one or two quite different design schemes in the archives of both the Schenectady and University Unitarian congregations. But the record of communication during this back-and-forth process is more complete. The first scheme was rejected solely on the basis that it far exceeded the budget, perhaps partly due to misunderstanding the scope and scale of the building. The second the committee objected to on design issues. Despite a substantial change in form from the first to the final scheme, Kahn held fast to two important concepts: a unified structure rather than one divided into distinct parts, and a centrally located auditorium surrounded by a spatial gap that he called an "ambulatory." In the first scheme, the ambulatory surrounds the seating area of the auditorium and is itself surrounded by a corridor. In the final scheme, there is just the auditorium and corridor. Although the layering is reduced, the complete ring of the corridor is maintained. Kahn was taken with the Unitarian practice of providing space for making a choice on whether to join in worship or not: he placed the social hall on the direct path of entry, not the auditorium, and he amplified the corridor/ambulatory to surround the auditorium completely.[42]

In the end, Kahn produced a project that met the requirements of being both functional and imaginative, and of being modern but also having a sense of spirituality and emotion through simplicity and intimacy at a time when modern architecture was often thought to be cold. His exterior forms suggest a gathering of individuals and the unified sense of place of a medieval town, an Italian *commune*. Architectural historians have recognized that the successful design arose in part due to "intense collaboration" with the congregation. Kahn himself was quick to describe the project as the one in which he discovered new clarity about a design philosophy that he had been searching for—the relationship of form and design—and Sarah Williams Goldhagen writes that "the Unitarian Church was the first building Kahn built that gave an indication of his mature style."[43] This resonates with similar assessments of unique creative moments in the Unitarian church projects of H. H. Richardson, Frank Furness, and Frank Lloyd Wright.[44] These were architects with personal knowledge of Unitarian beliefs; as artists they found resonance with the unique qualities of the Unitarian communities with their own expressive dispositions.

Not all of the architects dove as deeply into the meaning of Unitarianism and its possibilities for architectural expression as Goodman and Kahn. But they always connected some aspect of the design to an idea such as "unity." Congregations that chose a well-known architect sometimes got a custom design that was nevertheless similar in fundamental ways to other works—that is, the architect's idea of architecture at that time shone through somewhat stronger than the ideas of Unitarianism. For instance, Edward Durrell Stone did not engage all that much with the Schenectady congregation, and the building looks much like several of his other designs of that time, especially the Stuart Pharmaceutical Company in Pasadena, California (1956).[45] However, it should be noted that Stone tried a very different scheme before settling on the concept that was developed and built. And he did take the general ideas of Unitarianism to meaningful architectural ends—the skillful and rational planning and the spatial relationships make it a good fit for its congregation, and the custom-designed block with interlocking circles make it unique. Other architects whose concurrent formal interests are particularly strong in their Unitarian church designs include Wright's design for Madison and Paul Rudolph's design for First Boston, which is clearly related to his Tuskegee Chapel at Tuskegee University, Alabama, completed in 1969.

In contrast, Pietro Belluschi worked with three Unitarian congregations, and the results have little similarity. In the case of May Memorial in Syracuse, New York, eighty church members working on eleven committees were involved in the new building planning. In addition to committee meetings, there were six full congregational meetings from which a brief was prepared for the architect. This included the desire to use natural materials and for an overall simplicity. Congregational historians noted, "They asked for an architecture marked by beauty, dignity, serenity, strength, stimulation, and challenge."[46] The committee interviewed fourteen architects, and architectural historian Meredith Clausen perceived that "the democratically minded congregation ... wanted nothing more than a simple, quiet, functional place for communal worship."[47] They were satisfied with their choice of Pietro Belluschi. The minister's dedication sermon on October 10, 1965, described the character of the building, asserting that it expressed "the truth that makes men free ... the spirit of liberty ... brotherhood, ... the worship of God and the service of man; a sanctuary for every seeking, questing soul, ... an open door to all truth and all men."[48]

"If ever a church building came close to being built by a committee of the whole, surely this must have been it!"[49] This sentiment, expressed by a congregation member in the Unitarian Fellowship of Ames, Iowa, accurately describes their process as among the most participatory. But there were others that might have had a similar impression from their own congregation's experiences with the process of creating a new congregational home. Congregational votes on the major issues were universally expected. Keeping the congregation informed about the basis of decisions through published committee reports was a standard practice. Often there were many committees and many meetings. In some cases, congregation members even participated in construction. A participatory design process does not in itself mean that a democratic architecture will follow; like originality, participatory design is often a part of the intersection of democracy and architecture, but not itself enough. But in all cases, congregations went to great lengths to state their needs, their vision, and their values—in words. Throughout the process, they recorded their deliberations in words. When the building was completed, they assessed the results in words. These words were important, and no architect could fail to show the impact of the congregation's words in some tangible way.

Sullivan described democracy as a process, the result of which must capture the collective will or the collective imagination. However, he believed that the ability to represent it in physical form, to move from idea or spirit to a design, required

the creative genius of an individual. Unitarian congregations used a variety of processes that sought to state, as best they could, the collective will of the congregation,
and then asked the architect to interpret it in built form. The creative genius of the
architect was trusted to simultaneously envision the building that served its inhab-
itants' pragmatic daily needs and touched their humanity with emotion and beauty.
In Sullivan's own work, this was explicitly the role of ornament, which offered a
visual feast. In Unitarian churches, it consisted most often of the radical simplicity
that causes one to see the architecture itself as a carefully delineated thought.

ARCHITECTURE FOR . . . : "EVANGELICAL HUMANISM"

The early nineteenth-century Unitarian theologians of Harvard and Boston did
not identify themselves as humanists, but they shared important ideas with
Renaissance humanism: belief in the dignity of humans, "confidence in man's freedom and potential . . . [and] the Renaissance world view of a unified, hierarchical
cosmos, presided over by a beneficent deity who revealed himself through nature
and Scripture alike." They encouraged development of education and the arts as
both necessary for individual self-fulfillment and as a way to improve the social culture of early America. Democracy depends on education so that citizens have the
means and desire to seek information; to assess opinions; and to evaluate, judge,
and decide. From the earliest time, Unitarians were open-minded about education's
goals. Harvard president James Walker asserted that "education . . . does not consist
in putting things into the mind, but, as the name implies, in bringing things out."
Furthermore, while Unitarians did believe in the importance of a class of leaders
in society, they did not believe in limiting the education of laborers, mechanics, or
professionals to the extent of their jobs. Democratic principles of education were
not instrumental—aimed at the provision of economic improvement or "upward
mobility"—but at the fulfillment of every individual's human nature and intelligence: for fuller realization of their human-ness. The historian Daniel Walker Howe
observed that Unitarians believed that the "New World might be the place where
man would find his greatest fulfillment," and so advocated to advance education
toward this end through an "evangelical humanism."[50] Their passion was not to win
converts to their denomination; their passion was to improve the general population, to create a more literate society. They preferred to speak on issues of ethics and
morality on Sundays rather than biblical passages.[51] The Boston area congregations
were focused by their ministers on the human condition.

Broad notions of humanism, unfortunately simplistic for an historically complex term, involve an understanding of the world, inclusive of human and other life forms, based in reason and science but also in human compassion. The Latin *humanus* means both "benevolent" and "learned."[52] Many Protestant Christians in nineteenth-century America would have considered themselves "humane" through virtues such as compassion and charity, but Unitarians made the practice of "service to man" a central tenet of their congregational life. And in the later nineteenth century, the continuous insistence that new scientific knowledge be accepted and any contradictory religious belief altered as necessary contributed to a humanistic progressivism. In the twentieth century, the dignity of humans was no longer understood as their likeness to God; it was a belief in the inherent goodness of people. In all of these ways, Unitarianism was inherently humanistic.

Humanism came to the foreground as a more formal philosophy in the twentieth century as a growing number of atheists felt the need to define a religion without God. Unitarian ministers preaching from an atheistic perspective were still a minority, but their numbers were growing even before World War I. No position was taken nationally by the AUA, but individual ministers eventually joined forces to codify their shared views. By forming an independent organization, they joined with theologians of other religions and philosophers to create an alternative idea to belief in God in "A Humanist Manifesto," completed in 1933.[53] There were fifteen points framed as religious humanism with no mention of a deity. Among the thirty-four signers, almost half were Unitarian ministers. It was controversial to many Unitarians at the time, and the national organization never adopted the humanism defined by this movement. Belief in God remained common as a matter of individual conscience, but the ideas articulated by the humanists were accepted widely among Unitarians after World War II.

A general account of what twentieth-century humanism meant within the broader cultural landscape was written by Harvard professor Howard Mumford Jones in a slim volume that was part of the same series, Harper & Row's World Perspectives, as *Scope of Total Architecture* by Walter Gropius.[54] The title of Jones's 1957 contribution gives one pause—*American Humanism: Its Meaning for World Survival*. Jones described humanism in lay terms rather than from a religious or philosophical framework. To him, it was a theory of knowledge that focused on the nature of human beings individually and collectively, humanity. In America, it serves our separation of church and state by offering validity to knowledge formed outside of religion and faith—a humanistic knowledge that is aimed at the dignity of humans.[55] That is, seeking knowledge can only be considered a humanistic endeavor if it is serving a noble purpose. There is an insistent ethical and moral ground to humanism.

Humanism is related to humanities and to the human need for stories as a way to comprehend human experience. Unitarian congregations routinely record their histories, and there is often a volunteer from the members serving as historian. Chronological milestones, such as the fiftieth or one hundredth anniversary of the founding of a congregation, often inspire a major effort to create or update a congregational history through recorded narratives in printed booklets, assembled photographic timelines, videos, or other means of story-telling. The sequence of ministers often provides the backbone of a narrative. Such histories often highlight activist ministers and members who have been influential in some way beyond the congregational community, and conversely world events that have impacted the congregation. Examples include abolitionist ministers and Progressive Era leaders in social causes such as women's suffrage, child labor, and public health issues. In the 1960s, Unitarian congregations were more broadly active in the civil rights and antiwar movements. While these stories are a reminder that every congregation is completely independent and thus has a need to remember where they have come from, they also reveal much about the connected nature of the relatively small denomination. The tracings of ministers moving from one congregation to another form an image of a living network of relationships. For instance, the minister of the Schenectady congregation during the planning and construction of their new building in the early 1960s, Reverend William Gold, was leading the Richmond, Virginia, congregation when they built their new building at the end of the decade.

The sequence of buildings that a congregation built and occupied over time is another important element in congregational histories and is sometimes produced as an independent record. Churches with histories stretching back two centuries and beyond may have a string of six or more buildings that have served as their homes. Even some twentieth-century congregations have had four or five different churches. Many of the older congregations even display their architectural heritage in an entry area or narthex as an important part of their identity. It is a record of fires, growth, and changing contexts. It is a remembrance of continuity that seems to be particularly important to a denomination whose continued existence is not insured by a centralized form of governance and economic stability. Along with written histories, church building "genealogies" are a reminder of strong roots even though congregations experience periods of precarious membership and resources. More importantly, they celebrate change over permanence, change rather than constancy. For Unitarians, there is nothing holy about their building in the religious or secular sense of the word.

The example of First Boston's architectural genealogy in the introduction spans the entire timeline of American Unitarianism and illustrates one version of continuity and change in the place it developed. The story of the Atlanta Unitarian congregation, founded in 1882, illustrates a more complicated community and a common enough story of growth and decline and even rupture in a democratically constituted congregation. They built their first home in the mid-1880s on the prominent corner of North Forsyth and Church Streets.[56] The Carnegie Foundation bought it at the turn of the century for the development of a full-scale central library. The congregation subsequently built a neoclassical building just a few blocks to the north, which they occupied from 1900 until 1914. They then moved to a new church farther north on West Peachtree, a building that remained their home until 1951, when the congregation briefly dissolved. The congregation had been divided in attitudes toward race in the 1940s, causing membership to steadily decline. A new minister arrived in 1952 and was able to rebuild the membership on the grounds of core Unitarian values, including the belief in universal fellowship.

At that point, they purchased an existing church just to the east of their former home. Although the integrated congregation remained predominantly white, African American families occasionally attended, and in the mid-1950s Whitney Young and his wife were the first Black people to join as members. He was soon serving on the board, encouraging activities that would promote greater integration and making connections with Ebenezer Baptist Church. Dr. Martin Luther King Jr. was among several civil rights leaders that were occasional guests to the pulpit, and the Unitarian youth group met together regularly with the Baptist youth group, which was led at the time by Coretta Scott King. The Unitarians started a capital fund drive and were in a position to look for a suitable new property by 1961. But in 1962 the congregation was denied the right to purchase a property north of midtown on Shady Valley Drive. It was not merely the owner or the neighbors that objected; the purchase was blocked by a vote of the Atlanta City Council in agreement with the local alderman, Buddy Fowlkes. He felt it would "lower the moral tone of the neighborhood" if the Unitarians moved in.[57] It was a full year before the congregation was able to successfully purchase a suitable lot further to the east, on Cliff Valley Drive. But the site they purchased put the church, still the only Unitarian congregation in the state at the time, about a mile outside of the city limit on a less desirable lot adjacent to a new interstate highway.

It was apparently their only option to evade the political machinery of the city of Atlanta. Each building in the congregation's history has some significance to their identity, through its architecture, its location, and its stories (fig. 6.3).

The Unitarian humanistic worldview has had significance for American architec-

FIGURE 6.3. Architectural heritage of the First Unitarian Church, Atlanta.

FIGURE 6.3a. Second building, 1900. Photographs of Unitarian Universalist Churches, bMS 15001, Andover-Harvard Library, Harvard Divinity School, Cambridge, Massachusetts.

FIGURE 6.3b. Third building, 1914. Photographs of Unitarian Universalist Churches, bMS 15001, Andover-Harvard Library.

FIGURE 6.3c. Fifth building, 1965. Permission of the Georgia Institute of Technology Library and Information Center, Archives and Records Management Department, Atlanta, Georgia.

ture and our cultural landscape beyond the churches they built. Wright's Unitarian heritage was a fundamental constituent of his philosophies and values. His original thinking about the house and the place of work in a changing world were widely influential. Bernard Maybeck and Buckminster Fuller are examples of other Unitarian free-thinkers that experimented with new possibilities. And we have also seen that in the nineteenth century, some Unitarians were influential patrons whose contributions were a benefit in the public sphere, not solely in the private. The work that H. H. Richardson did for the Ames family of North Easton gave him the chance to execute a suite of public buildings, perfecting his ability to express a noble civic character. Similarly, Frank Furness's Unitarian clients gave him creative freedom and steady work that amounted to an impact on the development of the Philadelphia School. And there was also significant cultural influence through political power. Justin Smith Morrill was a Unitarian congressman from Vermont from 1855 to 1898. His legacy includes sponsorship of the Land Grant College Act in 1862, which led to the establishment of 106 new college campuses across the country. Many of these were established in rural areas that would not have otherwise been likely places for educational institutions but have developed into important places and remain significant educational and cultural centers to this day.

At the culmination of the nineteenth century, the time of the greatest cultural influence of Unitarian "evangelical humanism," there was distinct Unitarian influence on the last federal government building of the century, the first independent building of the Library of Congress. Founders James Madison, Thomas Jefferson, and John Adams knew Congress would need recourse to independent and up-to-date sources of knowledge which would be pertinent to their political debates and decisions. It was President Adams, a Boston Unitarian, that established the congressional library with the first allocation of funds for purchasing books and maps. Jefferson donated his substantial personal library when he died. The library remained housed within the U.S. Capitol building throughout the nineteenth century. But the collection grew substantially after the Civil War, and by the 1870s the first steps were taken toward the provision of an independent structure. Now known as the Thomas Jefferson Building, it was finally built in the 1890s. It was Senator Justin Morrill who understood the library project to be an important cultural priority, one that would place knowledge itself, physically and ideologically, at the center of American government. As chair of the Senate Committee on Buildings and Grounds, he pushed Congress to fund the project and oversaw its administration. In the process, the idea of the library was transformed from providing Congress with resources pertinent to its duties to a comprehensive collection of universal

scope. The scale of the enterprise was therefore much grander, and it would need
to serve not only Congress but the American people—a national library. This transformation resulted from the combined efforts of Ainsworth Spofford, the head
librarian who devised various means of expanding the collection to a global scale,
and Morrill, who saw it as essential to democracy. Such a library would also serve
as proof that the United States, far from being a provincial or commercially driven
country, was in fact a fully enlightened culture equal to any Old World country.

Like other public buildings undertaken in the "American Renaissance" of the
1880s and 1890s, the library was conceived as a complete work of art. It was modeled on Charles Garnier's design of the Paris Opera, and the grand interiors were
similarly finished with the classical orders and ornament, sculptures, mosaics,
and paintings. Fifty-five painters and sculptors contributed to the completion
of the interiors under the direction of Edward Pearce Casey, who had replaced
the original architects during construction, and Bernard Green, the engineer in
charge of construction. Casey was a graduate of Columbia University and the
École des Beaux-Arts; Green, a Unitarian, was a graduate of Harvard University.
The extensive program of murals and sculpture that they conceived and implemented conveyed a message that went further than asserting America had "come
of age" as an important nation; it portrays an America conscious of its destiny as
"heir" to the great Western cultural traditions.[58]

Art historian Sally Webster believes that this message at the heart of a central
icon of American democracy is "a reflection of the teachings and humanitarian
tenets of Unitarianism."[59] In particular, it reflects the influential narrative of history
that Harvard University president Charles Eliot had developed for a new graduate
curriculum at Harvard, still a Unitarian institution though no longer only a divinity
school. Eliot was an influential public figure who lectured, published, and actively
promoted educational reform nationally. He was consulted formally on the central
reading room of the Library of Congress—he was asked to provide eight inscriptions for the drum of the dome. In doing so, he may well have also influenced other
aspects of the whole iconographic program (fig. 6.4). He was the sole attributed
contributor to the decorative scheme of the library outside of Casey and Green and
the individual artists that executed their visions.[60] It is not hard to imagine that he
was asked because Casey and Green had conceived the iconography with reference
to Eliot's influential ideas, or that in providing the inscriptions, Eliot also exerted
some direct influence on the whole. In any case, the result was an expression of "the
ethical humanitarianism of Unitarianism, which advanced a modern conception of

FIGURE 6.4a. Thomas Jefferson Building, Library of Congress, Smithmeyer & Pelz; completed by Edward Pearce Casey, 1896, view of main reading room. Library of Congress, Prints & Photographs Division, LC-DIG-det-4a17345.

FIGURE 6.4b. View of one of the eight inscriptions at the base of the dome: "ONE GOD, ONE LAW, ONE ELEMENT, AND ONE FAROFF DIVINE EVENT TO WHICH THE WHOLE CREATION MOVES," from Tennyson's *In Memoriam*. Photograph by Carol M. Highsmith, Library of Congress, Prints & Photographs Division, LC-DIG-highsm-11601.

civilization that . . . became the underpinnings for the construction of a democratic, civic iconography."[61] The Library of Congress represents in architectural terms an embodiment of the intersection of Unitarian humanistic values and American democracy, and in a certain sense culminates the importance of Unitarian cultural leadership in America's first 125 years.

UNITARIAN CHURCHES AS A (HU)MAN-SEARCH: DEMOCRACY AND IMAGINATION

American Unitarianism as a separate denomination was born side by side with the United States as an independent republic. The ideas that propelled the Unitarians' need to separate from their established theological traditions were the same as those that drove the American colonies to separate themselves from the imperial British government. Individual freedom and dignity, the capacity for self-determination, and the basic moral goodness of humanity were shared beliefs in the founding documents of each. The moral basis of the Declaration of Independence was a foundation on which the secular and religious aspects of society rested: "If church and state operate independently under U.S. charter, American democracy is none-theless founded on a moral pediment."[62] Unitarianism of the twentieth century, having left any conception of a god or of a godless cosmos up to the individual, became an even more explicit "religious analogue to the country's founding prin-ciples." The "American Creed" is a universal faith in individual liberties tempered by the higher cause of the common good. William Ellery Channing's Unitarian Christianity placed the responsibility for virtue with the individual's moral nature or conscience, not in holding any particular religious belief.[63] Individual self-determination within the larger social and natural realms were a common element. Separation from the British Crown required the determination to mount a war, a revolution. Separation of liberal Congregationalists from conservative Calvinist Congregationalists required a social process, a steady turnover of clergy and sub-sequent congregational votes on a liberal or conservative replacement. It also required the construction of new churches.

Democratic principles and values have been either inherent or explicit in explanations of a Unitarian worldview, along with or as a natural part of its radi-cally humanistic outlook, from the start. Channing believed that "the best of all revolutions . . . would culminate in the marriage of Christianity and democracy."[64] The essential shared principles of Unitarianism and democracy can be found in ministers' sermons and essays throughout the nineteenth century. For instance, Theodore Parker's 1850 antislavery sermon on the American "idea" was both an affirmation of democracy and a critique of the actual distribution of power in America in the 1840s. It called for a government that was more truly "over all the people, for all the people, by all the people."[65] Evidence of the democratic spirit and of American individualism is seen as well in the difficulties of organizing the Unitarian denomination experienced throughout the entire nineteenth century. Many feared that a national organization would compromise congregational autonomy and might lead easily to corruption, compromise, or sectarianism.

Humanism and democracy are frequently paired: Modern humanism, also called naturalistic, scientific, ethical and democratic humanisms, is "a naturalistic philosophy that rejects all supernaturalism and relies primarily on reason and science, democracy, and human compassion."[66] Democracy is based on a premise of equal rights and, similarly to humanism, inheres the notion of the dignity of the individual. Richard A. Etlin's book *In Defense of Humanism* underscores the same observation.[67] His purpose was to reaffirm the importance of artworks that have been devalued by recent literary and cultural theories and the questions they raised. His argument for their value rests in their capacity to capture and intensify some particular, and sometimes peculiar, experience, emotion, or perception that touches a central nerve of our human-ness. He defended an idea of humanism as "an aggregate of moral principles and cultural values inherited from the Enlightenment that exalts the rights and dignity of the individual."[68] Although many shared concepts might be enumerated, humanism is a theory of knowledge and a value system, while democracy is a way of ordering human relationships.

Unitarians practice democracy as a way of life. The denomination has always functioned by the self-determination of each congregation, whose way of being together and reasons or values mutually agreed to are articulated in a covenant. New members of the congregation must affirm the covenant in order to join. All members vote in annual elections for officers who take responsibility for leadership and management. As Andrea Greenwood and Mark W. Harris explain, "Each of the congregations controls its property and is financially autonomous. This local and independent freedom and individual autonomy is reflected also in the principles of the UUA, where the fifth principle is: 'the right of conscience and the use of the democratic process within our congregations and in society at large.'"[69] Elected officers are answerable to the congregation, and there are full congregational meetings at least once a year. In services and in other groups and events, everyone has a voice; in important decisions, everyone gets a vote.

Democratic principles and values have been at the forefront of Unitarian social positions and actions. Unitarians feel responsible for securing and defending the

democratic rights of others, not just demanding their own. They have no missionary impulse in doing so, no wish to persuade the beliefs of others, and no drive to
increase membership for the purpose of sociopolitical power. The earliest service
impulse that looked outward from established congregations aimed at social work
as an extension of ministry: rather than trying to change minds, they were trying
to improve the material conditions of urban poverty. Joseph Tuckerman called
himself a "minister-at-large," concentrating in the 1830s on visitation and coun-
seling rather than preaching. He was innovative for the time in his focus on individual circumstances rather than broad categories of social problems. Tuckerman
represents a Unitarian pattern of leading reforms; while the denomination's
efforts were not of a magnitude to instigate broad change, their impulses "sowed
the seeds of social progress." More conventionally, Ezra Stiles Gannett founded
a mission for the poor in Boston around the same time.[70] In the Victorian Era,
social service became more widely valued and practiced by ministers and congregations. With the Progressives at the end of the nineteenth century, it became a
central tenet of the denomination. In the 1880s, James Freeman Clarke counted
among his five principles central to Unitarianism "the brotherhood of man." This
meant that it was not enough to recognize that each individual had rights and
dignity, but that inherent to those rights was also a responsibility to others. This
was made more explicit by William Channing Gannett in his statement of "Things
Commonly Believed among Us."[71] His declaration confirmed individual freedom
of belief as opposed to recognizing any authority. He also made service the central
purpose of religion, that is, the salvation of others rather than the salvation of self.
While freedom of belief is explicitly democratic, service to others is inherently so
because it is predicated on the worth of all. A. Powell Davies in the 1940s repeated
the centrality of individual freedom of belief and made explicit the "democratic
process in human relations" in his core principles of Unitarianism.[72]

In addition to social service, activism for social justice has a strong tradition.
Unitarians were at the forefront of equal regard and rights for women, including
activism for voting rights. There has always been a strong pacifist and environmental justice sentiment among Unitarians as well. There was strong support for
civil rights, and in more current times support and welcome to LGBTQ individuals. There is an active sanctuary movement to support undocumented immigrants in need. Many of the churches visited for this book in the summer of 2016
had "Black Lives Matter" banners hanging on the church. According to Reverend
John Buehrens, a former president of the UUA, "That sense that religion must be

practical and influence the moral and spiritual context in which we live remains absolutely central to Unitarian Universalism today."[73]

This democratic identity can be traced loosely in the architecture of Unitarian churches over time. The first widespread church form was the third style of New England meetinghouse, the Bulfinch synthesis of the earlier frame meetinghouses with a Wren- and Gibbs-inspired classically detailed facade. These proliferated at the same time that early American government buildings were being designed to recall the democracies of antiquity. Their relatively small scale fit them to their place, and their identity with the New England civic life was a direct fact of democratic openness.

Later nineteenth-century churches fell into two major groups: the domestic ideal and the Gothic Revival. Churches falling within the domestic ideal had a wide range of physical features and overall character, but they were inherently calculated to fit in their place and to be open and welcoming—not just on Sundays but all week. Gannett's published sermon on the philosophy that drove these buildings expressed deep reverence for the human act of using materials wrought from the earth and shaped to provide not just shelter but the space for the social relationships of the family to flourish. In rooms of "simplicity and repose," kindness is more readily practiced. In seeking to connect congregation members meaningfully with the reality of humanity's place in the wider scope of nature and with each other in positive, caring, and responsible communities, these churches were an overtly democratic architecture.

The Gothic Revival churches were not, taken as whole, obviously democratic in architectural character. For the most part, Unitarian Gothic Revival structures were comparatively small in scale and usually devoid of monumental flourishes. Gothic verticality was replaced with wider and heavier grounded elements. There may be small gestures that express a less hierarchical order than a traditional church, such as the number or position of entry doors. But none of these can be seen to have been adopted broadly as a rule or habit. Interiors were plain, not meant to influence ideas through mood or symbol. Although Gothic Revival did achieve some sense of populism through the theories of Pugin and Ruskin, it was not by its nature a democratic architectural expression. However, the early innovative designs of Richardson in Boston and Furness in Philadelphia took imaginative liberties with the standards of the style that began to express an authentic American architecture. Any connection to a known style was broken altogether by Schweinfurth, Wright, and Maybeck at the start of the twentieth century. These surprisingly unique designs (for Berkeley, Oak Park, and Palo Alto) were a preview of the modern architecture of the 1950s and 1960s.

In the post–World War II self-consciousness of American identity, the anxiety about finding or defining an authentic American architecture arose again. Architectural historian Karla Cavarra Britton observed that "many architects, artists, and historians were engaged with . . . questions about the relationship of design to a democratic society."[74] The Unitarian churches of this period were conceived by leading architects for whom this topic was in the foreground of their creative search. Having a Unitarian congregation as a client, and perceiving its democratic practices directly in the process of commissioning a new building, gave those architects a perfect opportunity. By asking for a building reflective of their passionate fidelity to democracy, and by using democratic processes, the congregations built churches that were distinctly American, expressing confidence in democracy: they felt compelled to build. By allowing their architects freedom of artistic imagination, Unitarians built churches that were creative and authentic.

For Unitarians, the postwar period was a fortunate time to fulfill their desire to work with highly regarded architects and to produce innovative buildings. The profession had not yet outgrown an atelier mode of operating, had not yet begun to emulate the corporate clients that would soon become a dominant force in shaping American cities. And the expanding vocabularies of modernism could be built relatively economically—due to interest in everyday materials, a compositional minimalism, and common, straightforward construction methods of the time. An award-winning building was within the means of a congregation because architectural ideas and construction methods were tuned to simplicity, at least in smaller scale production, which would not be the case by the 1980s. They were designed by architects with the ambition to be aesthetically distinctive, which would by some definitions imply "high culture" over "popular culture," in somewhat reductive terms. Although many were regarded by "average people" as somewhat strange, the high design of midcentury modernism was by definition architecture as a critique of the elitism of the International Style. Its tendencies toward simplicity and clarity gave it a direct and straightforward quality.

The churches of the 1950s and 1960s can be difficult to generalize because there is, in a twenty-five-year span, a great variety of architecture. Chronologically, this period begins and ends with two extremely different expressions of democracy. Wright's church for Madison embodied his nineteenth-century view of American individualism connected to the land; his "church in the country" was a prairie schooner in constant search of freedom. Rudolph's design for First Boston was an urban opposite. It was slightly recessive, echoing the humanistic design vision he had explored in his Boston Government Services building. At First Church, Rudolph extended the Unitarian program of social space in partnership with worship into the public realm. The churches built between these two were mostly made of everyday materials, and they were generally not grand in scale; they tended to be more horizontal than vertical. Rationality and clarity, seen in elements such as exposed structure and minimal additional finishes, were common. Some elaboration of the entry sequence, including courtyards, arcades or porticos, and bridges, was also common. Asymmetrical compositions were favored, simplicity generally ruled. While these physical characteristics tend to express openness and a humanistic/democratic presence, they can be subtle and are not universal.

The most consistent affirmations of democracy in the architecture of the Unitarians rests on two foremost points. One is the drive for creativity and imagination in the architecture, a building of its time and place in America. They wanted architecture that was forward-thinking, progressive, not traditional. They wanted to make a positive contribution to the idea of a shared culture, one that was recognized as dynamic. The other is the openness represented in the combination of a worship space of seeking and reflecting on the universal questions, a social space for discourse and conversation, and spaces for education, a vital element of a democracy. Their buildings were designed with a priority on social interaction placed ahead of spiritual expression, and a desire to not only feel welcoming but to instill some sense of ease and belonging. Congregations sometimes interpreted the social function in their own unique way, so that it might not have an equivalent architectural footprint. Other congregations multiplied the social spaces to have options for fit. There is also often a library.

As an architecture for a democratic religion, Unitarian spaces are relatively nonhierarchical. Generally, the auditorium or sanctuary is distinguishable as the primary space, but often it is by quite subtle degrees of difference from the social space or spaces. Education spaces are different in size and often depended on phased construction budgets, thus they frequently rank somewhat lower in architectural importance. But their importance to the social realm should not be underestimated. Religious education was not a matter of indoctrination but of sparking the "essential element" of a liberal church, the need to grow unhindered.[75] And plenty of examples such as Rochester, Schenectady, Concord, and Plandome show that they were of equal importance. Education as a vital part of social interaction was a primary value: there were ample daylit rooms for smaller groups to explore their own questions, often with outdoor space readily at hand. Still, it must be recognized that the greater variety in providing spaces for education leaves the impression that the core idea of worship space and social space are the essential and complementary parts of the Unitarian church. It is the most consistent basis for the building design and the key expression of an architecture for a democratic religion.

These paired spaces can be more fully appreciated by reflecting on similar couplings at a slightly larger scale. Thomas Jefferson's campus in Charlottesville and James Killian's MIT campus in Cambridge demonstrate a kind of democratic architecture that achieves the representation of Dewey's creative democracy as a way of life. Ockman further suggests that democratic architecture needs to express something of "what holds us together as citizens and human beings."[76] In Jefferson's design for the University of Virginia, the combination of the elements is expressive of democracy because they create an "open forum for human development." The Rotunda houses the library, the repository of knowledge; it is paired with the Lawn, a space for discussion and debate. The public space is defined on its two long edges by the individuals who join in the collective conversation of the Lawn. Opposite the Rotunda, the fourth side of the Lawn was left open to nature, the true source of knowledge. Theorist Sylvain de Bleeckere maintains that "the Lawn symbolizes the great freedom of seeing and thinking. For Jefferson the irreplaceable power of democratic thinking lies within a great openness of the human mind. This mind stands in constant dialogue with living nature, source of knowledge and cradle of the open space."[77]

The theme of library and forum was repeated by the Ames family's bequest to their company town, North Easton, Massachusetts. The heart of the town is not their factory or even the church but the free library and Memorial Hall—what we would call today a community center. Once again there is access to knowledge and the importance of using that knowledge in social exchange. The town, to support a healthy democratic citizenry, needed more than the provision of knowledge and ideas; it needed an open exchange of those ideas to thrive. A similar provision can be seen once again on the campus of MIT. The Rotunda and the Lawn were echoed 150 years later by the construction of the Chapel and Auditorium at MIT. Intellectual reflection was replaced with spiritual reflection in accordance with the needs of the time but still balanced with open discourse in the auditorium. The pairing of spaces serving related but distinct needs, different parts of human nature, is a gift in itself. Embedded into Unitarian churches is exactly this recognition and this gift, and it makes them profoundly democratic.

The recognition of the dual needs of the individual—spiritual seeking or reflecting and enrichment through an ongoing communal exchange of thoughts and ideas—makes every Unitarian church true to the *idea* of a meetinghouse, if not the shape or form of one (fig. 6.5). It is a place for citizen participation. Louis Sullivan, fiercely devoted to the vision of a democratic architecture, rejected any inherited forms of architecture. He saw in them centuries of various social orders in which a relatively small number of religious or secular rulers held power over all others. He demanded new forms that would fit the realities of a society that was created on a different basis of human relations—a democratic society. It required new imagination, and new architecture, to fit the way of life of free individuals who were fundamentally different than the subjects of the past. Sullivan called democracy a "man-search"; it seems to follow that we may call American Unitarianism, in its persistent allegiance to humanism and democracy, a human-search.

FIGURE 6.5. Unitarian Church, Rockford, Illinois, Pietro Belluschi, 1966, views of the sanctuary and the social hall. Photographs by author.

NOTES

INTRODUCTION

1. Joan Ockman, "What Is Democratic Architecture? The Public Life of Buildings," *Dissent* 58, no. 4 (October 2011): 65–72; Sylvain de Bleeckere, "Style and Architecture in a Democratic Perspective," *Enquiry* 4, no. 1 (November 2007): 13–20; J. C. Berendzen, "Institutional Design and Public Space: Hegel, Architecture, and Democracy," *Journal of Social Philosophy* 39, no. 2 (Summer 2008): 291–307.
2. Mark W. Harris, *Historical Dictionary of Unitarian Universalism* (Lanham, MD: Scarecrow Press, 2004), xx.
3. 1784: James Freeman was the first minister to call himself Unitarian; he altered the liturgy of his Anglican church, King's Chapel, Boston. 1796: Joseph Priestley founded a Unitarian congregation in Philadelphia on his arrival from Britain. 1804: Liberal Congregationalists gained control of Harvard Divinity School. 1819: William Ellery Channing delivered a defining sermon on Harvard-based New England liberal beliefs, using the name "Unitarian Christianity."
4. Virginia Dejohn Anderson, "Migrants and Motives: Religion and the Settlement of New England, 1630–1640," *New England Quarterly* 58, no. 3 (September 1985): 339–83.
5. David Robinson, *The Unitarians and the Universalists* (Westport, CT: Greenwood Press, 1985), 23.
6. Mark A. Noll, *America's God: From Jonathan Edwards to Abraham Lincoln* (Oxford: Oxford University Press, 2002), 285.
7. Stow Persons, *American Minds: A History of Ideas* (New York: Holt, Rinehart, and Winston, 1958), 180–82.
8. Lawrence Buell, "The Literary Significance of the Unitarian Movement," *ESQ* 33, no. 4 (1987): 212–23.
9. Sally Webster, "Unitarianism and the Iconography of Democracy: Decorations for the Library of Congress," *Library Quarterly* 80, no. 4 (2010): 357–83.
10. F. Forrester Church, *Cathedral of the World: A Universalist Theology* (Boston: Beacon Press, 2009), 121. See also Andrea Greenwood and Mark W. Harris, *An Introduction to the Unitarian and Universalist Traditions* (Cambridge: Cambridge University Press, 2011), 1–13.
11. Unitarian Universalist Association, "UUA Membership Statistics, 1961–2020," Demographics and Statistical Information about Unitarian Universalism, www.uua.org.
12. Paul Goldberger, "Housing for the Spirit," *New York Times*, December 26, 1982.
13. Joseph Siry, *Unity Temple and the Architecture of a Liberal Religion* (Cambridge: Cambridge University Press, 1996); Sarah Williams Goldhagen, *Louis Kahn's Situated Modernism* (New Haven, Conn.: Yale University Press, 2001).
14. Vincent Scully, *Louis I. Kahn* (New York: George Braziller, 1962), 24.
15. There is a survey of British Unitarian churches: Graham Hague, *The Unitarian Heritage: An Architectural Survey of Chapels and Churches in the Unitarian Tradition in the British Isles* (Sheffield, UK: Unitarian Heritage, 1986).

16. Albert Christ-Janner and Mary Mix Foley, *Modern Church Architecture: A Guide to the Form and Spirit of 20th Century Religious Buildings* (New York: McGraw-Hill, 1962), 265–79.
17. Greenwood and Harris, *Unitarian and Universalist Traditions*, 207.
18. "The Story of First Church Boston," First Church Boston, www.firstchurchbostonhistory.org.
19. Greenwood and Harris, *Unitarian and Universalist Traditions*, 140.
20. Persons, *American Minds*, 164–66.
21. Stow Persons, *Free Religion: An American Faith* (New Haven, CT: Yale University Press, 1947), 55.
22. Peter Benes, *Meetinghouses of Early New England* (Amherst: University of Massachusetts Press, 2012).

CHAPTER ONE: THE MYTH OF THE MEETINGHOUSE

1. There are numerous sources on the meetinghouse; I relied most heavily on Peter Benes, *Meetinghouses of Early New England* (Amherst: University of Massachusetts Press, 2012), and Edmund W. Sinnot, *Meetinghouse and Church in Early New England* (New York: McGraw Hill, 1963).
2. The term "church" is being used in a colloquial sense. Religiously speaking, "church" is an equivalent of "meetinghouse"—a place of assembly for worship, not the house of a god. But most Christian churches tend to blur the line between "house of the people of God" and "house of God." See Harold W. Turner, *From Temple to Meeting House: The Phenomenology and Theology of Places of Worship* (The Hague: Mouton, 1979).
3. Sinnot, *Meetinghouse and Church*. Sinnot identifies four types, but the third and fourth are a matter of how the pedimented portico is treated—the difference in style between Federal and Greek Revival but not a substantial change in form. Benes agrees with Sinnot's classification for the most part.
4. Benes, *Meetinghouses*, 21.
5. The current name of the congregation is the First Parish in Hingham, Unitarian Universalist.
6. Nina Wellford Price, "Rediscover the Meeting House," Friends of the Old Ship Meeting House, October 2015, http://oldshipfriends.org.
7. Sinnot, *Meetinghouse and Church*, 71. Writing in 1963, Sinnot described the original Europeans in New England and their direct descendants as "indigenous" to distinguish them culturally from the expansion of the population by later immigrants. That expansion brought diversity of denominations to New England towns.
8. Peter Williams, *Houses of God: Region, Religion, and Architecture in the United States* (Urbana: University of Illinois Press, 1997), 8.
9. Sinnot, *Meetinghouse and Church*, 71.
10. Sinnot was somewhat equivocal; he said that the change is not attributable to any single source, but having noted Bulfinch's importance, he also pointed to the Pittsfield design as displaying the essential elements and called them "new ideas" that others noticed. Benes states it more plainly: "Bulfinch's success in Taunton [nearly identical to Pittsfield] and in the Berkshires gradually changed the equation for towns and parishes planning new meetinghouses in the early Federal Republic." Benes, *Meetinghouses*, 213.
11. Stow Persons, *American Minds: A History of Ideas* (New York: Holt, Rinehart, and Winston, 1958), 179.
12. John Stilgoe, *Common Landscape of America, 1580–1845* (New Haven, CT: Yale University Press, 1982), 57.
13. Benes, *Meetinghouses*, 1.

14. Harold Kirker, *The Architecture of Charles Bulfinch* (Cambridge, MA: Harvard University Press, 1969), 282.

15. Graham Hague, *The Unitarian Heritage: An Architectural Survey of Chapels and Churches in the Unitarian Tradition in the British Isles* (Sheffield, UK: Unitarian Heritage, 1986), 62–63.

16. Charles Bulfinch and Ellen Susan Bulfinch, *The Life and Letters of Charles Bulfinch, Architect* (New York: Houghton, Mifflin, 1896), 240.

17. Roger W. Moss, *Historic Sacred Places of Philadelphia* (Philadelphia: University of Pennsylvania Press, 2005), 200.

18. John M. Bryan, *Robert Mills, America's First Architect* (New York: Princeton Architectural Press, 2001), 81–86.

19. Moss, *Sacred Places of Philadelphia*, 203.

20. Robert Alexander, *The Architecture of Maximilian Godefroy* (Baltimore: Johns Hopkins University Press, 1974), 132–56.

21. Latrobe had initially submitted a plan for the church but withdrew, giving Godefroy a favorable recommendation.

22. W. Brown Morton, "First Unitarian Church," National Register of Historic Places Inventory Nomination Form (Crownsville, MD: Maryland Historic Trust, 1971), n.p.

23. Charles Percier and Pierre François Léonard Fontaine, *Palais, maisons, et autres edifices modernes, dessines à Rome* (Paris: P. Didot L'Aîné, 1798).

24. Alexander, *Maximilian Godefroy*, 132–57.

25. John Allen Macaulay, *Unitarianism in the Antebellum South: The Other Invisible Institution* (Tuscaloosa: University of Alabama Press, 2001), 39.

26. This building was recognized as a National Historic Landmark in 1976.

27. Marian C. Donnelly, *The New England Meeting Houses of the Seventeenth Century* (Middletown, CT: Wesleyan University Press, 1968), 108.

28. Williams, *Houses of God*, 8.

29. Ibid., 1.

30. Massachusetts Cultural Resource Information System, Inventory No. GRO.22, First Parish Church Report, June 2, 2014, https://mhc-macris.net.

31. Unfortunately, the interior of the dome is no longer visible; a plaster barrel vault was suspended beneath it in the 1890s to improve the acoustics.

32. Conrad Wright, *A Stream of Light: A Sesquicentennial History of American Unitarianism* (Boston: Unitarian Universalist Association, 1975), 24.

33. Howard Mumford Jones, *American Humanism: Its Meaning for World Survival* (New York: Harper and Brothers, 1957), 101.

34. Mark A. Noll, *America's God: From Jonathan Edwards to Abraham Lincoln* (Oxford: Oxford University Press, 2002), 284, 287.

CHAPTER TWO: ORIGINALITY, NOT ORIGINS

1. Stow Persons, *American Minds: A History of Ideas* (New York: Holt, Reinhart, and Winston, 1958), 201–13.

2. Conrad Wright, *A Stream of Light: A Sesquicentennial History of American Unitarianism* (Boston: Unitarian Universalist Association, 1975), 30.

3. Biographic information on Emerson is primarily from David Robinson, *The Unitarians and the*

Universalists (Westport, CT: Greenwood Press, 1985), 252–53, and Harold Bloom, *Ralph Waldo Emerson* (New York: Chelsea House, 1985).

4. Robinson, *Unitarians and Universalists*, 28.

5. Lawrence Buell, "The Literary Significance of the Unitarian Movement," *ESQ* 33, no. 4 (1987): 212–13.

6. John A. Buehrens, *Conflagration: How the Transcendentalists Sparked the American Struggle for Racial, Gender, and Social Justice* (Boston: Beacon Press, 2020). Buehrens suggests an equally important sociopolitical impact.

7. Robinson, *Unitarians and Universalists*, 76. Robinson is quoting historian Perry Miller, *The Transcendentalists: An Anthology* (Cambridge, MA: Harvard University Press, 1950), 8.

8. Theodore Parker, "The Transient and Permanent in Christianity (1841)," in *Three Prophets of Religious Liberalism: Channing-Emerson-Parker*, ed. Conrad Wright (Boston: Beacon Press, 1961), 118.

9. Persons, *American Minds*, 210.

10. Arthur S. Bolster Jr., *James Freeman Clarke, Disciple to Advancing Truth* (Boston: Beacon Press, 1954). This is my primary source for biographical information. See also Buehrens, *Conflagration*, 269–77.

11. James Freeman Clarke, *Vexed Questions in Theology: A Series of Essays* (Boston: George H. Ellis, 1886), 9–18. See also Robinson, *Unitarians and Universalists*, 105.

12. Daniel Walker Howe, *Unitarian Conscience: Harvard Moral Philosophy, 1805–1861* (Cambridge, MA: Harvard University Press, 1970), 287.

13. Elizabeth M. Geffen, "William Henry Furness: Philadelphia Antislavery Preacher," *Pennsylvania Magazine of History and Biography* 82, no. 2 (July 1958): 259–92.

14. Lewis Perry and Matthew C. Sherman, "What Disturbed the Unitarian Church in This Very City?" *Civil War History* 54, no. 1 (2008): 8.

15. Theodore Parker, "Of Justice and the Conscience," in *Ten Sermons of Religion* (Boston: Crosby, Nichols, 1853), 66–101. King used slight variations of his paraphrase in numerous speeches in the 1960s, and President Barack Obama memorialized it in the Oval Office. See Jamie Stiehm, "Oval Office Rug Gets History Wrong," *Washington Post*, September 4, 2010.

16. John Allen Macaulay, *Unitarianism in the Antebellum South: The Other Invisible Institution* (Tuscaloosa: University of Alabama Press, 2001), 162.

17. David T. Van Zanten, "Jacob Wrey Mould: Echoes of Owen Jones and the High Victorian Styles in New York, 1853–1865," *Journal of the Society of Architectural Historians* 28, no. 1 (March 1969): 44.

18. Stow Persons, *Free Religion: An American Faith* (New Haven, CT: Yale University Press, 1947).

19. Robinson, *Unitarians and Universalists*, 88–89.

20. Howe, *Unitarian Conscience*, 302, 270.

21. Glenna Matthews, *The Golden State in the Civil War: Thomas Starr King, the Republican Party, and the Birth of Modern California* (New York: Cambridge University Press, 2012), 231.

22. James Early, *Romanticism and American Architecture* (New York: A. S. Barnes, 1965), 112–13. Early noted that there were Gothic chapels among the early Anglican churches of the middle and southern colonies but none in the eighteenth century.

23. Jeffrey W. Howe, *Houses of Worship: An Identification Guide to the History and Styles of American Religious Architecture* (San Diego: Thunder Bay Press, 2003), 143. This source has images of both designs.

24. Harold Kirker, *The Architecture of Charles Bulfinch* (Cambridge, MA: Harvard University Press, 1969), 249.

25. Early, *Romanticism*, 118.

26. Phoebe Stanton, *The Gothic Revival and American Church Architecture* (Baltimore: Johns Hopkins University Press, 1968), 31–125.

27. Early, *Romanticism*, 84–108.

28. This observation is a matter of resemblance without knowledge of the architects' or their clients' sources or inspirations. The adoption of Gothic Revival reflected some confusion about medieval English Gothic styles. However, these two churches and the contemporary Eastern State Penitentiary outside Philadelphia resemble the "castles" of English picturesque architects Richard Payne Knight and John Nash more than English churches of the same time. See Michael J. Lewis, *The Gothic Revival* (New York: Thames and Hudson, 2002), 34, 47.

29. "New Church in Salem," *Christian Register*, January 3, 1846, 2.

30. "Unitarian Church—New Bedford Mass," *Christian Register and Boston Observer*, June 30, 1838, 1.

31. Peter W. Williams, *Houses of God: Region, Religion, and Architecture in the United States* (Urbana: University of Illinois Press, 1997), 111.

32. William Robert Ware and Henry Van Brunt were both pupils in William Morris Hunt's New York atelier before starting their firm in Boston in 1863.

33. Stanton, *Gothic Revival and American Church Architecture*, 331.

34. Henry Van Brunt, "Cast Iron in Decorative Architecture (1859)," in *Architecture and Society: Selected Essays of Henry Van Brunt*, ed. William A. Coles (Cambridge, MA: Belknap Press of Harvard University Press, 1969), 78.

35. Lewis, *The Gothic Revival*, 135–55.

36. Peter Stiles, "From Discreet Chapel to Gothic Ostentation: Developments in 19th Century Unitarian Architecture as a Paradigm for the Problematic Nature of Elizabeth Gaskill's Fiction," Religion, Literature and the Arts Project Conference Proceedings (1994): 376–77, https://openjournals.library.sydney.edu.au.

37. Van Zanten, "Jacob Wrey Mould," 41.

38. Lewis, *The Gothic Revival*, 135–36.

39. Van Zanten, "Jacob Wrey Mould," 41. Van Zanten quotes Bellows's dedicatory sermon, which was printed in the *New York Journal of Commerce*, December 27, 1855.

40. Lewis, *The Gothic Revival*, 120.

41. Ralph Waldo Emerson, *Records of a Lifelong Friendship, 1807–1882* (Boston: Houghton Mifflin, 1910), 10.

42. George Thomas, Michael J. Lewis, and Jeffrey A. Cohen, *Frank Furness: The Complete Works* (New York: Princeton Architectural Press), 26–35. Emerson and Furness brought an American perspective to ideas such as those of English historian James Fergusson, whose history of architecture "in all countries" implied that architectural expressions were singular and distinct to individual countries. After the Civil War, American art forms fulfilled the dream of an "American" expression in every category, but in architecture there was later a turning back that was "ratified" by the 1893 World's Fair in Chicago (35n62). See James Fergusson, *A History of Architecture in All Countries, from the Earliest Times to the Present Day* (London: John Murray, 1862).

43. Furness had apprenticed in an office in Philadelphia before moving to New York, but apprenticeships were not generally instructive in design.

44. James F. O'Gorman, *The Architecture of Frank Furness* (Philadelphia: Philadelphia Museum of Art, 1973), 23–30. See also Thomas, Lewis, and Cohen, *Frank Furness*, 99.

45. Stanton, *Gothic Revival and American Church Architecture*, 113. See also Thomas, Lewis, and Cohen, *Frank Furness*, 146.

46. Van Zanten, "Jacob Wrey Mould," 47, 56. Van Zanten quotes an 1884 history of Brooklyn. Regarding the reconstructed plan, I have not been able to find any other church quite like this one. The closest are later, for instance Richardson's Emmanuel Episcopal Church, Pittsburgh (1886). See Howe, *Houses of Worship*, 214.

47. John Notman's Chapel of the Holy Innocents in Burlington, New Jersey (1845), was also a simple space but much taller. Richard Upjohn's Christ Church in Elizabeth, New Jersey (1854), has some of the width but is more spatially complex and is ruled by piers supporting pointed arches.

48. Thomas, Lewis, and Cohen, *Frank Furness*, 77–78.

49. Ibid., 69.

50. Ibid., 246.

51. Van Zanten, "Jacob Wrey Mould," 48. The article provides a photograph (and plan) but no location for the chapel.

52. A subtle recessed panel set under the opening of the chimney pot contains the carved symbol of Jesus Christ—an interwoven "IHS." This, together with a cross carved into the front of the reading desk inside, is a good indicator of the complexities of Unitarian beliefs in the later nineteenth century. William Henry Furness, and presumably the congregation he steered for fifty years, maintained an "aesthetic Christology" even though he believed in the singularity of God. He still held Jesus and Jesus's teaching as "the paradigm of humanity fully in touch with that larger spiritual reality" that is called God, and that Jesus was the example of the "ultimate union of the individual life with the eternal truth toward which it is directed and in which it has its being." So even though Furness was aligned with the Transcendentalists, it does not automatically signal an easily summarized view. Joseph R. Hoffman, "William Henry Furness: The Transcendentalist Defense of the Gospels," *New England Quarterly* 56, no. 2 (1983): 247–48.

53. Furness used the same circulation and shallow transepts fifteen years earlier in Germantown.

54. Thomas, Lewis, and Cohen, *Frank Furness*, 246. In the 1930s photograph, it appears that the trusses were stripped of paint.

55. Michael J. Lewis, *Frank Furness: Architecture and the Violent Mind* (New York: Norton, 2001), 160–61.

56. Ibid., 160.

57. O'Gorman, *Architecture of Frank Furness*, 55.

58. James F. O'Gorman, "Then and Now: A Note on the Contrasting Architectures of H. H. Richardson and Frank Furness," in *H. H. Richardson: The Architect, His Peers, and Their Era*, ed. Maureen Meister (Cambridge: MIT Press, 1999), 76–101.

59. Some sources call it the Brattle Street Church.

60. Henry Russell Hitchcock, *The Architecture of H. H. Richardson and His Times* (Cambridge, MA: MIT Press, 1936), 111. Hitchcock calls it "definitely Romanesque" but goes on to point out many details that fail to conform.

61. Margaret Henderson Floyd, *Henry Hobson Richardson: A Genius for Architecture* (New York: Monacelli Press, 1997), 41.

62. Ibid., 40–41.

63. Aline Kaplan, "Brattle Square Angels," The Next Phase Blog, http://aknextphase.com.

64. Hitchcock, *The Architecture of H. H. Richardson*, 115.
65. William H. Pierson, Jr., "The Beauty of a Belief: The Ames Family, Richardson, and Unitarianism," in Meister, ed., *H. H. Richardson*, xviii.
66. Floyd, *Henry Hobson Richardson*, 189–92.
67. Pierson, "The Beauty of a Belief," xxxii, xxxix.
68. Clubs such as the Saturday Club and the Metaphysical Club were a common feature of social life for Harvard intellectuals in the nineteenth century. See Louis Menand, *The Metaphysical Club: A Story of Ideas in America* (New York: Farrar, Straus and Giroux, 2001).
69. Jeffrey Karl Ochsner, *H. H. Richardson: Complete Architectural Works* (Cambridge, MA: MIT Press, 1982), 74.
70. Floyd, *Henry Hobson Richardson*, 176.
71. Jeanne Halgren Kilde, *When Church Became Theater* (Oxford: Oxford University Press, 2002), 108–10.
72. Bolster, *James Freeman Clarke*, 300.

CHAPTER THREE: ". . . AND THE SERVICE OF MAN"

1. Edwin Scott Gaustad and Philip L. Barlow, *New Historical Atlas of Religion in America* (New York: Oxford University Press, 2001), 245. By contrast, Presbyterians, among the larger Protestant denominations, had 500 churches by 1840, 1,250 by 1853, and approximately 3,000 in 1906.
2. Ibid., 248.
3. Ibid., 245.
4. Mark W. Harris, *Historical Dictionary of Unitarian Universalism* (Lanham, MD: Scarecrow Press, 2004), 513.
5. At that time, Chicago had three ongoing congregations. A fourth on the south side had recently faltered; Jones stepped into the void.
6. Wanda A. Hendricks, *Fannie Barrier Williams: Crossing the Borders of Region and Race* (Chicago: University of Illinois Press, 2013), 72, 83. Williams also delivered a speech at the World's Congress of Representative Women.
7. Jenkin Lloyd Jones, *The Ideal Church: A Discourse* (Chicago: Colegrove Books, 1882), 8–9.
8. Jenkin Lloyd Jones, "The New Problems in Church Architecture," *Unity*, May 1885, 202–5.
9. Silsbee was the son of a Unitarian minister. Henry Russell Hitchcock, *In the Nature of Materials* (New York: Duell, Sloan, and Pearce, 1942), 4.
10. Joseph Siry, *Unity Temple: Frank Lloyd Wright and Architecture for a Liberal Religion* (Cambridge: Cambridge University Press, 1996), 15, 19.
11. William C. Gannett, *The House Beautiful* (River Forest, IL: Auvergne Press, 1896), n.p.
12. Elinor Sommers Otto, Pauline Eichten, and Ellen Green, "Unity Church History," Unity Church–Unitarian, St. Paul, Minnesota, www.unityunitarian.org.
13. Edward Searl, "Many Histories of the Unitarian Church of Hinsdale," UU Essentials, https://sites.google.com.
14. "Visitors: What is UU / History," Unitarian Church of Hinsdale, www.hinsdaleunitarian.org.
15. "Our Roots," First Unitarian Church of Chicago, https://firstuchicago.org.
16. Cynthia Tucker, *Prophetic Sisterhood: Liberal Women Ministers of the Frontier, 1880–1930* (Boston: Beacon Press, 1990), 104.
17. Ibid., 101.

18. Susan Eberly, "The Little Church That Looks Like a House," in *From Within These Walls: 100 Years at 10 South Gilbert*, ed. Susan Eberly (Iowa City: Unitarian Universalist Society, 2008), 25.

19. Tucker, *Prophetic Sisterhood*, 112.

20. "Co-Creating the 'Greenest Church in Iowa,'" Unitarian Universalist Society, www.uusic.org.

21. Renee Ruchotzke, "Caroline Bartlett Crane," Dictionary of Unitarian and Universalist Biography, https://uudb.org.

22. Lynda J. Rynbrandt and Mary Jo Deegan, "The Ecofeminist Pragmatism of Caroline Bartlett Crane, 1896–1935," *American Sociologist* 33, no. 3 (Fall 2002): 58–68.

23. Charles R. Starring, "Caroline Bartlett Crane," in *Notable American Women, 1607–1950: A Biographical Dictionary*, ed. Edward T. James (Cambridge, MA: Belknap Press of Harvard University Press, 1971), 401–2.

24. Caroline Bartlett Crane, "The Story of an Institutional Church in a Small City," *Charities* 14, no. 6 (May 6, 1905): 723–31.

25. "Nichols, Minerva Parker, (1860–1943)," Harvard Square Library Biographies, www.harvardsquare library.org. Nichols was the second to own a firm, but Louise Blanchard Bethune had a partnership with her husband, while Nichols was a sole proprietor.

26. Elizabeth G. Grossman and Lisa B. Reitzes, "Caught in the Crossfire: Women and Architectural Education," in *Architecture: A Place for Women*, ed. Ellen Perry Berkeley (Washington, DC: Smithsonian Institution Press, 1989), 32.

27. Edwin J. Lewis, J. Enoch Powell, and Albert Walkley, *Plans for Churches* (Boston: American Unitarian Association, 1902), 30.

28. Sharon Grimes, "Women in the Studios of Men: Gender, Architectural Practice, and the Careers of Sophia Hayden Bennett and Marion Mahony Griffin, 1870–1960" (PhD diss., East St. Louis University, 2007), 97.

29. Margaret Shaklee, "A History of the Unitarian Church of Evanston," Unitarian Church of Evanston, https://ucevanston.org.

30. Grimes, "Women in the Studios of Men," 97.

31. Tucker, *Prophetic Sisterhood*, 104, 101.

32. John Sears, *Sacred Places: American Tourist Attractions in the Nineteenth Century* (New York: Oxford University Press, 1989), 127–28.

33. Glenna Matthews, *The Golden State in the Civil War* (Cambridge: Cambridge University Press, 2012), 231.

34. Maybeck is known for a mix of styles, displaying imagination even in his neoclassical monumental works. His unique capacity to blend influences and create something unique is best known in the 1910 First Church of Christ, Scientist, Berkeley.

35. Betty Marvin, "First Unitarian Church," National Register of Historic Places Inventory Nomination Form (Berkeley Architectural Heritage Association, 1981), n.p.

36. Ibid.

37. Leland Roth, *Shingle Styles: Innovation and Tradition in American Architecture, 1874 to 1982* (New York: H. N. Abrams, 1999), 143.

38. Marvin, "First Unitarian Church."

39. "Our History," Unitarian Universalist Church of Palo Alto, www.uucpa.org.

40. Kenneth H. Cardwell, *Bernard Maybeck: Artisan, Architect, Artist* (Santa Barbara, CA: Peregrine Smith, 1977), 120.

41. "The Palo Alto Church (1907)," *Pacific Unitarian* 15, no. 6 (April 1907): 187.

42. Cardwell, *Bernard Maybeck*, 120.

43. Joseph Siry, "The Abraham Lincoln Center in Chicago," *Journal of the Society of Architectural Historians* 50, no. 3 (September 1991): 237. Siry's in-depth analysis describes the evolution of the project in detail and points to numerous complications in the design process.

44. Jenkin Lloyd Jones, *All Souls Seventeenth Annual* (Chicago: All Souls, 1900), 75.

45. Siry, "The Abraham Lincoln Center," 242.

46. Siry, *Unity Temple*, 80–98.

47. Frank Lloyd Wright, "Designing Unity Temple," in *Writings and Buildings*, ed. Edgar Kaufmann and Ben Raeburn (New York: Horizon Press, 1960), 81.

48. Frank Lloyd Wright, *Frank Lloyd Wright: An Autobiography* (New York: Duell, Sloan and Pearce, 1943).

49. Wright never had formal training in art or architecture; his genius for design is largely attributed to his mother's home schooling in his youth. A central element was the comprehension of geometry through manipulation of blocks designed by educational reformer Friedrich Froebel.

50. Jones, "New Problems," 202.

51. Wright, "Designing Unity Temple," 75.

52. Jones, *The Ideal Church*, 2. The full passage makes the meaning clear: "The great helpers of old were called seers, because when others looked into vacancies, they saw realities and caught their inspiration therefrom. Jesus is the highest of teachers because he saw settling down over bigoted Jerusalem and ignorant Gallilee 'the good time coming.' While his ears were filled with the dissonance of strife . . . he had a dream . . . that has become, I trust, an abiding hope in the hearts of most of us. All of us I suspect are now beginning to think that a time will come when the rich will cease to curse the poor, when the wise will teach and not scorn the ignorant, and the good will cease to dread the contaminating touch of the wicked, as they hasten to help and to heal them. Perhaps we all believe that in some way the church is to have something to do in bringing about this good time, this 'kingdom of heaven,' and our ideal church is that church best calculated to hasten the realization of this *popinae* of the prophet, this dream of the poet . . ."

53. Jones, "New Problems," 203.

54. Jones, *The Ideal Church*, 5.

55. Frank Lloyd Wright, "In the Cause of Architecture," in Kaufmann and Raeburn, eds., *Writings and Buildings*, 181–96.

56. Gannett, *The House Beautiful*.

57. Siry, *Unity Temple*, 80–85.

58. Ibid., 110.

59. Sidney K. Robinson, foreword, in David M. Sokol, *The Noble Room: The Inspired Conception and Tumultuous Creation of Frank Lloyd Wright's Unity Temple* (Oak Park, IL: Top Five Books, 2008), xxvii–xxix. Robinson describes Wright's liberal use of images from the past as "nutrients" rather than as precedents.

60. Jones, "New Problems," 203.

61. Siry, *Unity Temple*, 77.

62. Barr Ferree, "Art in the Modern Church I–III: On Un-Christian Churches," *American Architect and Building News*, October 19, 1895, 50.

63. Sokol, *The Noble Room*, 14.

64. Vincent Scully, *Louis I. Kahn* (New York: Braziller, 1962), 24. Sidney K. Robinson agrees: "The discussion that calls the building a 'temple' is evidence of this effort to go back to origins." Robinson, foreword, xxix.

65. Charles Goodman, "Report of Charles M. Goodman, FAIA; The Unitarian Church of Arlington:

the New Building," 1960, Unitarian Universalist Church of Arlington Archives, Arlington, Virginia.

66. Meredith Clausen, *Spiritual Space: The Religious Architecture of Pietro Belluschi* (Seattle: University of Washington Press, 1992), 122–25.

67. Wright, "Designing Unity Temple," 80.

68. Robinson, foreword, xxxiv.

69. Jones, "New Problems," 102.

70. Andrea Greenwood and Mark W. Harris, *An Introduction to the Unitarian and Universalist Traditions* (Cambridge: Cambridge University Press, 2011), 92.

CHAPTER FOUR: FROM COMMONS TO CAMPUS

1. David Robinson, *The Unitarians and the Universalists* (Westport, CT: Greenwood Press, 1985). This the primary source for the general history in this chapter. See also David B. Parke, *The Epic of Unitarianism: Original Writings from the History of Liberal Religion* (Boston: Starr King Press, 1957), and Conrad Wright, ed., *A Stream of Light: A Sesquicentennial History of American Unitarianism* (Boston: Unitarian Universalist Association, 1975).

2. Arthur Cushman McGiffert, *Pilot of a Liberal Faith: Samuel Atkins Eliot, 1862–1950* (Boston: Beacon Press, 1976).

3. Samuel Eliot, "Two New Churches," *Christian Register* 90 (January 5, 1911): 4–5.

4. Ibid.

5. Daniel Kidd, "First Unitarian Church of Omaha," National Register of Historic Places Inventory Nomination Form (Nebraska State Historical Society, 1980), designed by John and Alan McDonald, https://npgallery.nps.gov; Carla Benka, "Second Unitarian Church," Massachusetts Cultural Resource Information System, Inventory No. BKL 612, Second Unitarian Church Report, December 1979, https://mhc-macris.net.

6. "Our History," All Souls Unitarian Church of Indianapolis, https://allsoulsindy.org, designed by Kurt Vonnegut Sr.; Dienna Danhaus Drew, Frieda Dege Marshall, and Lisa Wigoda, *Quincy Unitarian Church: 175 Years in Quincy, Illinois* (Quincy, IL: Priority One, 2014); Rodney Cobb et al., *In Good Times and in Bad: The Story of Sacramento's Unitarians, 1968–1984* (Sacramento, CA: Society, 2008). See also Andover-Harvard Theological Library, Flickr Photostream, Albums, www.flickr.com.

7. Bruce T. Marshall, *Unitarians and Universalists of Washington, DC* (Charleston, SC: Arcadia, 2010).

8. Ibid., 41.

9. McGiffert, *Pilot of a Liberal Faith*, 122. Now listed on the National Register of Historic Places, the Arlington Street Church was designed by Arthur Gilman and Gridley James Fox Bryant.

10. Laurence C. Staples, *Washington Unitarianism: A Rich Heritage* (Washington, DC: N.p., 1970), 81.

11. Marshall, *Unitarians and Universalists of Washington*, 65.

12. "First Unitarian Church, Los Angeles," *Architectural Forum* 3 (March 1929): 395–96.

13. The church also shares some basic features with a more overt mission revival, the United Liberal Church in St. Petersburg, Florida, completed in 1929. This building was designed by Boston architect Philip Smith, whose firm, Smith & Walker, was then a consultant to the AUA. See "Church History," Unitarian Universalist Church of St. Petersburg, http://uustpete.org.

14. Mission Santa Cruz has a replica of the original mission church.

15. David Gebhard and Robert Winter, *An Architectural Guidebook to Los Angeles* (Salt Lake City, UT:

Gibbs Smith, 2003), 221: "You have a feeling that the architects *cast a quick glance* at northern Italian churches." This source also describes one element as "somewhat Islamic."

16. Marshall, *Unitarians and Universalists of Washington*, 34.

17. *Types of Unitarian Churches* (N.p.: N.p., 1915?).

18. Two from Canada are included; statistics are for congregations so the number of churches may be lower.

19. Edwin J. Lewis Jr., J. Enoch Powell, and Albert Walkley, *Plans for Churches* (Boston: American Unitarian Association, 1902).

20. Edward Everett Hale, "The Unitarians," *The Independent . . . Devoted to the Consideration of Politics, Social and Economic Tendencies, History, Literature, and the Arts (1848–1921)* 50 (January 6, 1898): 13.

21. Lewis, Powell, and Walkley, *Plans for Churches*, 8.

22. Ibid., 17.

23. There was some indication that Peabody & Stearns was also a consultant, but I have not found further evidence of this.

24. Philip Horton Smith Architectural Papers, Massachusetts Historical Society, www.masshist.org.

25. Paul Eli Ivey, *Prayers in Stone: Christian Science Architecture in the United States, 1894–1930* (Urbana: University of Illinois Press, 1999).

26. Elizabeth Curtiss, "Samuel Atkins Eliot II," Dictionary of Unitarian and Universalist Biography, http://uudb.org.

27. Parke, *The Epic of Unitarianism*, 132.

28. David B. Parke, "'A Wave at Crest,'" in Wright, ed., *A Stream of Light*, 109.

29. Robinson, *Unitarians and Universalists*, 143–62.

30. Parke, "A Wave at Crest," 108.

31. Ibid., 111. Parke identified the genesis of Unitarian humanism in the ideas shared among John H. Dietrich, Charles Francis Potter, and Curtis W. Reese even before World War I.

32. Vito R. Giustiniani, "Homo, Humanus, and the Meanings of 'Humanism,'" *Journal of the History of Ideas* 46, no. 2 (April–June 1985): 178.

33. American Unitarian Association Commission of Appraisal, *Unitarians Face a New Age: The Report of the Commission of Appraisal to the American Unitarian Association* (Boston: American Unitarian Association, 1936).

34. Carol R. Morris, "It Was Noontime Here . . . ," in Wright, ed., *A Stream of Light*, 130–33.

35. This effort was chronicled by filmmaker Ken Burns in the 2016 documentary "Defying the Nazis: The Sharps' War."

36. Matt Crawford, "Third Unitarian Church Building," Landmark Designation Report, City of Chicago (July 2007), 3, https://ia800702.us.archive.org.

37. "The Third Unitarian Church, Chicago, Illinois," *Architectural Record* 80 (December 1936): 441–44.

38. Alan Seabury, "Frederick May Eliot," Dictionary of Unitarian and Universalist Biography, http://uudb.org.

39. Munroe Husbands, "Unitarians to Meet Here at Boys Club," *North Westchester Times* (Katonah, NY), March 21, 1957.

40. Robinson, *Unitarians and Universalists*, 167.

41. The only exceptions I have found in my research are the First Unitarian Church of Cleveland, Ohio, 1950, and All Souls Unitarian Church of Tulsa, Oklahoma, 1955, both neoclassical buildings. See Virginia P. Dawson, *A History of the First Unitarian Church of Cleveland, 1867–2017* (Shaker Heights, OH: First Unitarian Church of Cleveland, 2017), and "All Souls Unitarian Church," Wikipedia, https://en.wikipedia.org.

42. Miles David Samson, *Hut Pavilion Shrine: Architectural Archetypes in Mid-Century Modernism* (New York: Routledge, 2016), 1–14.

43. "First Church History," First Unitarian Universalist Church of Houston, accessed by author on a congregational website; this history is no longer available in their new website design.

44. "The Nature of Unitarianism," *Architectural Forum* 99 (December 1953): 94–96.

45. Sally Wilkinson and Rolfe Gerhardt, "A Centennial History," First Unitarian Church of Richmond, Virginia (1994); Pat Vaughn, "The Little Church on Council Chamber Hill and the Conflicts of Belief in a Southern Community" (undated booklet), copy in author's possession, obtained from the congregation archive in Richmond.

46. The courtyard was recently renovated, eliminating the fountain and creating a new main entrance to the building.

47. F. D. Cossitt, "An Architectural Critic," *Richmond [VA] Times-Dispatch*, December 2, 1972. The review noted, "When a dinner was given in the building, many people remarked that it seemed to have been made just for that, and, at last week's big art exhibit, they once again found themselves saying it seemed to have been designed just for exhibitions."

48. Wilkinson and Gerhardt, "A Centennial History," 20.

49. Kathryn Hale Embury, "History of the First Unitarian Church of Memphis from 1893 to 1983" (September 1985), 16–18.

50. Kathryn Boyd Rice, "How Our Church Came to Be Where It Is," Church of the River, www.church oftheriver.org.

51. Urban renewal was undertaken in Memphis from the mid-1950s to the mid-1970s. As elsewhere, a central motive was the clearance of substandard (derelict) housing. One African American neighborhood among those effected was just to the north of the site later acquired by the congregation. Their site, however, had been occupied by rail lines coming from the east and making a turn at the river. See R. Alan Sigafoos, *Cotton Row to Beale Street: A Business History of Memphis* (Memphis: Memphis State University Press, 1979).

52. Susan Ellis, "Church of the River Celebrates 50th Anniversary," *Memphis: The City Magazine*, January 8, 2016, https://memphismagazine.com. See also "P/A Awards—Citation," *Progressive Architecture* 46 (January 1965): 154–55.

53. Rice, "How Our Church Came to Be Where It Is."

54. Kathleen LaFrank, "First Unitarian Society Church," National Register of Historic Places Registration Form (December 2013), 7–1, New York State Historic Preservation Office, Waterford. Stone's design dates from 1958; construction took place in 1960–61. This was Stone's first design for a church.

55. John Garber, "Architecture—Structure," Dedication Festival Pamphlet, 1960, 6, St. John's Unitarian Church Archives, Cincinnati, Ohio.

56. Various qualities of the architecture at the time were seen as humanistic due to engagement of the body by both Vincent Scully and William H. Jordy. See Scully, "Modern Architecture: Towards a Redefinition of Style," *Perspecta* 4 (1957): 4–11, and Jordy, "Humanism in Contemporary Architecture: Tough- and Tender-Minded," *Journal of Architectural Education* 15, no. 2 (1960): 3–10. More recently, Miles David Samson identifies the midcentury "new monumentality" as part of an interest in more scenographic effects, while Renata J. Hejduk and Jim Williamson identify some of the same qualities as evidence of "religious imagination." Samson, *Hut Pavilion Shrine*; Renata J. Hejduk and Jim James Williamson, "Introduction," in *The Religious Imagination in Modern and Contemporary Architecture*, ed. Renata J. Hejduk and Jim James Williamson (New York: Routledge, 2011), 1–9.

57. In my inventory, only the church in Grosse Pointe, Michigan (1963), could be included; there may be others, but it could not be many.

58. Conrad Cherry, *Nature and Religious Imagination: From Edwards to Bushnell* (Philadelphia: Fortress Press, 1980), 1–4.

59. Bart Verschaffel, "(Sacred) Places Are Made of Time," in *Loci Sacri, Understanding Sacred Places,* ed. Thomas Coomans et al. (Leuven, Belgium: Leuven University Press, 2012), 55.

60. Susan Power Bratton, *Churchscape: Megachurches and the Iconography of Environment* (Waco, TX: Baylor University Press, 2016), 255.

61. "UUCP History—The 1950's," and "Handbook and History: The Unitarian Church of Princeton New Jersey: 1948–1965," Unitarian Universalist Congregation of Princeton, www.uuprinceton .org.

62. David Weissbard, "History of the Unitarian Universalist Church," Unitarian Universalist Church, Rockford, IL, https://uurockford.org.

63. The full quotation reads, "Trying to define ourselves. . . . Trying to establish our church's scale of values. We want leadership, but not too much. . . . A place where our children have at least a fighting chance to find out why their parents are the kind of people they are. A quiet spot in a confusing world, a haven for people who will always love the unending search for their own certainties about God, Man and the Universe." Ken Wells (board president in 1958), "UUCP History—The 1950s," www.uuprinceton.org.

64. Sally Easter and Raj Nigam, "UUCP Grounds, Gardens, and Memories" (Princeton, NJ: N.p., 2015), www.uuprinceton.org.

65. "Grounds," Unitarian Universalist Congregation, Blacksburg, VA, https://uucnrv.org.

66. Meredith Clausen, *Spiritual Space: The Religious Architecture of Pietro Belluschi* (Seattle: University of Washington Press, 1992), 122. Clausen quotes Belluschi from a personal interview.

67. Reyner Banham, "The New Brutalism," *Architectural Review* 118 (December 1955): 354–61. See also Jordy, "Humanism in Contemporary Architecture," 3–10.

68. Bratton, *Churchscape,* 47.

69. "Washington Goes Unitarian," video recording, YouTube, www.youtube.com.

70. Donald E. Skinner, "Cedar Lane's Modernist Auditorium," *UU World* (Summer 2008), www.uuworld.org.

71. Ibid.

72. "Program of Building Requirements, Preliminary Report," June 16, 1960, Fairfax Unitarian Church, Fairfax, Virginia.

73. "Stories about Church Buildings," excerpted from Betty Gorshe, *Unitarian Church, Davenport, Iowa—For 125 Years, A Place to Grow,* Unitarian Universalist Congregation of the Quad Cities, www.uucqc.org.

74. "Program of Building Requirements, Preliminary Report."

75. J. B. Jackson, "From Monument to Place," *Landscape* 17, no. 2 (Winter 1967–68): 22–26.

76. Penelope Reed Doob, *The Idea of the Labyrinth from Classical Antiquity through the Middle Ages* (Ithaca, NY: Cornell University Press, 1990), 117–33.

77. "Introduction to Labyrinths," People's Church, Kalamazoo, MI, http://peopleschurch.net.

78. McGiffert, *Pilot of a Liberal Faith,* 75.

79. Sarah Williams Goldhagen, *Louis I. Kahn's Situated Modernism* (New Haven, CT: Yale University Press, 2001), 137.

80. John Fuller, "The Religion We Built It For," unpublished MS (sermon), October 4, 1964, https:// roghiemstra.com. Pietro Belluschi, the architect, was in attendance.

81. "Fifty Years of NSUU, Part II," North Shore Unitarian Universalist Congregation, Danvers, MA, https://nsuu.org.

82. Florence Van Straten, "An Anecdotal History of the Early Years of the River Road Unitarian Church," n.d., copy in author's possession from church archives, Bethesda, Maryland.

83. Clausen, *Spiritual Space*, 114.

84. Jean M. Hofer and Irene Baros-Johnson, "May No One Be a Stranger" (Syracuse, NY: May Memorial Unitarian Society, 1988), 40–41, https://roghiemstra.com: "After numerous committee sessions and six congregational meetings, the committees prepared 16 pages of background data and information for the architect, including a request for the use of natural materials and simplicity of design. They said the congregation required a feeling of space, inviting spiritual reaching out and growth. 'The creative principle of organic evolution, of form evolving from inner necessity, growth, and movement, is fundamental to Unitarian belief.' They asked for architecture marked by beauty, dignity, serenity, strength, stimulation, and challenge."

CHAPTER FIVE: CHURCH WITHOUT CROSS OR CREED

1. Renata J. Hejduk and Jim James Williamson, "Introduction," in *The Religious Imagination in Modern and Contemporary Architecture*, ed. Renata J. Hejduk and Jim James Williamson (New York: Routledge, 2011), 2.

2. John C. Fuller, "The Religion We Built It For," unpublished manuscript, October 4, 1964, https://roghiemstra.com; emphasis added.

3. Monica Penick, "'Modern but Not Too Modern': *House Beautiful* and the American Style," in *Sanctioning Modernism: Architecture and the Making of Postwar Identities*, ed. Vladimir Kulic et al. (Austin: University of Texas Press, 2014), 219–43.

4. Sarah Williams Goldhagen, *Louis I. Kahn's Situated Modernism* (New Haven, CT: Yale University Press, 2001), 143.

5. Margaret M. Grubiak, *White Elephants on Campus: The Decline of the University Chapel in America, 1920–1960* (Notre Dame, IN: University of Notre Dame Press, 2014), 97–98.

6. Ibid., 95. See also Joseph M. Siry, "Tradition and Transcendence: Eero Saarinen's MIT Chapel and the Nondenominational Ideal," in *Modernism and American Mid-20th Century Sacred Architecture*, ed. Anat Geva (New York: Routledge, 2019), 275–95.

7. Grubiak, *White Elephants*, 99.

8. James R. Killian, "'The Obligations and Ideals of an Institute of Technology,' Inaugural Address, April 2, 1949," *Technology Review* 51 (May 1949): 429–40.

9. The nearby dormitory designed by Alvar Aalto and completed in 1949 was named Baker House in his honor.

10. Grubiak, *White Elephants*, 106.

11. Conrad Wright, *A Stream of Light: A Sesquicentennial History of American Unitarianism* (Boston: Unitarian Universalist Association, 1975), 149.

12. Robert B. Tapp, *Religion among the Unitarian Universalists: Converts in the Stepfather's House* (New York: Seminar Press, 1973), 12–17.

13. Ibid., 226.

14. Charles M. Goodman, "Report of Charles M. Goodman, FAIA; The Unitarian Church of Arlington: The New Building," 1960, The Envelope, 1, Unitarian Universalist Church of Arlington Archives, Arlington, Virginia. Goodman was quoting Reverend Ross Weston, "The Vocation of the Liberal Church, April 12, 1959."

15. "Paul Kirk Turns to Church Design," *Western Architect and Engineer* 21 (April 1961): 20–29.

16. John Garber, "Architecture—Building as a Whole," Dedication Festival Pamphlet, 1960, 7, St. John's Unitarian Church Archives, Cincinnati, OH.

17. "Churches: East Shore Unitarian Church, Bellevue, WA," *Architectural Record* 122 (December 1957): 186–88.

18. "A Unitarian Church by Belluschi," *Architectural Record* 138 (December 1965): 118–19.

19. Meredith L. Clausen, *Spiritual Space: The Religious Architecture of Pietro Belluschi* (Seattle: University of Washington Press, 1992), 125.

20. Goldhagen, *Kahn's Situated Modernism*, 159.

21. Richard Kieckheffer, *Theology in Stone: Church Architecture from Byzantium to Berkeley* (Oxford: Oxford University Press, 2004), 15.

22. Andrea Greenwood and Mark W. Harris, *An Introduction to the Unitarian and Universalist Traditions* (Cambridge: Cambridge University Press, 2011), 147; emphasis added.

23. Florence Van Straten, "An Anecdotal History of the Early Years of the River Road Unitarian Church," 7, River Road Unitarian Church Archives, Bethesda, Maryland.

24. Wesley I. Shank, "How the Strange Looking Original Building for the Unitarian Fellowship of Ames Came About," March 2013, 6, Unitarian Fellowship of Ames Archives, Ames, Iowa.

25. Goodman, "Report of Charles M. Goodman, FAIA," The Envelope, 3.

26. Rudolf Wittkower, *Architectural Principles in the Age of Humanism* (London: Warburg Institute, 1949). This book explores the meaning of ideal geometries and proportions used by Renaissance architects in terms of Renaissance humanist philosophies. Although it is a scholarly publication, it sparked interest in these topics among many professional architects as well. These topics were further popularized by James Ackerman, *Palladio* (London: Pelican Books, 1966).

27. William J. Gold, "Miracle on Wendell Street," unpublished manuscript, October 3, 1971, Archive of First Unitarian Church, Schenectady, NY.

28. "New Ideas of Victor A. Lundy," *Architectural Record* 131 (February 1962): 119.

29. "The site lies on a gently sloping hillside overlooking Hartford, approached from on up the slope. It gives one the feeling of being able to see from all directions and to see out from it in all directions. The concept is that many points of view draw together and become united in the center. One may start in one of many directions to reach the unity of the center; a unity of equality. The congregation specifically asked for a 'closed' sanctuary; one that directs attention inward rather than outward. From outside, there is a sense of being able to enter from any directions; which is so. The building rises towards the center, the high points forming a ring of reverse skylights, which will throw colored light backwards upon the white walls of the sanctuary. A delicate ceiling tapestry of radiating thin wood members will further diffuse the light." Christopher Domin, "Sacred Spaces," in *Victor Lundy: Artist Architect*, ed. Donna Kacmar (New York: Princeton Architectural Press, 2019), 107.

30. David Robinson, *The Unitarians and the Universalists* (Westport, CT: Greenwood Press, 1985), 154–55. Perry Miller asked in 1942, "After [Unitarianism] made men free to choose, what did it leave for them to choose?" Perry Miller, "Individualism and the New England Tradition," in *The Responsibility of Mind in a Civilization of Machines*, ed. John Cromwell and Stanford J. Searl Jr. (Amherst: University of Massachusetts Press, 1979), 42. Robinson explains further that in the twentieth century, "individualism had come to mean, all too often, irresponsibility to any larger whole, to any enterprise larger than the self."

31. "New Ideas of Victor A. Lundy," 105.

32. Victor Alfred Lundy, First Unitarian Congregational Society Church Building, Hartford, Connecticut, Sections, Plans, and Elevations, 1962, www.loc.gov. This drawing is in a of collection of Lundy

drawings held by the Library of Congress; the digital file is not reproducible in print but can be viewed online.

33. Neil Levine, *The Architecture of Frank Lloyd Wright* (Princeton, NJ: Princeton University Press, 1996), 45.

34. Goodman, "Report of Charles M. Goodman, FAIA," The Envelope, 3.

35. Ibid., The Plan, 1–2. Goodman's single cited precedent was a European medieval "Hall Church," Maria Wiese in Wisenkirche at Soest, Germany, a directional space without side aisles.

36. Ibid., The Envelope, 5.

37. John Toline, 1958–59 Year Book, 124, Unitarian Universalist Church of the Quad Cities Archives, Davenport, Iowa.

38. "A Brief History," Unitarian Universalist Church of Concord, New Hampshire, https://concorduu .org; emphasis added.

39. The current name is the Unitarian Universalist Church of Annapolis. The architect was George Van Fossen Schwab of Baltimore; the original design dates to 1967. Schwab's design credits of the 1960s included the Kuwait Embassy in Washington, DC, and the Maryland Pavilion at the 1964 World's Fair.

40. Joseph M. Siry, *Beth Shalom Synagogue: Frank Lloyd Wright and Modern Religious Architecture* (Chicago: University of Chicago Press, 2012), 247–307, 285 (quotation). Siry's in-depth investigation of the design and construction of this Unitarian church is the best source on this building.

41. Ibid., 269–71.

42. Albert Christ-Janer and Mary Mix Foley, *Modern Church Architecture: A Guide to the Form and Spirit of 20th Century Religious Buildings* (New York: McGraw-Hill, 1962), 279.

43. For instance, the golden rectangle was used as a structural module in Evanston, Illinois, and determined the dimensions of the sanctuary in Cedar Falls, Iowa.

44. Hejduk and Williamson, "Introduction," 5.

45. Kahn quoted in Goldhagen, *Kahn's Situated Modernism*, 148.

46. "Unitarian Church," *Progressive Architecture* 37 (October 1956): 107.

47. The congregation that built this church moved in 1986. The building now belongs to the Reconstructionist Synagogue of the North Shore.

48. Margaret Shaklee, "A History of the Unitarian Church of Evanston," Unitarian Church of Evanston, Illinois, 2012, 7, https://ucevanston.org.

49. Peter Blake, "A Modern Church for a Modern Faith," *Architectural Forum* 110, no. 5 (May 1959): 131.

50. Goldhagen, *Kahn's Situated Modernism*, 151, fig. 6.8.

51. Garber, "Architecture—Building as a Whole," 5.

52. Goldhagen, *Kahn's Situated Modernism*, 159.

53. Christ-Janer and Foley, *Modern Church Architecture*, 279.

54. Juhani Pallasmaa, "The Aura of the Sacred: Art, Architecture, and Existential Sacredness," in Hejduk and Williamson, eds., *The Religious Imagination in Modern and Contemporary Architecture*, 236–38.

55. Karsten Harries, "Transcending Aesthetics," in *Transcending Architecture: Contemporary Views on Sacred Space*, ed. Julio Bermudez (Washington, DC: Catholic University Press, 2015), 222.

CHAPTER SIX: ARCHITECTURE OF, BY, AND FOR THE PEOPLE

1. Richard A. Etlin, *In Defense of Humanism: Value in the Arts and Letters* (New York: Cambridge University Press, 1996), 48–54.

2. Sylvain de Bleeckere, "Style and Architecture in a Democratic Perspective," *Enquiry: The ARCC Journal* 4, no. 1 (April 2007): 13–20, 17 (quotation).

3. John Dewey, "Emerson—The Philosopher of Democracy," *International Journal of Ethics* 13, no. 4 (July 1903): 411.

4. Lauren S. Weingarden, *Louis H. Sullivan and a 19th-Century Poetics of Naturalized Architecture* (Farnham, UK: Ashgate, 2009), 20–27. See also Louis H. Sullivan, *Kindergarten Chats and Other Writings* (New York: Dover, 1979), 135–42.

5. Louis H. Sullivan, *Democracy: A Man-Search* (Detroit: Wayne State University Press, 1961), 151, xix; Sullivan, *Kindergarten Chats*, 191–94.

6. Harry Francis Mallgrave, *From Object to Experience: The New Culture of Architectural Design* (London: Bloomsbury Visual Arts, 2018), 9–13.

7. Claude Bragdon, *Architecture and Democracy* (New York: Knopf, 1926), 145, 24.

8. Frank Lloyd Wright, *An Organic Architecture: The Architecture of Democracy* (Cambridge, MA: MIT Press, 1970), 1.

9. Joan Ockman, "What Is Democratic Architecture? The Public Life of Buildings," *Dissent* 58, no. 4 (Fall 2011): 65–72.

10. De Bleeckere, "Style and Architecture," 17.

11. Ockman, "What Is Democratic Architecture?" 65–72.

12. Vincent Scully, "Modern Architecture: Toward a Redefinition of Style," in *Modern Architecture and Other Essays*, ed. Neil Levine (Princeton, NJ: Princeton University Press, 2003), 74–87.

13. Geoffrey Scott, *The Architecture of Humanism: A Study in the History of Taste* (New York: Norton, 1974), 178.

14. Scully, "Modern Architecture," 85.

15. Sarah Williams Goldhagen, *Louis I. Kahn's Situated Modernism* (New Haven, CT: Yale University Press, 2001), 164–66; emphasis added.

16. Ockman, "What Is Democratic Architecture?" 65–72.

17. J. C. Berendzen, "Institutional Design and Public Space: Hegel, Architecture, and Democracy," *Journal of Social Philosophy* 39, no. 2 (Summer 2008): 305.

18. Ockman, "What Is Democratic Architecture?" 72.

19. Jan-Werner Mueller, "Can Architecture Be Democratic? The Tension between the People and Their Places," *Public Seminar* (June 22, 2015), https://publicseminar.org.

20. Mark D. Morrison-Reed, *Black Pioneers in a White Denomination* (Boston: Beacon Press, 1984), 168.

21. Gideon Kramer, "Response to Building Committee Survey," April 15, 1954, University Unitarian Church Archives, Seattle.

22. Rev. Chabourne Spring, "A Look to the Future," Dedication Program, 1956, East Shore Unitarian Universalist Church Archives, Bellevue, Washington.

23. "Building Philosophy—1959," Unitarian Universalist Church of Concord Archives, Concord, New Hampshire.

24. Rev. William Gold, "Our Building at 1221 Wendell Ave," Dedication Pamphlet, First Unitarian Universalist Church Archive, Schenectady, New York.

25. Kramer, "Response." This is just one example; Kramer said, "It should not be said of this congregation that we did not know what time it was."

26. For instance, the University Unitarian Building committee decided, after making inquiries to Charles Eames, that they would only interview local firms. Meeting Minutes, January 23, 1955, University Unitarian Church Archives, Seattle.

27. Jennifer Walkowski, "First Unitarian Church," National Register of Historic Places Registration Form (Waterford, NY: New York State Historic Preservation Office, 2014), 8.10.

28. Rev. Jon Luopa, conversation with author, May 15, 2015.

29. Scott Theodore Mulder, "Congregational Health in Unitarian Universalist Churches: A Grounded Theory Approach to Leadership, Systems, and Processes" (PhD diss., Niagra University, 2018), 39.

30. Kathryn Ritson, "Unitarian Universalist Church of Arlington," National Register of Historic Places Registration Form (Richmond: Virginia Department of Historic Resources, 2014), 8.19.

31. Charles Goodman, "Architecture and Society" in *The People's Architects*, ed. Harry S. Ransom (Chicago: University of Chicago Press, 1964), 112–120. Goodman wrote, "I believe that architecture is an art . . . but an art for the many" (113).

32. Charles M. Goodman, "Report of Charles M. Goodman, FAIA: The Unitarian Church of Arlington: The New Building," 1960, Unitarian Universalist Church of Arlington Archives, Arlington, Virginia.

33. Ibid., The Site, 5–6.

34. Ibid., The Envelope, 1–2, 3–4.

35. Ronald W. Marshall and Barbara A. Boyd, "Charles Goodman: Production, Reputation, Reflection," *Modernism Magazine* 2, no. 3 (1999): 46; Elizabeth Lampl, "Charles M. Goodman and 'Tomorrow's Vernacular,'" in *Housing Washington: Two Centuries of Residential Development and Planning in the National Capitol Area*, ed. Richard W. Longstreth (Chicago: Center for American Places at Columbia College, 2010), 234.

36. Elsa Liles, congregation member, quoted in Walkowski, "First Unitarian Church," 8.28.

37. In addition to Goldhagen, *Kahn's Situated Modernism*, see Robin Williams, "First Unitarian Church and School," in *Louis I. Kahn: In the Realm of Architecture*, ed. David Brownlee and David DeLong (New York: Rizzoli, 1991), 340–45.

38. Williams, "First Unitarian Church and School," 340.

39. Goldhagen, *Kahn's Situated Modernism*, 149–50.

40. Mulder, "Congregational Health in Unitarian Universalist Churches," 64.

41. Ibid., 46–47.

42. Goldhagen, *Kahn's Situated Modernism*, 142. Goldhagen reasonably attributes this conception to his exploration of a common problem of the 1950s, a university nondenominational chapel. This is a different problem: the religious building is part of a public campus where only a small percentage of students and faculty will attend services in the chapel. Kahn's intention in that case was to create multiple layers of space to act as a spatial filter. It likely disposed him toward an amplification of the Unitarian practice of offering a choice by means of multiple doors, narthex, arcade, and alternative paths at the entry to their churches. Lundy would repeat the use of a continuous corridor ringing a central sanctuary in Hartford.

43. Ibid., 136.

44. Looking further back, though without any inference regarding the architect-client relationship, their Unitarian church projects were judged to be the most successful work of both Maximilian Godefroy in Baltimore and Jacob Wrey Mould in New York City.

45. There were two architects on the building committee who facilitated much of the process in his place.

46. Jean M. Hofer and Irene Baros-Johnson, "May No One be a Stranger" (Syracuse, NY: May Memorial Unitarian Society, 1988), 40.

47. Meredith Clausen, *Spiritual Space: The Religious Architecture of Pietro Belluschi* (Seattle: University of Washington Press, 1992), 114.

48. Rev. John C. Fuller, "The Religion We Built It For," unpublished manuscript, October 4, 1964, https://roghiemstra.com.

49. "Brief History 1946–1985," Unitarian Fellowship of Ames, unpublished manuscript, Unitarian Fellowship of Ames Archives, Ames, Iowa.

50. Daniel Walker Howe, *The Unitarian Conscience: Harvard Moral Philosophy, 1805–1861* (Cambridge, MA: Harvard University Press, 1970), 202, 258.

51. Lawrence Buell, "The Unitarian Movement and the Art of Preaching in 19th Century America," *American Quarterly* 24, no. 2 (May 1972): 175. See also Howe, *The Unitarian Conscience*, 7.

52. Vito R. Giustiniani, "Homo, Humanus, and the Meanings of 'Humanism,'" *Journal of the History of Ideas* 46, no. 2 (April–June 1985): 167–95.

53. American Humanist Association, *Humanist Manifestos I and II* (Amherst, NY: American Humanist Association, 1973).

54. Walter Gropius, *Scope of Total Architecture* (New York: Collier Books, 1962).

55. Howard Mumford Jones, *American Humanism: Its Meaning for World Survival* (New York: Harper Brothers, 1957), 103.

56. "Unitarian and Universalist Atlanta History Summary 1879 to 2003," Unitarian Universalist Digital Archive, https://nwuuc.org.

57. "Aldermen Deny Beer License, Reject Church Zoning," *Atlanta Constitution*, August 21, 1962.

58. Sally Webster, "Unitarianism and the Iconography of Democracy: Decorations for the Library of Congress," *Library Quarterly* 80, no. 4 (2010): 357–83, 372 (quotations).

59. Ibid., 357.

60. Helen Dalrymple and Charles A. Goodrum, *Guide to the Library of Congress* (Washington, DC: Library of Congress, 1982), 11–13. Edward Casey and Bernard Green determined the pictorial content and hired the artists. Artists proposed their visions of how to portray whatever was requested, and Casey and Green approved or amended.

61. Webster, "Unitarianism and the Iconography of Democracy," 357.

62. Forrest Church, "The American Creed: US Values Rest Historically on a Spiritual Foundation Grounded in Nature," *Nation* 275, no. 8 (September 16, 2002): 27.

63. William Ellery Channing, *A Sermon Delivered at the Ordination of the Rev. Jared Sparks to the Pastoral Care of the First Independent Church in Baltimore, May 5, 1819* (Boston: Hews & Goss, 1819).

64. Stow Persons, *American Minds: A History of Ideas* (New York: Holt, Rinehart, and Winston, 1958), 182.

65. Theodore Parker, "Speech at the New England Anti-Slavery Convention in Boston, May 20, 1850," in *Speeches, Addresses, and Occasional Sermons* (Boston: Ticknor and Fields, 1861), 3:41. Abraham Lincoln had read Parker's sermon and marked this passage, which he improved and immortalized in his Gettysburg Address.

66. Fred Edwords, "What Is Humanism?" American Humanist Association, https://americanhumanist.org.

67. Etlin, *In Defense of Humanism*.

68. John Beldon Scott, review of *In Defense of Humanism*, by Richard Etlin, *Art Bulletin* 80, no. 2 (1998): 399–400.

69. Andrea Greenwood and Mark W. Harris, *An Introduction to the Unitarian and Universalist Traditions* (Cambridge: Cambridge University Press, 2011), 128.

70. David Robinson, *The Unitarians and the Universalists* (Westport, CT: Greenwood Press, 1985), 46, 44.

71. Rev. William Channing Gannett, "Things Commonly Believed among Us," in *The Epic of Unitarianism*, ed. David B. Parke (Boston: Starr King Press, 1957), 129–31.

72. Robinson, *Unitarians and Universalists*, 167.

73. Daniel Burke, "Can Unitarian Universalists Make It Another 50 Years?" *HuffPost*, June 29, 2011, www.huffpost.com.

74. Karla Cavarra Britton, "Robert Damora and the Mission of American Architecture," *Journal of Architecture* 21, no. 7 (2016): 995–1011.

75. Robinson, *Unitarians and Universalists*, 165–66. Robinson quotes Frederick May Eliot describing the liberal church as a "company of seekers" who have in common the "need to grow." Although not spoken in respect to the Unitarian approach to religious education, it expresses their expectation for all social structures of the congregation.

76. Ockman, "What Is Democratic Architecture?" 65–72.

77. De Bleeckere, "Style and Architecture," 17.

INDEX

Page references in *italics* refer to figures and photographs.

ANN MARIE BORYS was born in Massachusetts and grew up in Maryland. She has architecture degrees from the University of Maryland, Syracuse University, and the University of Pennsylvania. She is a licensed architect in several states. Her first book, *Vincenzo Scamozzi and the Chorography of Early Modern Architecture* (2014), was the first English-language study of the last Italian Renaissance architect and theorist. She teaches architectural design and cultural studies at the University of Washington in Seattle.